I0795769

IMAGES
of America

HAMPTON

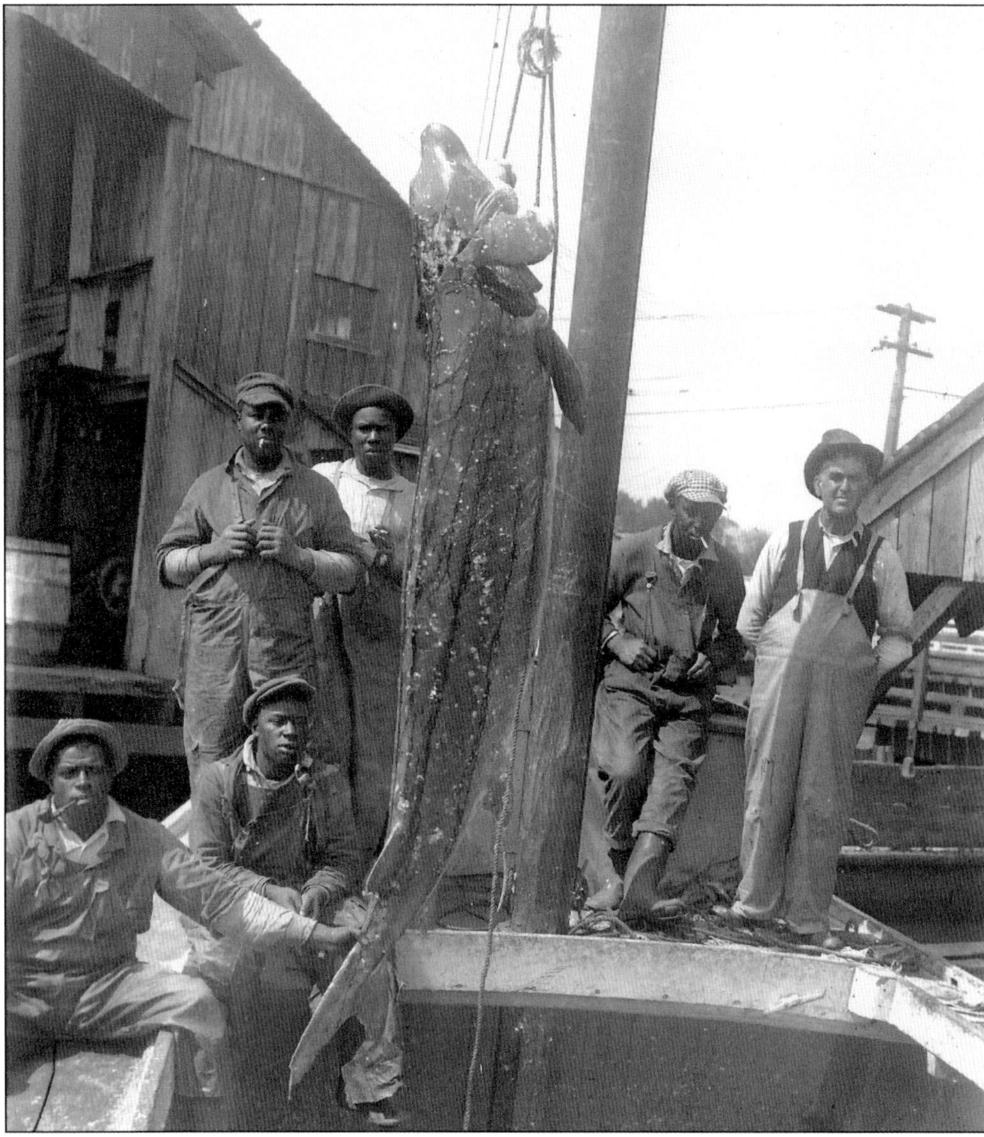

WHEN SEAFOOD WAS KING. Hampton's greatest modern claim to fame and the engine of its prosperity was seafood. Here rubber-booted watermen proudly display a huge sturgeon they have caught. No longer plentiful, sturgeons have been harvested here since the 17th century.

ON THE COVER: Hampton's master photographer Ethelbert Cheyne has captured the intersection of King and Queen Streets in the town's heyday around 1930. Through the centuries, the "cross streets" have always formed the heart of Hampton. (Courtesy of the Hampton History Museum.)

IMAGES
of America

HAMPTON

J. Michael Cobb and Wythe Holt
on behalf of the Hampton History Museum

with Tim Smith and Ed Hicks, photo editors

ARCADIA
PUBLISHING

ISBN 978-0-7385-5381-8

Published by Arcadia Publishing
Charleston, South Carolina

Printed in the United States of America

Library of Congress Catalog Card Number: 2007941423

For all general information contact Arcadia Publishing at:
Telephone 843-853-2070
Fax 843-853-0044
E-mail sales@arcadiapublishing.com
For customer service and orders:
Toll-Free 1-888-313-2665

Visit us on the Internet at www.arcadiapublishing.com

To Girard Chambers Jr., a second-generation surveyor of Hampton and Elizabeth City County, whose knowledge of Hampton's history and environs is unsurpassed.

Contents

ACKNOWLEDGMENTS

All unattributed images are from material reposing in the various collections of the Hampton History Museum. We wish to thank Leslie E. Thomas and Bethany Austin of the museum staff for their daily help; Jim Wilson, director of Parks and Recreation in Hampton, for his sustained support; and the Hampton History Museum Association for its members' enthusiastic encouragement. Several Hamptonians have generously provided images. Thanks go to Libby Kendrick; Richard, Sandra, and Sherwood von Schilling; Robert Mclanahan Smith III; Brenda and Tommy Hutton; John R. Wilt; Cary Patrick; Eddie Williams; and David Hornsby Wallace. Several others have patiently helped us with identifications and have been of much other help too. Thanks go to Ernest Wilson, Ann Tormey, Frear and Carolyn Hawkins, and Girard Chambers Jr.

Several institutions have provided images, identifications, and other aid. In addition to attributions following some of the images below, we would like especially to thank Dale Neighbors of the Library of Virginia; Jason Lamb of Riggs Ward Design; Peggy Hale McPhillips of the Norfolk Public Library; Elizabeth Wilson of the Hampton Public Library; Brooks Johnson, curator of photography at the Walter P. Chrysler Museum; and Dorothy Rouse-Bottom and Terry Hammond of the William E. Rouse Research Library. There are friends and fellow workers who have given so generously of their time, expertise, and hard work that this book could not have been completed without them. Eirlys Barker did important groundwork, research, and organization; Ray Barker helped too. Tim Smith took much time from his marine railway work to put the images on disc and to help select the images. Ed Hicks worked with us daily, researching, writing, and providing consistently good advice and companionship—he should be listed as the third coauthor.

INTRODUCTION

This book is a labor of love.

Mike Cobb has been curator of the Hampton History Museum for a quarter century, engaging actively as downtown Hampton has been archaeologically excavated, collecting photographs, artifacts, documents, and other material donated by many Hampton residents who adore their town and its long, varied, and distinguished history, and creating a working public archive always open to interested Hamptonians.

Wythe Holt is a practicing historian, born in Hampton, whose family has been involved in Hampton's ups and downs for nearly two centuries and who shares his love of the town's heritage with many other Hamptonians.

Together we wanted to use the fascinating resources of the Hampton History Museum to produce a useful, interesting, historically accurate overview of Hampton's four centuries. Arcadia's photo-history approach has allowed us to accomplish our goal.

We have placed our primary focus on downtown, symbolized by "the crossing" streets of Queen and King. Arcadia titles have already dealt with other Hampton neighborhoods, such as Aberdeen, Fox Hill, and Wythe, and more are planned. In this book, we have reached out for bits of Phoebus, Fox Hill, Merrimac Shores, and Langley Field, and have included more on Fort Monroe, the Old Soldiers' Home (as Hamptonians call it), and Hampton University, but we have persistently emphasized the changing moods and faces of downtown Hampton. Too, the bulk of our visual sources is photographic, and thus the book mostly dates from the 1880s forward.

Some of these images have appeared elsewhere. Most, however, appear here in a Hampton history book for the first time. We have tried to bring to light photographs and drawings readers have not seen before. In addition, we wanted to write a history for all Hamptonians. We have been as inclusive as we could. This book depends upon the collections actually reposing in the Hampton History Museum, which in turn depend almost entirely upon the desires of those who have wished to deposit their valuable materials in it. The breadth and range of our images is directly a product of our sources. We are proud of our inclusiveness, but it could have been better.

We have selected images for their appeal. We have tried to draw the reader into the excitement, fun, difficulty, confusion, and complexity that life in this community has entailed. We have tried to capture interesting, important, sometimes just plain titillating stories, personalities, and memories—some of which might otherwise have been lost forever. We have also tried to connect Hampton people, buildings, and occurrences to their context, and to the broader currents and themes of American and world history within which they have existed and changed. Finally, we have included several of our predecessors as Hampton's historians, people whose work we admire and upon whose shoulders we are struggling to stand. One of the best of those is our dedicatee. History is a group process, a cooperative, contentious, and cross-referenced project in which no contribution is solely individual.

Some like their history upbeat—that is, emphasizing exclusively what they think of as the good and the positive. Some like their history Whiggish, that is, built around a theme of continuous improvement toward an apparently preordained goal, emphasizing the stories of the dominant.

Be warned that we view history differently. Hampton's history has blemishes too, and we believe that the principal theme has been one of struggle and constant change, of ups and downs, of the need for Hamptonians constantly to reinvent their economy, their primary activities and endeavors, and indeed what it is that Hampton meant. For example, Hampton produced George Wythe, who worked hard for and signed the Declaration of Independence, and Hamptonians owned slaves; and as economic and political changes occurred, so too did Hampton rise, fall, and become rebuilt and re-thought. We strove to present it all here. We recognize that we have taken positions, some of them disputed, and that others differ from us. We welcome it. Thank goodness that people see things differently. Such is the nature of history.

A word on our chief sources: the City Directories for Hampton, commencing with *Chataigne's* of 1896–1897, republished by Dorothy Rouse-Bottom, and continuing with *Hill's* from 1898 forward, have been fundamental. The special business editions of the *Hampton Monitor* of August 1907 and July 1918 proved invaluable. We have extensively relied upon the published archaeological reports on downtown Hampton excavations by the William and Mary Center for Archaeological Research and the James River Institute for Archaeology; here we would particularly mention Joe Benthall, Tom Higgins, and Hank Lutton.

For the early national period, we have depended upon the first-rate College of William and Mary dissertation of Sarah Shaver Hughes, "Elizabeth City County, Virginia, 1782–1810." For Hampton's black history, Robert F. Engs's *Freedom's First Generation* is indispensable, and we have also consulted Colita Nichols Fairfax's *Hampton Virginia*, an Arcadia black history volume. Helen C. Rountree (a Hamptonian) and E. Randolph Turner III's *Before and After Jamestown: Virginia's Powhatans and Their Predecessors* is definitive on Hampton's Native American heritage. The coauthored collection *Hampton: From the Sea To the Stars* has been helpful, as has been Hamilton "Sis" Evans's *Lost Landmarks of Old Hampton, Revolutionary War Port Town*.

The Hampton History Museum wishes to start its own publication series. We hope that this volume is a step in that direction. We also want to welcome you to see the collections there and even to make your own contributions. By no means is Hampton's history finished.

One

The Founding of Hampton

Hampton seemed an excellent place for humans to dwell early in the 17th century. Its site, at the end of a fruitful peninsula on the banks of the Hampton River, was sufficiently close to the open waters of the Chesapeake and the Atlantic for a commercial entrepot.

When the Spanish attempted unsuccessfully to found a mission near present-day Yorktown around 1570, the place was known as Kecoughtan, and habitation was probably confined to the east bank. Native Americans had lived in the area for centuries, and by the late 1590s, Kecoughtan formed part of the Powhatan chiefdom, which encompassed much of the region.

In addition to harvesting the natural bounty of the area, the Kecoughtans grew maize, beans, and squash. When the English landed at Strawberry Banks on April 30, 1607, they were welcomed with food and dancing by the leader, Pochins, son of the great Powhatan and half-brother to Pocahontas.

Matters between the old and new populations soon grew hostile. By the fall of 1609, settling first at Jamestown in a more sheltered place up the James River, the English had established a military outpost, Fort Algernoune at Point Comfort. The next summer, the English attacked and routed the Kecoughtans, removing the survivors westward and building now-lost Forts Henry and Charles, probably astride the entrance to Hampton River.

English settlement soon expanded beyond the walls of these forts. Renamed Elizabeth City in 1619 in honor of King James's daughter, by 1625, it had the highest population of any Virginia settlement, with 359 people. Thirty-four of its 89 houses were fortified. It became one of the most important ports in Virginia; the early location of a customs house there indicates its commercial significance.

The first Africans in Virginia, taken as slaves by the Portuguese from what is now Angola, were offered for trade at Point Comfort in 1619, probably as indentured servants.

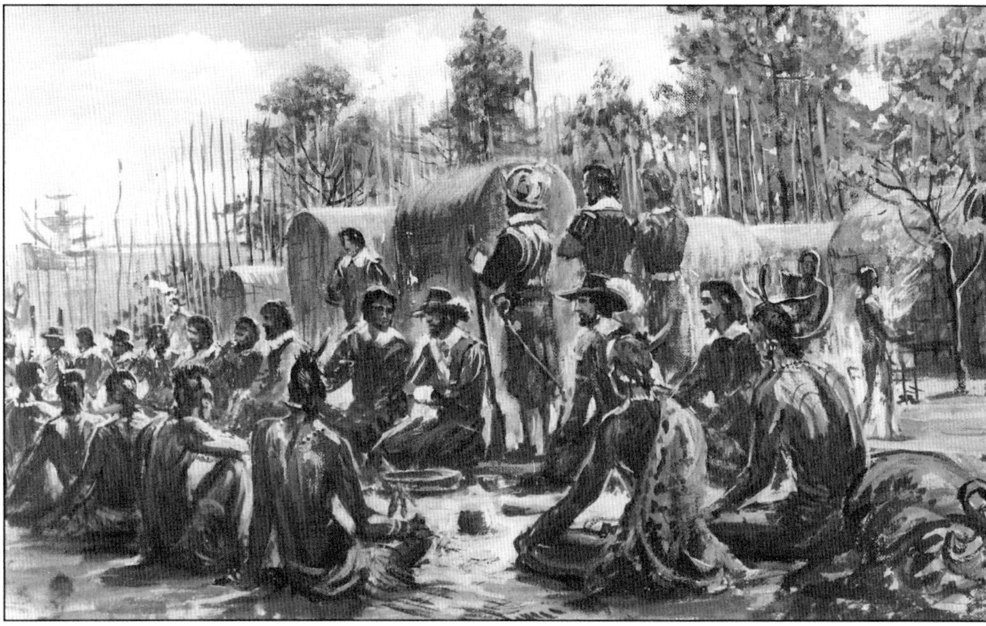

The First English Landing. This conjectural painting depicts the English landing at Kecoughtan, probably situated on the east bank of what is now Hampton River. A meal much like this ensued. The ships contained 104 sea-weary men and boys. The Virginia Company had charged them to search for gold and the elusive Northwest Passage, and to establish profitable industries. (Painting by Sydney King; courtesy of National Park Service, Jamestown.)

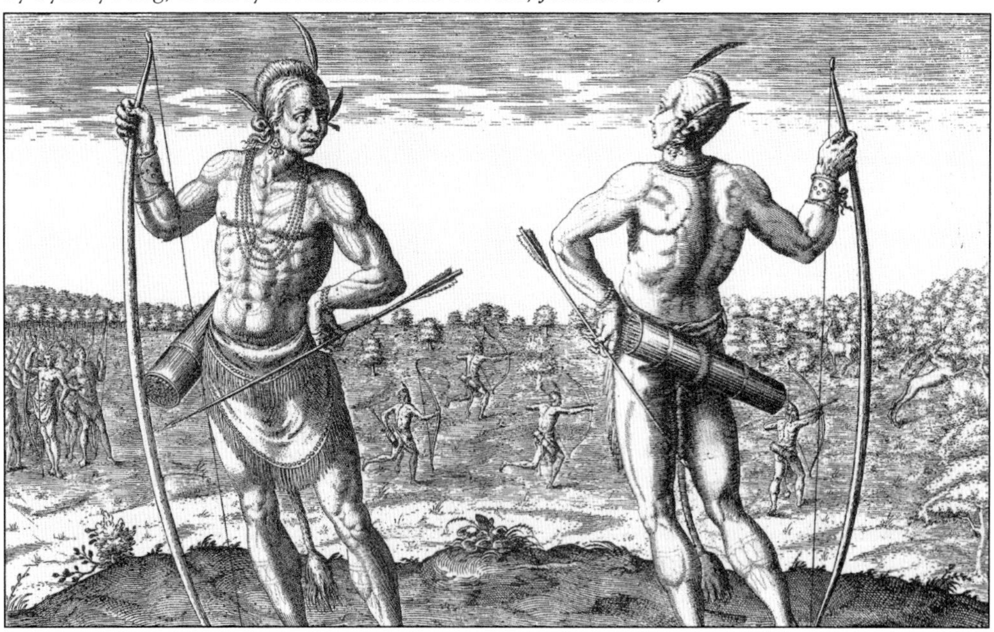

An Indian Warrior. Pochins, leader of Kecoughtan in 1607, despite prolonged drought, welcomed the English with food and again provided needed sustenance in December 1608. His refusal of food led to brief warfare in September 1607. Kecoughtan was a desirable location with the natives' reed lodges being placed amid thousands of cleared acres with much cultivation. (Engraving by Theodore deBry.)

INDIANS FISHING. Using fire to hollow out trees, Native Americans built sturdy log canoes for fishing. This engraving from the ill-fated Roanoke colony of 1586 shows the abundance of seafood of various recognizable varieties in the nearby waters. Hampton River's waters were equally fecund. A leader noted in 1611: "At all times this place yields the better relief by means of fishing than James Towne." (Engraving by Theodore deBry.)

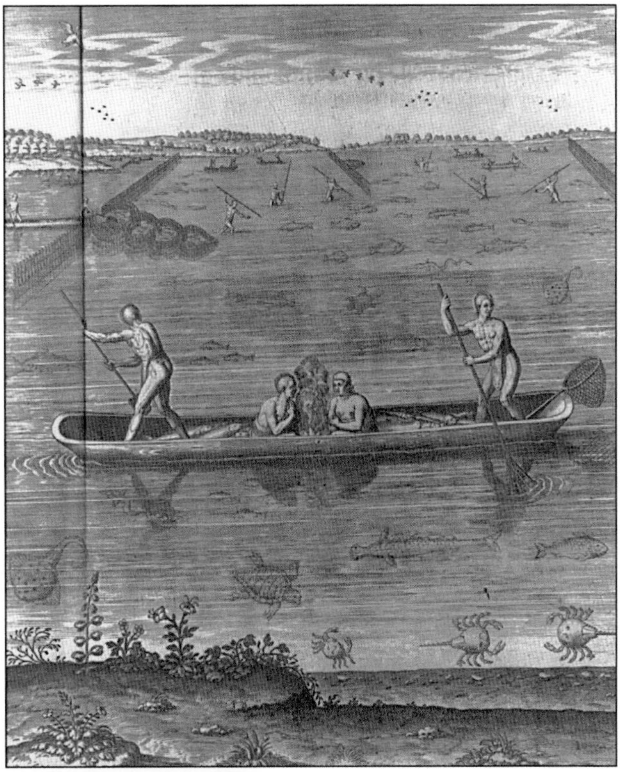

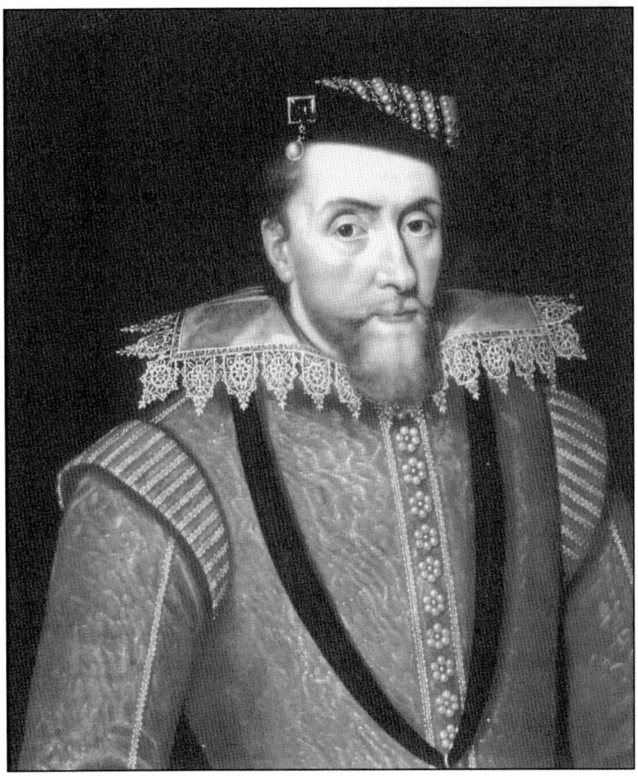

KING JAMES. James, the king of Scotland, became the king of England in 1603. He granted a charter to the Virginia Company of London to establish a permanent English colony in North America. It was a commercial venture, as the company was selling shares and anticipating profit. Later Forts Henry and Charles and Kecoughtan itself, renamed Elizabeth City, were given the names of James's children. (Artist unknown; courtesy of Colonial Williamsburg Foundation.)

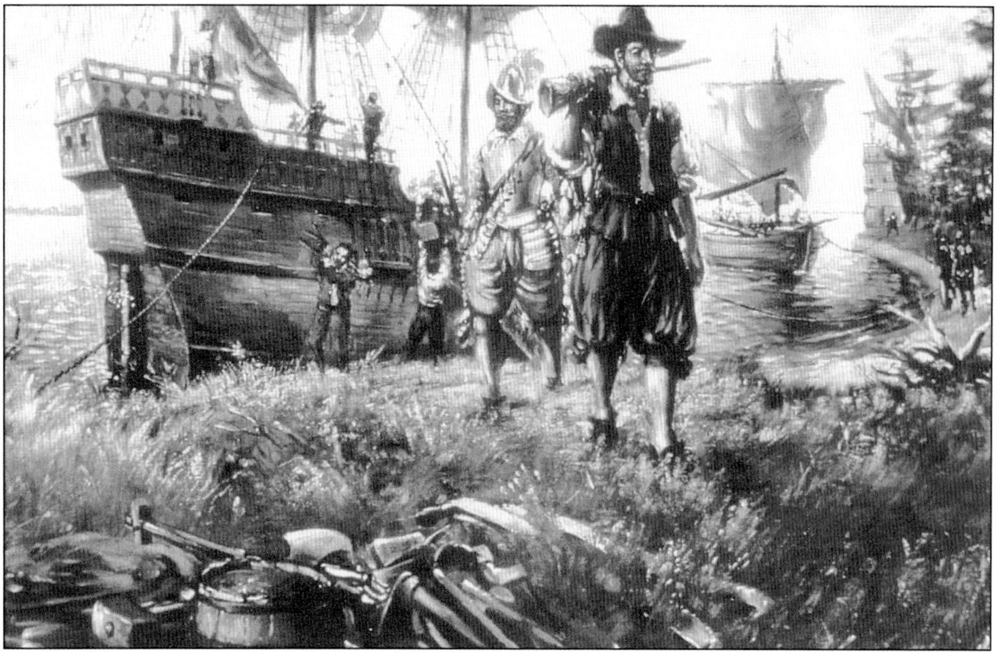

LANDING AT JAMESTOWN. The English fixed their principal settlement at Jamestown, an isolated isthmus 40 miles up the nearby James River. Their instructions required them to attempt to avoid depredations by the feared Spanish. They were also instructed to remove local inhabitants from their area of settlement. (Painting by Sydney King; courtesy of National Park Service, Jamestown.)

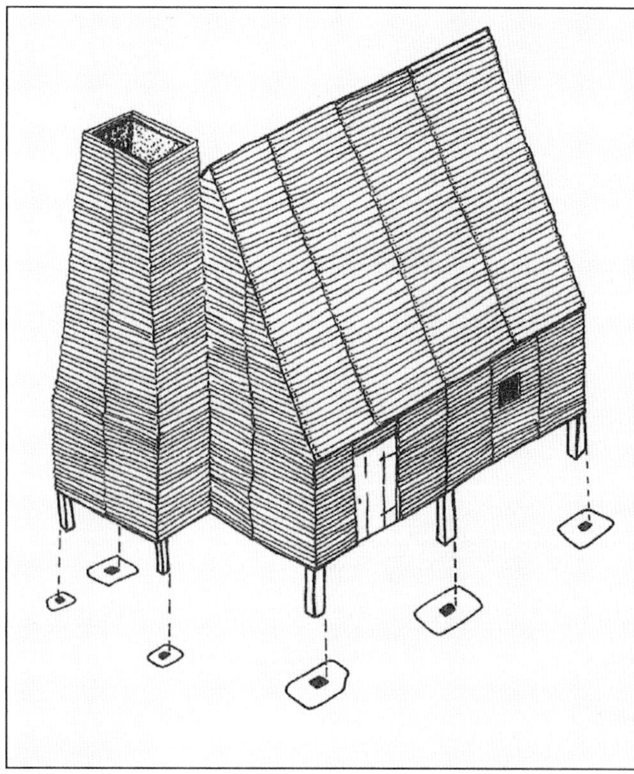

AN EARLY HOUSE. Primitive "earth-fast" structures affixed to posts dug into the ground were quickly fashioned and impermanent. They had dirt floors, while the walls and roof were rough-hewn clapboards and shingles. They sheltered people's meager possessions. The arrival of women in 1619 heralded increased stability. (Sketch by Eric Deetz.)

WILLIAM CLAIBORNE. Arriving in 1621, William Claiborne became a respected political and military leader, explored the Chesapeake, and helped to establish the Chesapeake region as a major source of the fur trade. By 1631, he had established a trading plantation at Kecoughtan, where he built a warehouse for trading with the Native Americans. (Copy of original painting by Mary R. Gilmer; courtesy of Virginia Historical Society.)

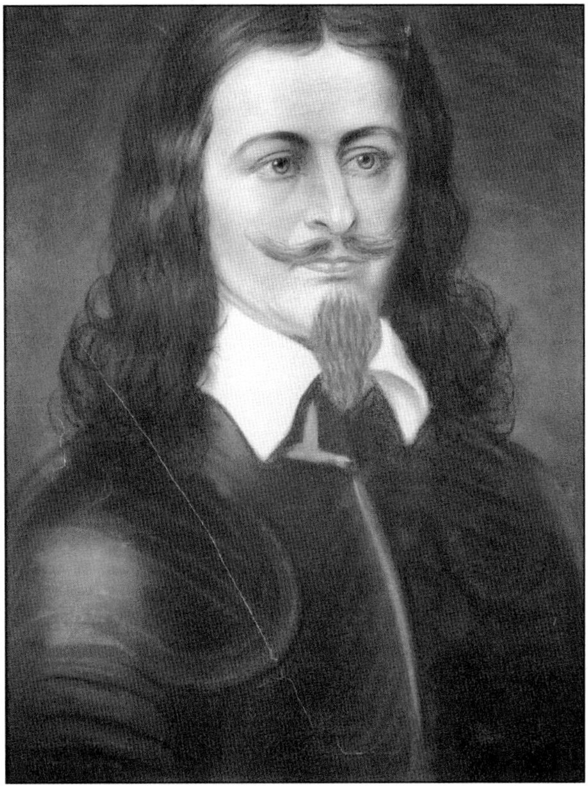

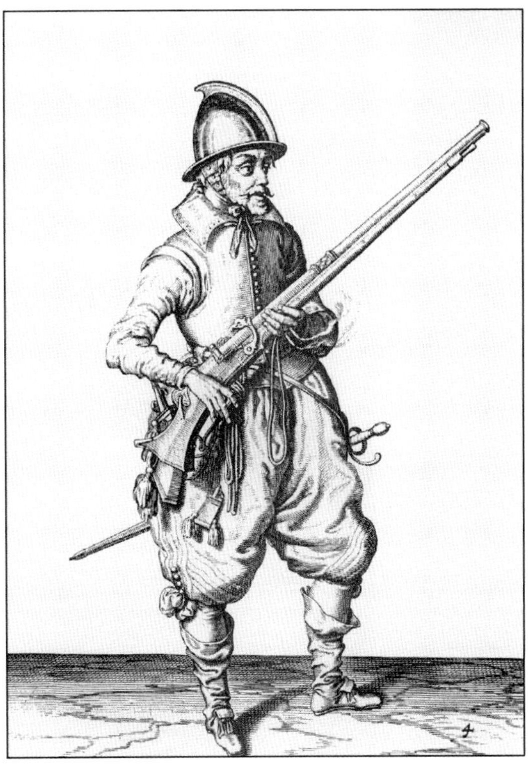

A 17TH-CENTURY SOLDIER. Fort Algernoune was a stockade built of rough-hewn posts at Point Comfort in 1609 to guard against Spanish attack from the sea. Capt. James Davies was in command of about 40 soldiers. When the Powhatans under Opechancanough attacked most of the English settlement in 1622, Kecoughtan was one of the eight designated places of refuge for the survivors. (Engraving by Jacob de Gheyn.)

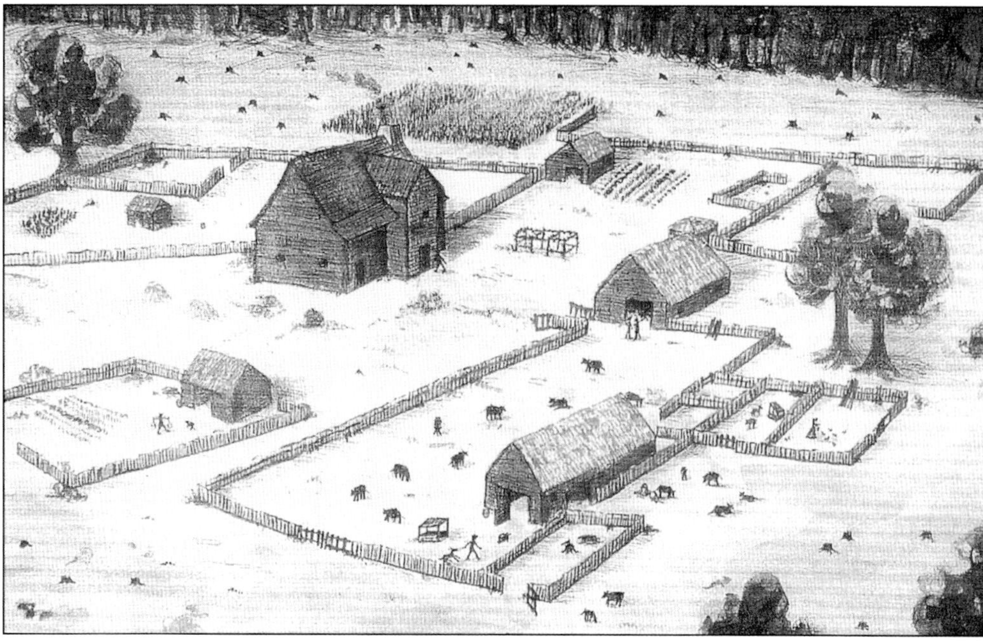

THOMAS JARVIS'S TRADING PLANTATION. Archeologists excavating near Hampton's present-day city hall uncovered what was probably the Jarvis plantation, dated to 1650–1690. Jarvis was a ship captain, merchant, tobacco planter, and Kecoughtan's representative in Virginia's House of Burgesses in the 1680s. The house had a distinctive medieval entrance and plastered walls, displaying far more opulence than most dwellings. (Courtesy of Virginia Department of Transportation; William and Mary Center for Archaeological Research.)

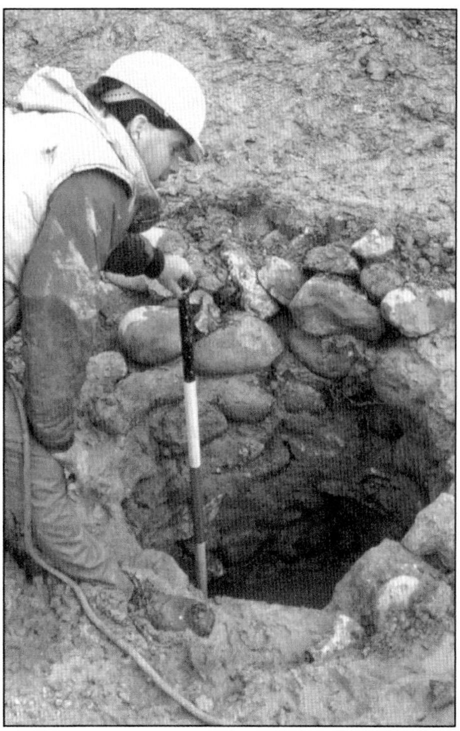

THE JARVIS PLANTATION WELL. Archaeologists here unearth a dry-laid well made partially of ballast stones from the hold of a transatlantic ship and partially of sea coral, probably from a West Indian reef. Wells are treasure troves of mislaid objects. Also found on the site was a silver thimble embossed with the likeness of King Charles I. (Photograph by J. Michael Cobb.)

Two

An Atlantic Tobacco Port

By the end of the 17th century, a formal town plan existed, featuring the "arrow" of Queen Street running east and west, intersected at right angles as if a bow or bowstring by King Street, which runs south to the docks. It was renamed Hampton in 1706 after the earl of Southampton.

Hampton prospered as a port, remaining one of Virginia's largest towns in the early 1700s. A stroll down its streets would reveal sailors, fishermen, excise agents, lawyers, merchants, innkeepers, farmers and planters who had come to town, and both enslaved and free blacks. Shipwrights, coopers, blacksmiths, and other "mechanics" important in the seafaring trades labored near busy wharves, taverns, and apothecaries' stores. Inbound ships were laden with consumer goods for the growing gentry. These goods were exchanged for tobacco. Virginia tobacco, introduced from the Caribbean by Pocahontas's English husband, John Rolfe, not only saved a struggling colony, but also became the engine that drove a burgeoning economy. An official tobacco warehouse had been constructed in Hampton in 1633. By the mid-1700s, half the population of the colony was black, indicating the labor-intensive nature of tobacco cultivation and the loathsomeness of such labor for whites.

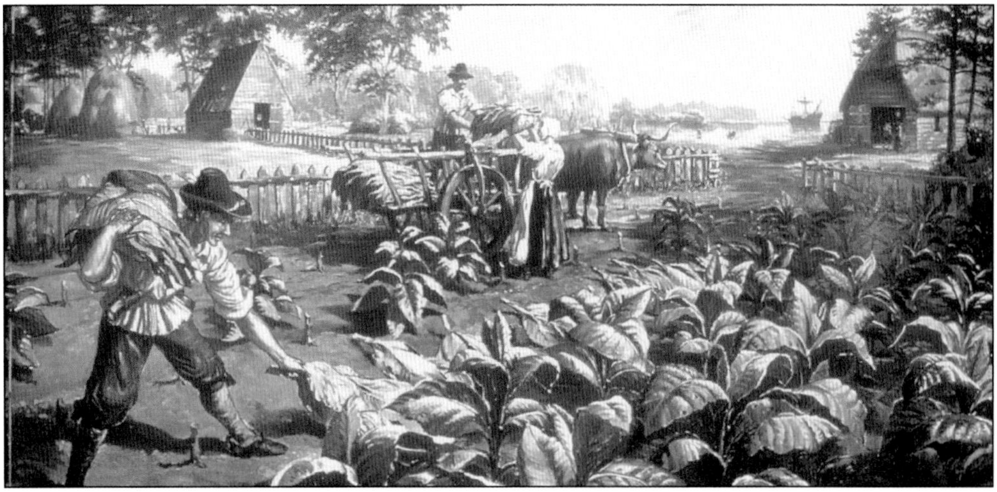

VIRGINIA'S GOLD. The fortunes of Hampton moved with the cycles of the tobacco trade. A most lucrative business with England and later with the Caribbean had Virginians growing the so-called weed in the streets. Tobacco exhausts the soil, depleting it of nitrogen. Elizabeth City County was the earliest Virginia locale to turn away from tobacco monoculture. (Painting by Sydney King; courtesy of National Park Service, Jamestown.)

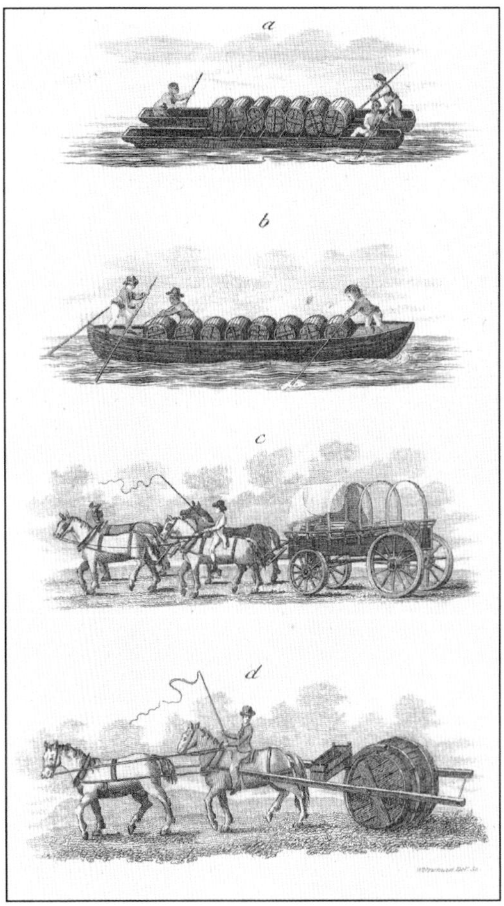

BRINGING TOBACCO TO MARKET. Tobacco was cut, dried, and pressed into half-ton barrels called hogsheads. As these engravings show, it was taken by water or land to Hampton's tobacco inspection warehouse. After bad leaves were removed, it was stored in the warehouse until spring shipment. Planters judged one's community standing by the quality of one's tobacco. Leaves were even used as currency. (Engravings by Basil Tatham; courtesy of Colonial Williamsburg Foundation.)

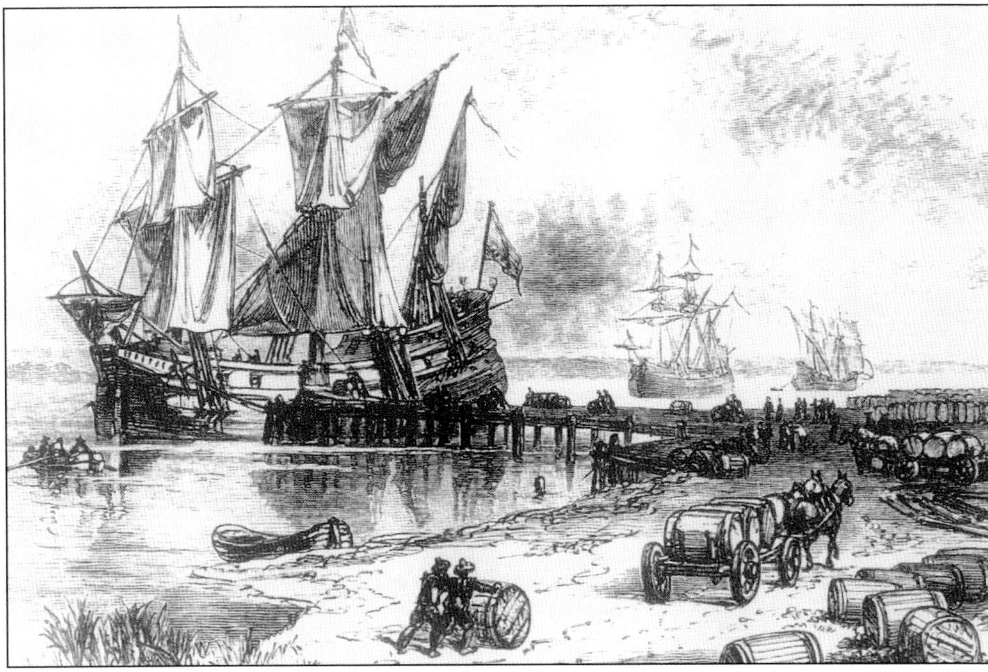

TOBACCO HOGSHEADS BEING LOADED. Planters gave possession of tobacco to "factors," or middlemen, working on commission. They in turn exchanged it in England for manufactured goods. The *Tristram and Jane*, a typical trading vessel landing in Hampton in 1636, had in its hold (among other items) Spanish wine, sugar, cheese, candles, nails, and a pair of scales. (Painting by Sydney King; courtesy of National Park Service, Jamestown.)

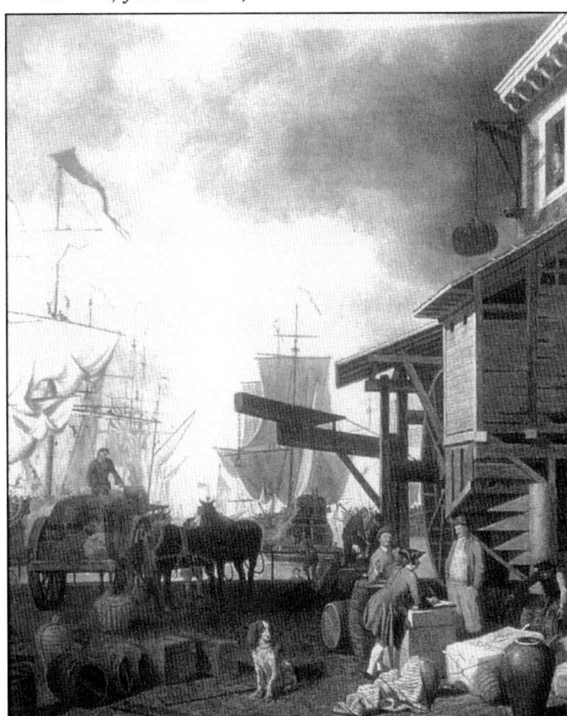

A BRITISH WHARF. The importance to trade of barrels, jars, wagons, hoists, chains, and warehouses is evident from this painting. Pictured is the process of dickering, plus draymen and warehousemen at work. Atlantic ports were cosmopolitan, with sea captains and merchants rubbing elbows with motley ship crewmen from all over the world. (Painting by Samuel Scott; courtesy of Colonial Williamsburg Foundation.)

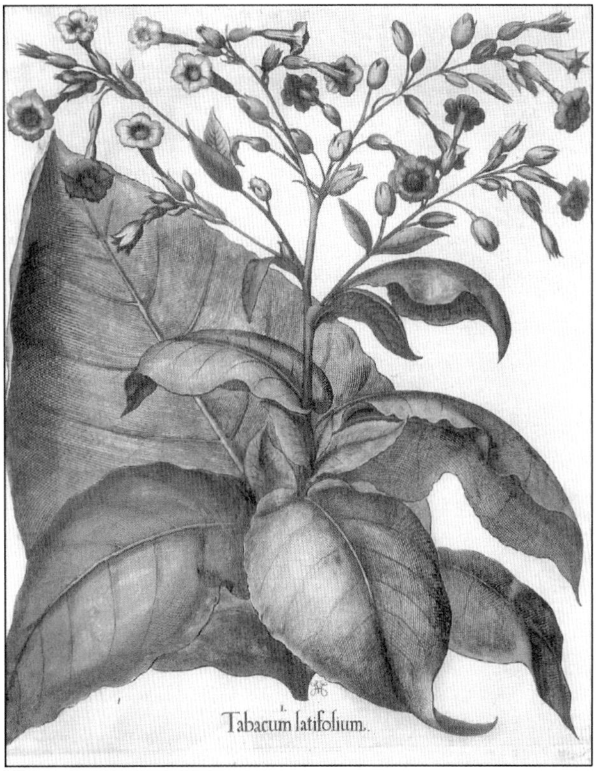

TOBACCO PLANT. The tobacco boom began with the first shipment to England in 1617. Kecoughtan became a bustling port as merchant fleets set sail in convoys to England that were manned by black and white crews. According to Ralph Hamor of the Virginia Company, "No country under the sun may, or doth afford a more pleasant, sweet, and strong tobacco than I have tasted here." (Courtesy of Colonial Williamsburg Foundation.)

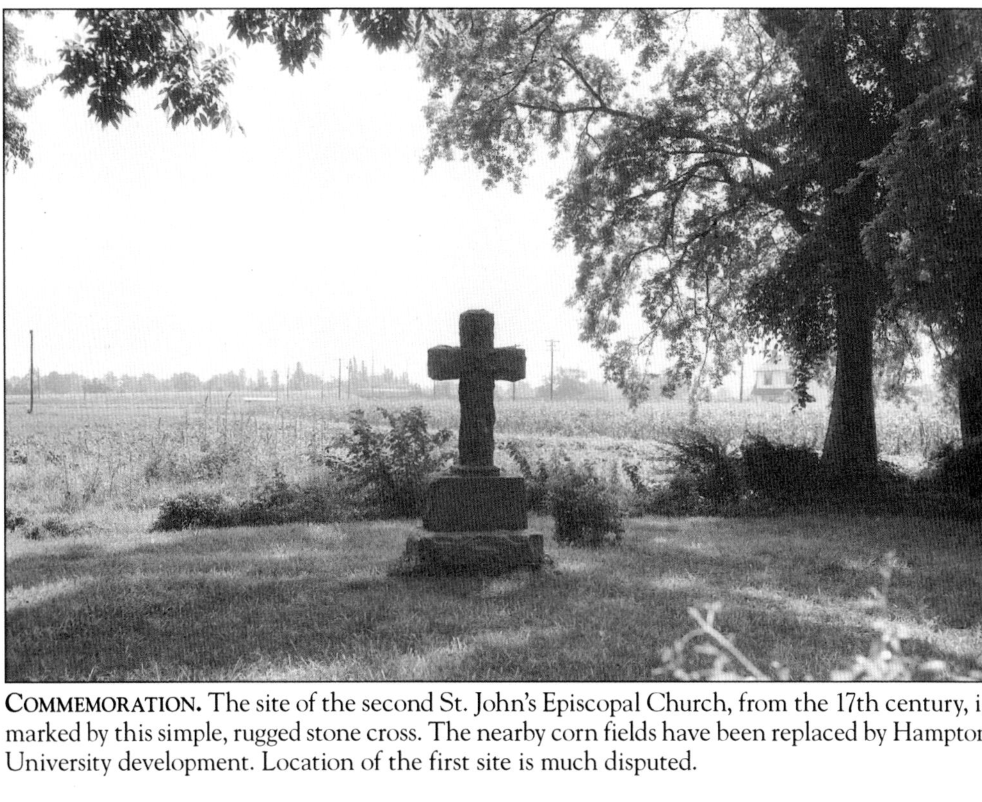

COMMEMORATION. The site of the second St. John's Episcopal Church, from the 17th century, is marked by this simple, rugged stone cross. The nearby corn fields have been replaced by Hampton University development. Location of the first site is much disputed.

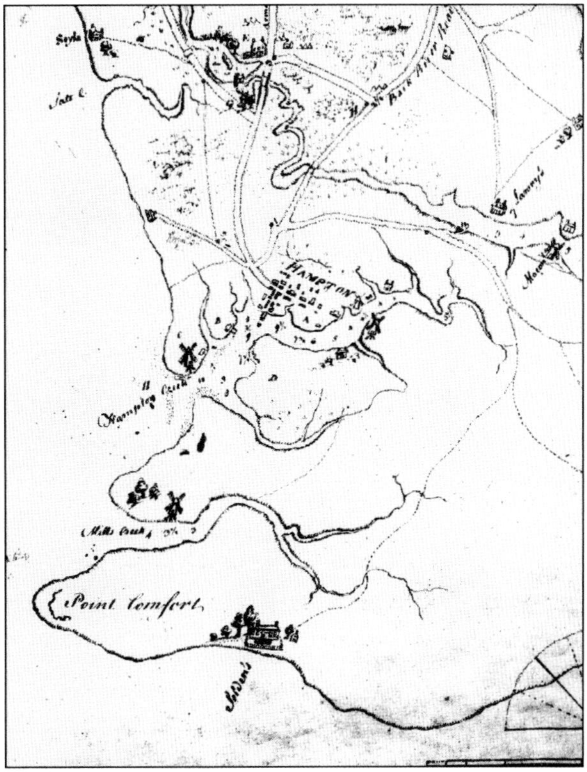

EARLY HAMPTON MAP. The crossing streets of Queen and King (note the town wharf) are visible in this mariner's map. Windmills, particularly the one on what is now Blackbeard's Point, and substantial houses on the shore would have been excellent mariners' aids. Point Comfort is shown as fortified.

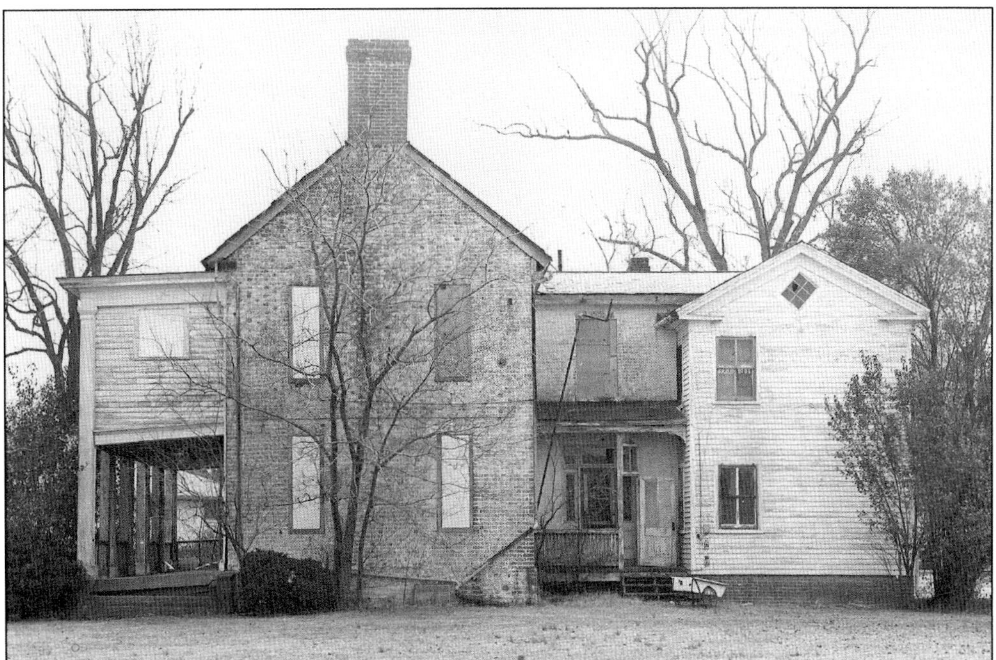

PASCO HERBERT HOUSE. Although this early 1980s photograph shows wooden additions in front and in back, the basic brick structure—the oldest dwelling still standing in Hampton—is visible. Built on what is now Armstrong's Point about 1753, the house has been stabilized and restored.

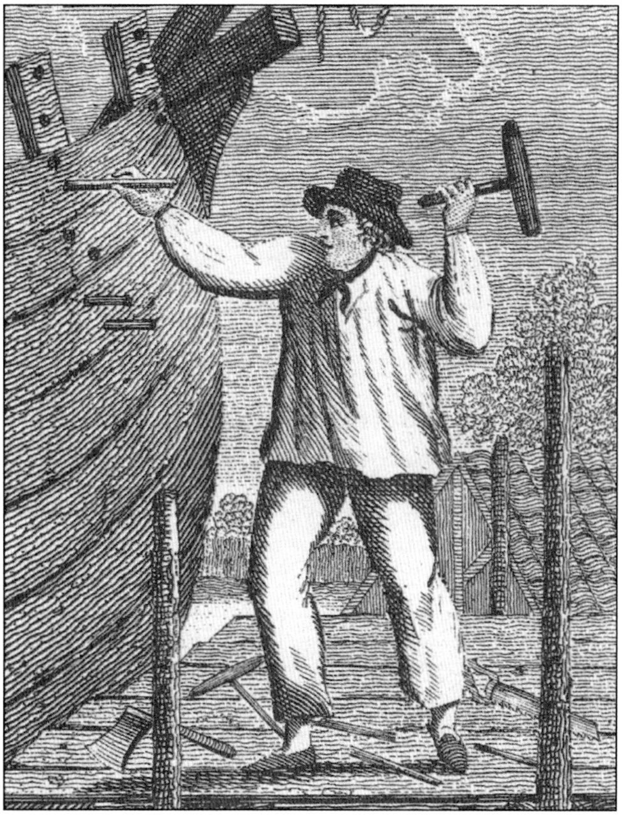

Keeping Commerce Afloat. A shipwright, the master of many trades needed to construct or repair a ship, knew how to design and build a sturdy, maneuverable, and watertight vessel tailored to the needs of its owner. George Hope's Hampton Shipyard built the 284-ton *Virginia Packet*, the largest ship constructed locally in the 1700s. (Image taken from *The Little Book of Trades.*)

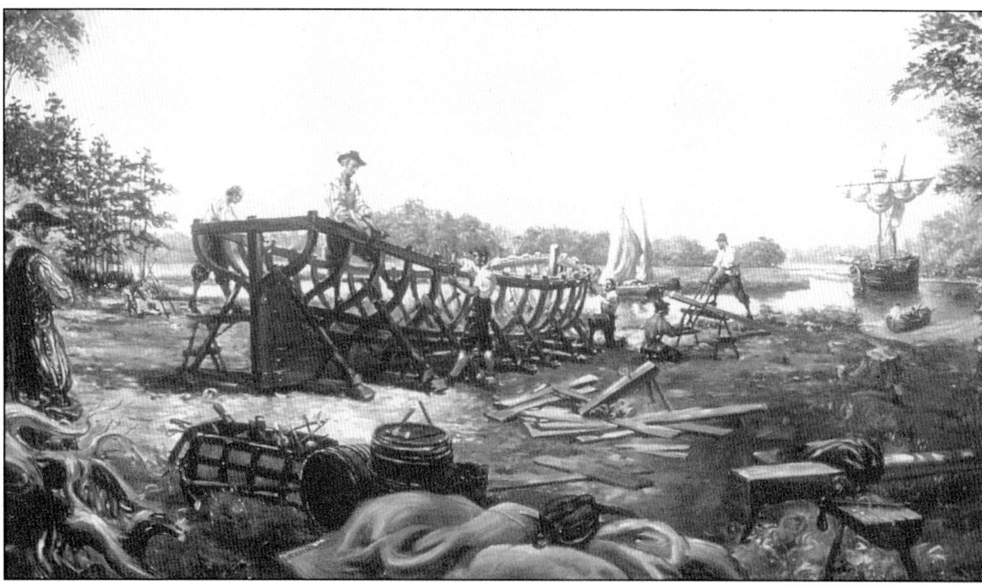

Shipbuilding. The sound of the adz shaping timber and the sight of men laboring along the waterfront fashioning watercraft essential for life became commonplace. The first recorded evidence of shipbuilding in the area occurred when the newly arrived colonial leader, Samuel Argyll, ordered the repair and construction of vessels for transportation and fishing at Point Comfort in 1619. (Painting by Sydney King; courtesy of National Park Service, Jamestown.)

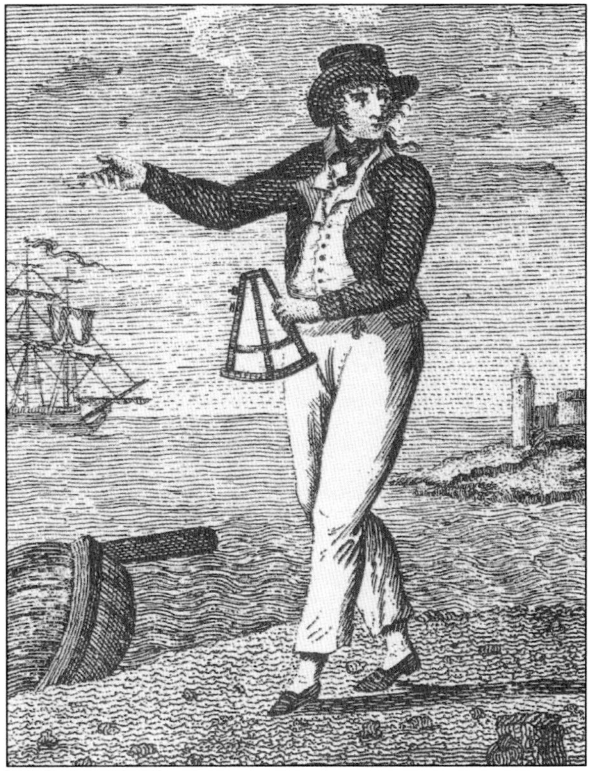

ABLE-BODIED SEAMEN. Seafaring men were part of both the upper and lower echelons of society. "Mariners" in Hampton, such as the man depicted here, were pilots. The highly skilled men who performed most of the dangerous and physically demanding work aboard ship, though well-paid, had low status, so few Virginians were seamen, and Hampton's waterfront was filled with foreigners. (Image taken from *The Little Book of Trades*.)

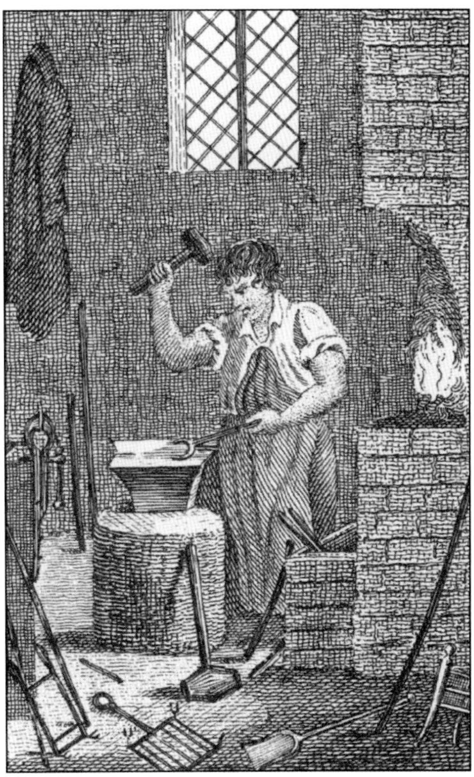

MEN WORKING WITH FIRE. Blacksmiths made and repaired tools used in the production of tobacco, as well as tools for use by coopers and other craftsmen. Importantly, they shod horses. They also forged door latches, pintles, and hinges for domestic use. Archaeologists have recovered many specimens of the work of blacksmiths from excavations in Hampton. (Image taken from *The Little Book of Trades*.)

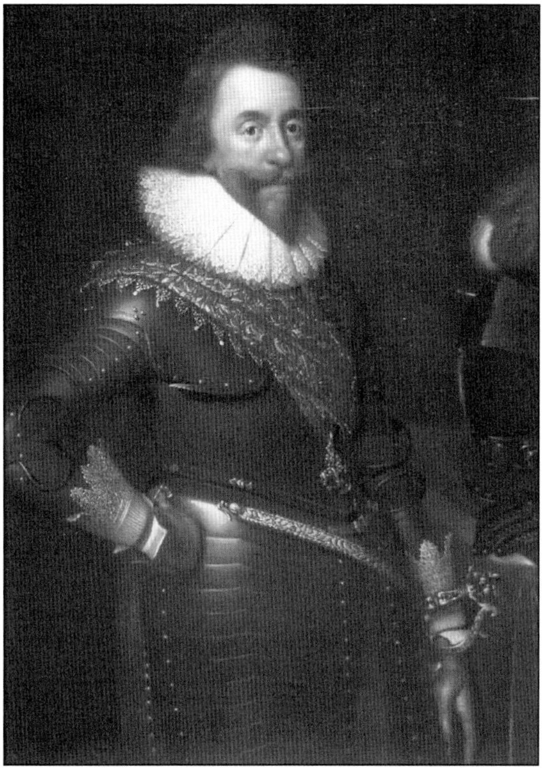

HAMPTON'S NAMESAKE. Hampton received its present name in 1706 after Henry Wriothesley, the third earl of Southampton. He was a steadfast supporter of English exploration and colonial expansion in the New World, though he never crossed the Atlantic Ocean. An investor in the Virginia Company, Wriothesley served as its treasurer. (Painting by studio of Michiel Merault; courtesy of Jamestown-Yorktown Foundation.)

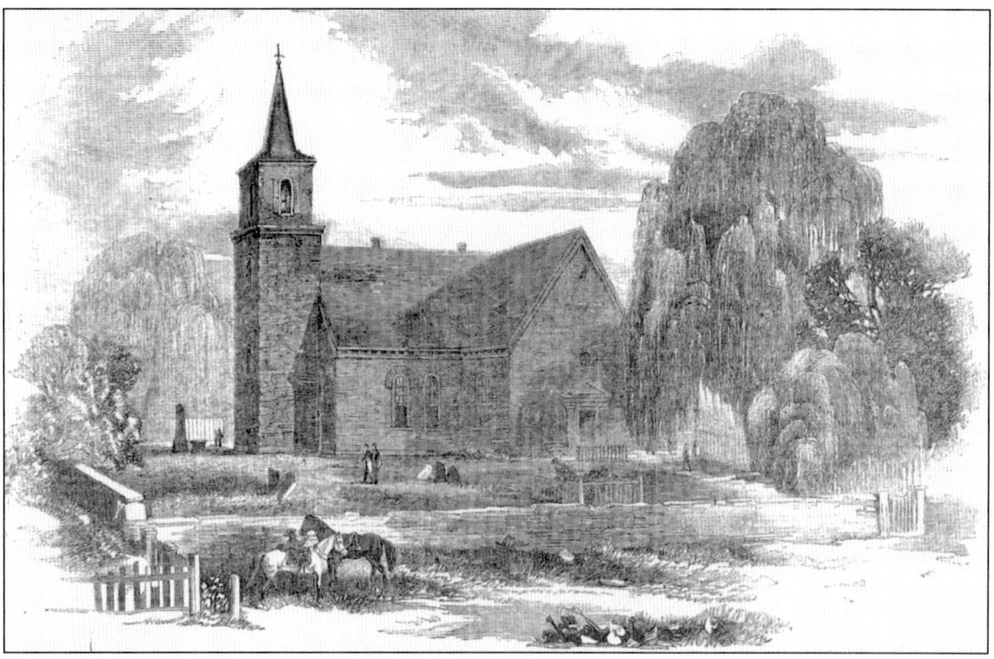

ST. JOHN'S EPISCOPAL CHURCH. In 1727, responding to the needs of the growing town, land on the west end of Queen Street was designated for the new church building. Bricks were made from clay dug on the site. The belfry was added in 1762. No other church or denomination was sanctioned in Hampton until the American Revolution. (Sketch in *Frank Leslie's*.)

BLACKBEARD. Pirates were rebels, escaping the strictures of a rigidly classed society to prey on commerce. Edward Teach, the most feared pirate of his day, was killed after a fierce battle in North Carolina waters. Teach's head was impaled on a pole near a spit of land in Hampton River as a warning to others. Today the site is known as Blackbeard's Point. (Courtesy of Virginia Historical Society.)

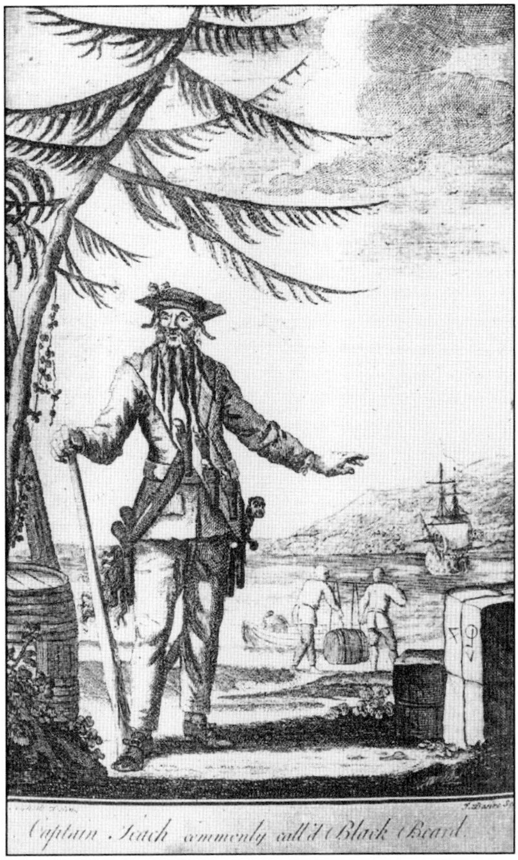

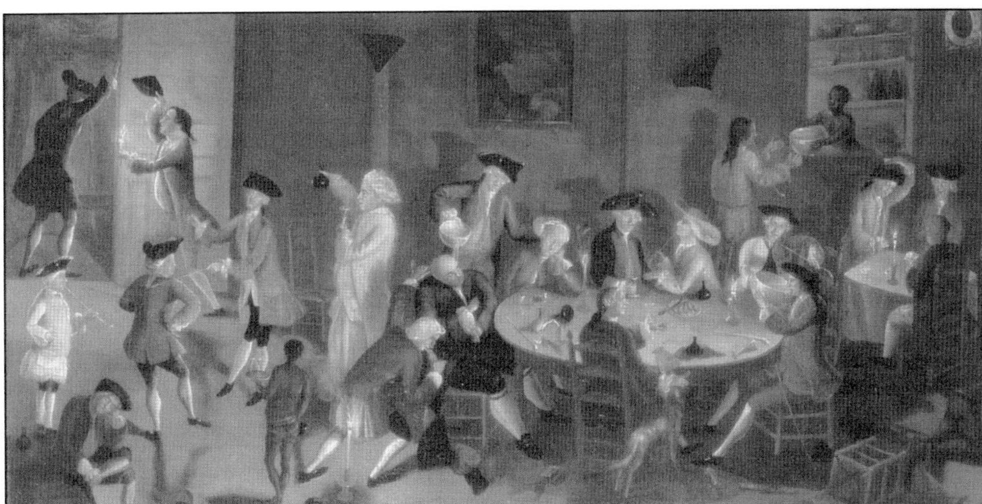

TAVERNS. Taverns were especially essential in ports. Finer establishments served sea captains, merchants, and planters, while more rough-and-tumble taverns offered spirits, food, and prostitutes to seamen, watermen, and other workers. All were cozy, dark, and boisterous. British sailors once threatened to burn Hampton down when they were denied what they thought was sufficient food and drink at a tavern. (Painting by John Greenwood; courtesy of St. Louis Art Museum.)

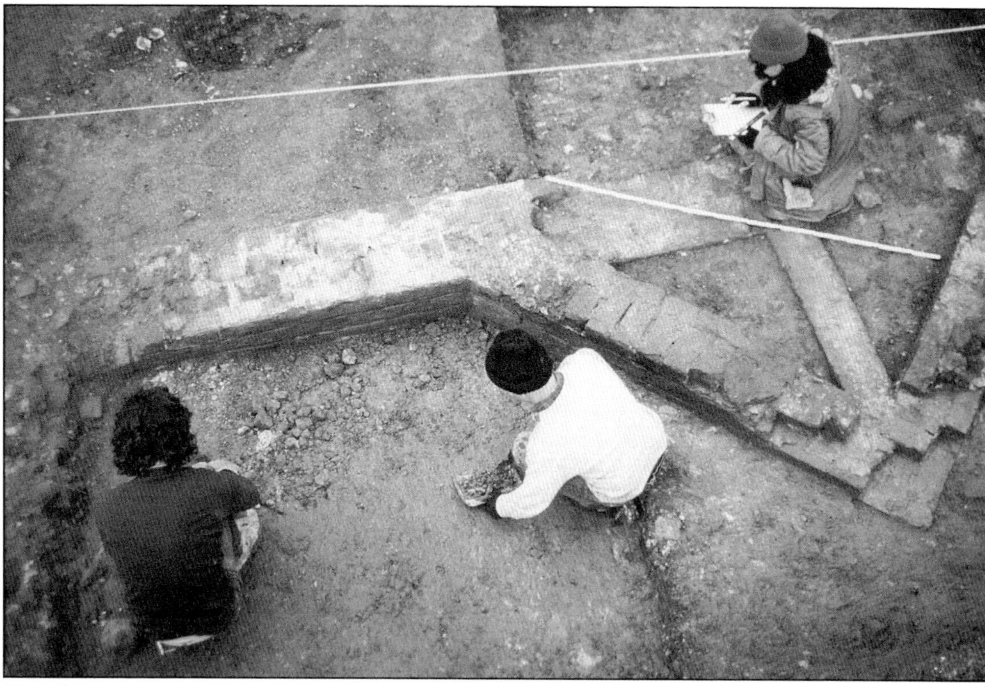

THE BUNCH OF GRAPES. This photograph shows the excavation of a corner chimney at the Bunch of Grapes Tavern. An advertisement in the *Virginia Gazette* in October 1767 described the tavern as: "A very convenient well furnished dwelling-house with four good rooms on the lower floor, and two above, with a fireplace in each room . . . it commands a very fine prospect [of] the [Hampton] River and the Bay."

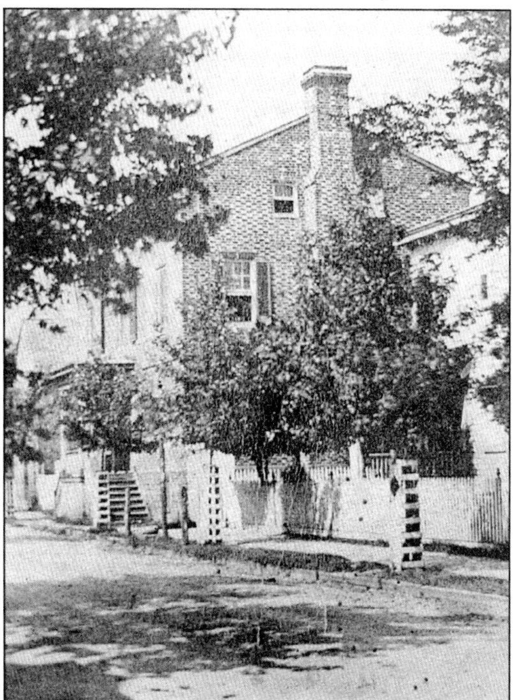

"THE OLD BRICK HOUSE." Two of its names were the Brick House Tavern and the King's Arms Tavern. Madame Brown, visiting Hampton in 1755, found it "a very agreable Place, and all the Houses extremely neat." She dined at the King's Arms, eating "ham and turkey, a breast of veal and oysters," and drank "Madeira wine, punch and cyder." The tavern-keeper was Mary Brough.

THE GROWTH OF SOUTH KING STREET. These are artists' reconstructions of the area that became south King Street in 1691. The upper picture bears a date of about 1680, while the lower one is dated perhaps 100 years later. Archaeologists provided the evidence from several excavations conducted to make way for modern structures. By about 1775, several substantial homes and business buildings existed along a well-defined street oriented, unlike the earlier structures, toward the wharf at the end of the street (not shown). The building at the left end of the street in the later drawing is the Bunch of Grapes Tavern, while the King's Arms Tavern is at the center on the other side of the street. (Drawings by Willie Graham and Jeffrey Bostetter; courtesy of William and Mary Center for Archaeological Research.)

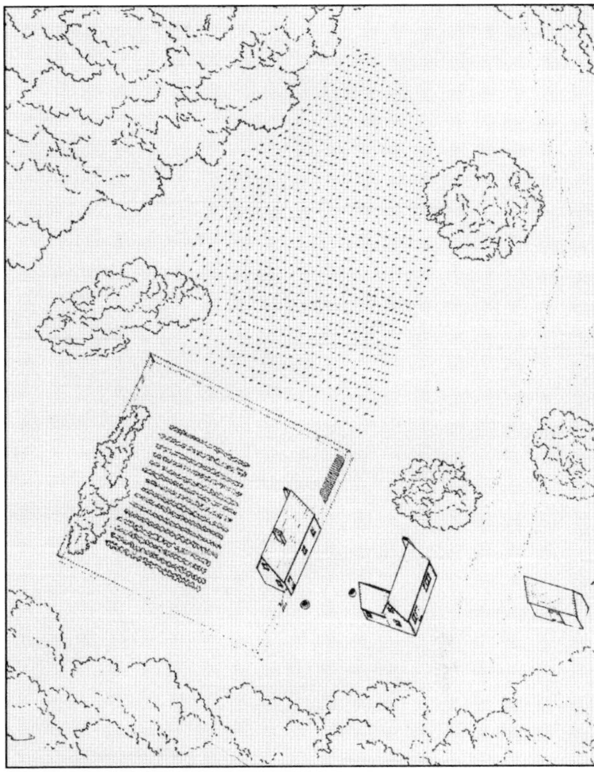

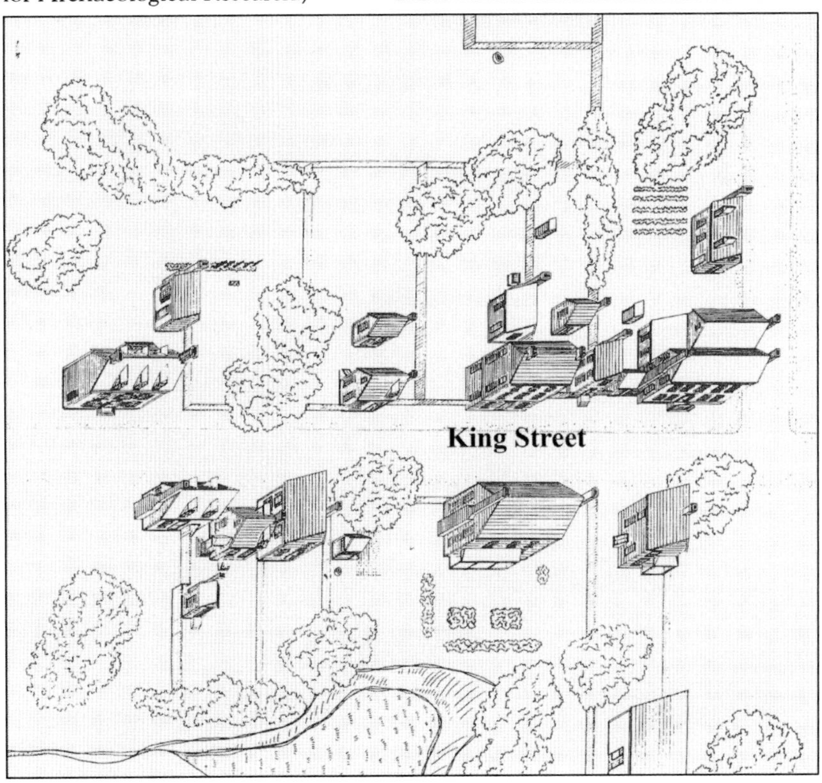

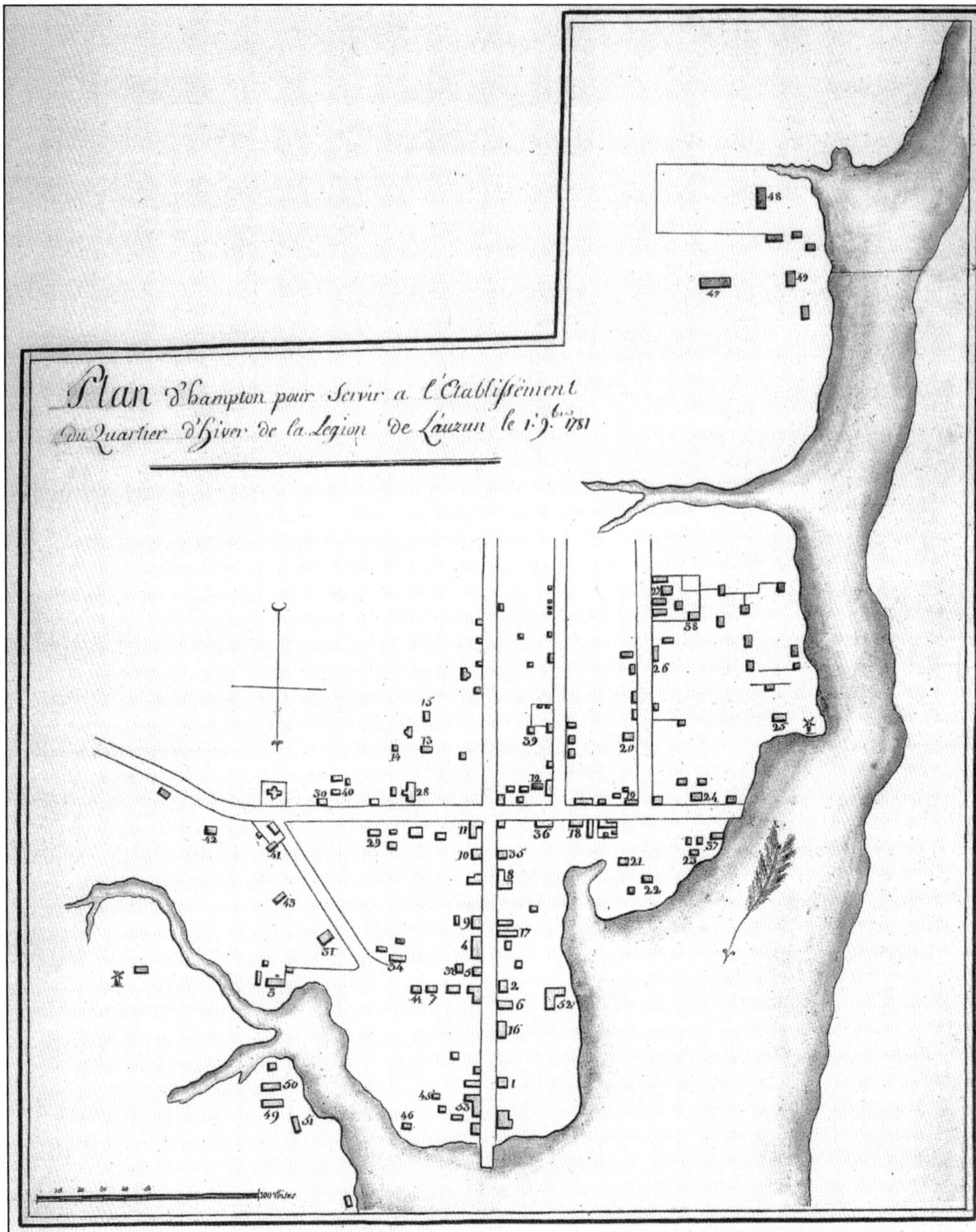

106 PLAN OF HAMPTON [IN VIRGINIA] TO BE USED FOR ESTABLISHING THE WINTER QUARTERS OF LAUZUN'S LEGION, 1 NOVEMBER 1781

FRENCHMAN'S MAP, 1781. This map was drawn by a cartographer named Berthier to identify quarters for French soldiers during the Yorktown campaign. About 100 shops, houses, and other buildings are shown, including St. John's Church (at the arrow). Building No. 53 is the Bunch of Grapes Tavern, building No. 16 is the King's Arms Tavern, and building No. 52 may have been the tobacco warehouse. (Courtesy of Princeton University.)

Three

Revolution; War of 1812

Hampton's most famous son, George Wythe, as a member of the Continental Congress spoke persuasively for freedom from Britain. Wythe signed the Declaration of Independence in 1776, was a delegate to the Constitutional Convention in 1787, was an important judge, and taught law to Thomas Jefferson, John Marshall, Henry Clay, and generations of American patriots.

A British naval squadron threatened to burn Hampton in October 1775, six months after the opening shots of the American Revolution reverberated from Lexington and Concord, Massachusetts. Hastily assembled local militiamen repulsed the British ships as they bombarded the town.

In the War of 1812, the town was pillaged after an unsuccessful attempt by overmatched local militias to save it. Ashamed of the ease with which the British stormed the American seacoast, presidents James Madison and James Monroe determined to fortify it. Fort Monroe was sited near where Fort Algernoune and its hurricane-ruined successor, Fort George, had stood on Point Comfort, and Fort Calhoun (later Fort Wool) was thrown up on the "Rip Raps," a man-made island guarding the entrance to Hampton Roads.

As ships grew larger and as a growing sandbar made river entry difficult, Hampton was in decline as a major port by 1812. Presidents Andrew Jackson and John Tyler each established temporary residences there, and tourists enjoyed the nationally famous Hygeia Hotel, built at Old Point Comfort in 1822.

The Chesapeake Female Seminary opened its doors to young women in 1854. Two schools named Hampton Academy appeared. The first was opened in 1805 to give free elementary education to poor and worthy boys and girls, consolidating separate schools established in Colonial times by bequests of Benjamin Syms and Thomas Eaton. The second, near the first, was opened by John B. Cary in 1852, charged tuition, had a military branch for the boys, attracted pupils from other states, and was sometimes known as the Hampton Military Academy.

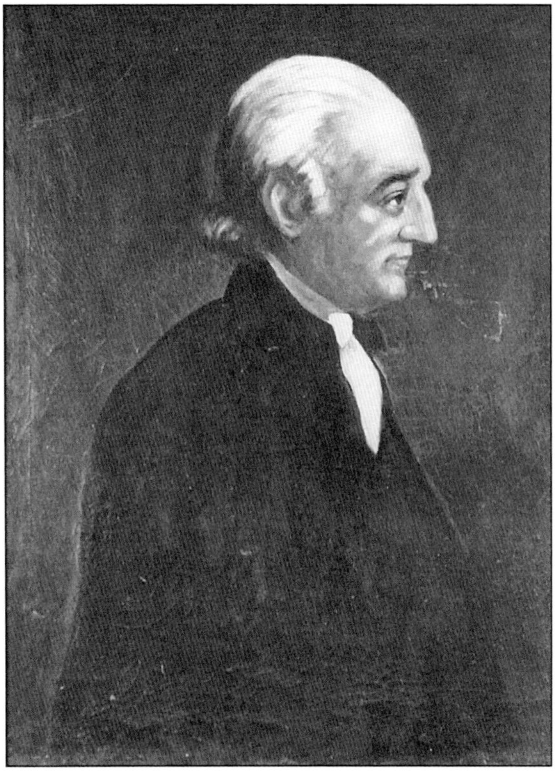

GEORGE WYTHE. The famous lawyer inherited Chesterville, a plantation now forming part of Langley Field. As a member of the local gentry, Wythe sat as a justice on the Elizabeth City County Court and represented the county and town in the General Assembly. Reputed to be the most erudite judge of his age, he had been schooled in the classics by his Quaker mother, Margaret.

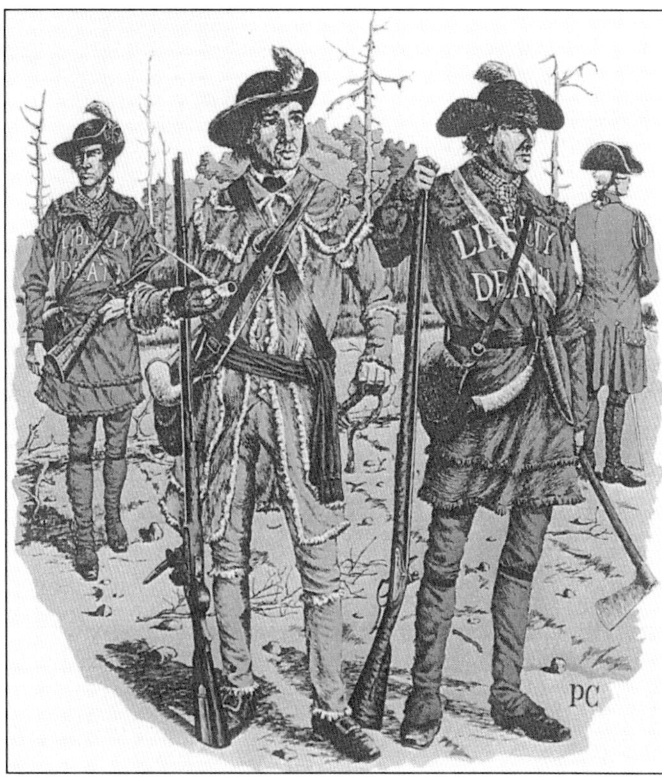

VIRGINIA MILITIAMEN. All free white males were required to serve in the militia for the community's defense. They had to provide their own weapons, and they elected lower-ranking officers. They defended Hampton in 1776, but were no match for the British in 1812. Gen. Andrew Jackson warned the inhabitants of New Orleans that they might share Hampton's fate. (Courtesy of the Company of Military Historians.)

VIRGINIA'S LEXINGTON AND CONCORD. This fanciful drawing of the Battle of Hampton appeared in a late 19th-century Virginia children's schoolbook, Mary Tucker Magill's *History of Virginia*, to teach about the beginning of the Revolutionary War. In the actual battle, local militiamen, reinforced by regulars from Williamsburg, so thoroughly raked the decks of the five British ships with their rifle fire that the British withdrew.

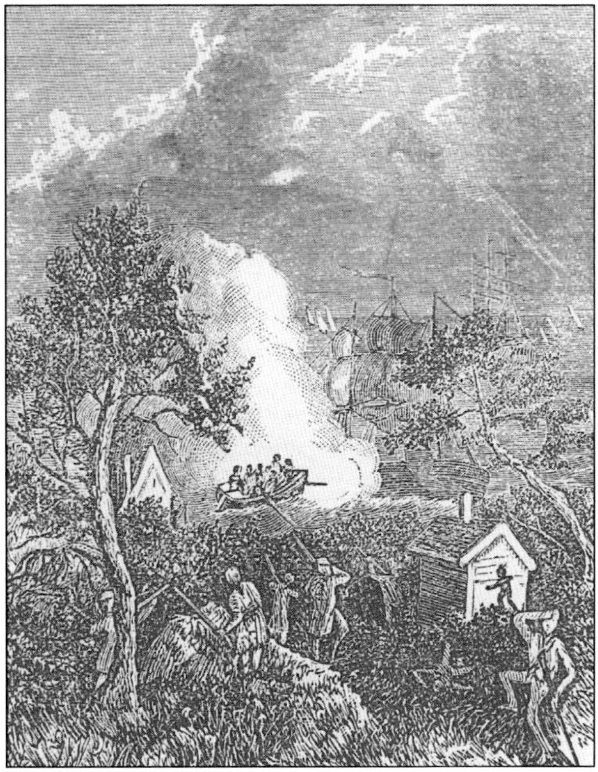

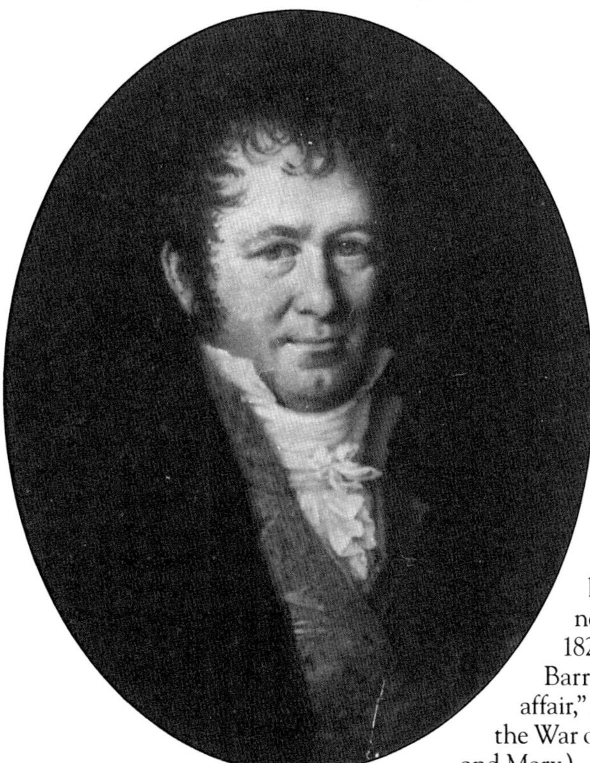

COMMODORE BARRON. The seafaring Barron family of Hampton produced notable naval captains in the American Revolution, the War of 1812, and the Civil War. British impressment of sailors from James Barron's ship *Chesapeake* in 1807 helped lead to the War of 1812. He became notorious for killing Stephen Decatur in 1820 in a duel over Decatur's criticism of Barron's conduct during "the Chesapeake affair," a controversial event that helped lead to the War of 1812. (Courtesy of College of William and Mary.)

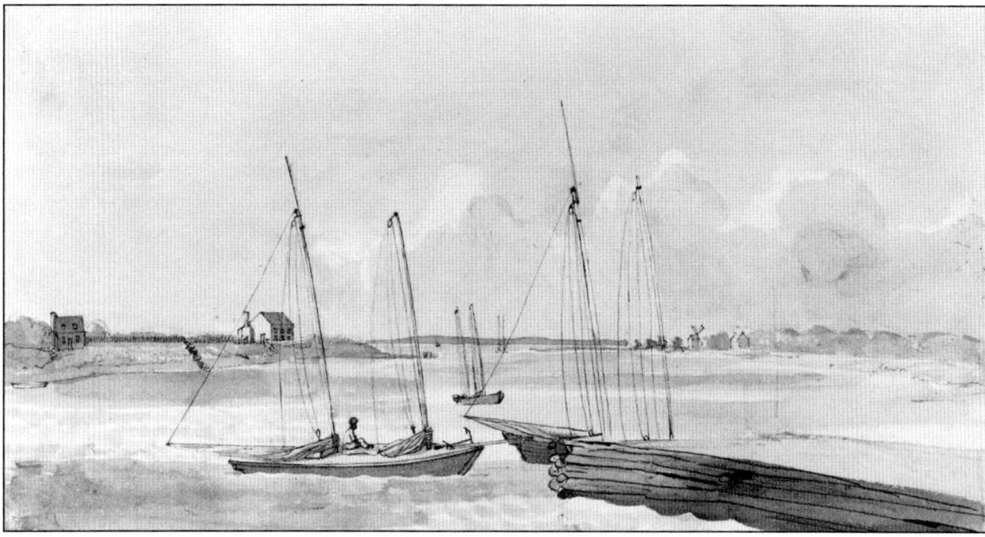

Hampton Harbor, about 1798. Benjamin Latrobe designed the U.S. Capitol. When visiting Hampton, the architect and watercolorist recorded this view of Hampton River from the foot of King Street. The Herbert House and windmill are at the top right with Blackbeard's Point stretching into the river. John and Judith Herbert's four sons served in the American Revolution. (Courtesy of Maryland Historical Society.)

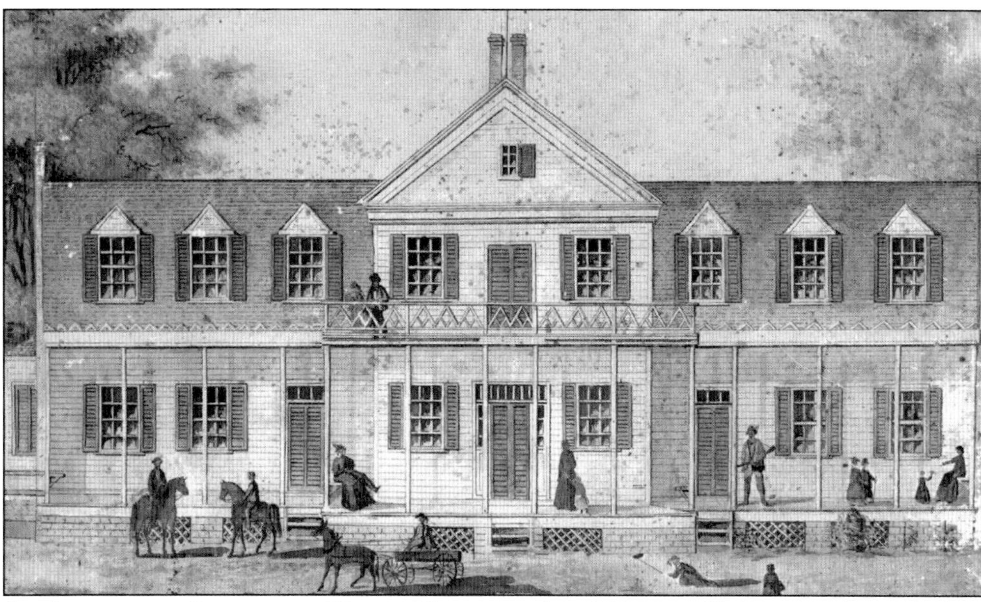

An Antebellum Plantation House. This watercolor of "Sherwood," George and Ann Booker's plantation on the present site of Langley Field, was supposedly drawn by a Union soldier. Booker, a William and Mary graduate, was a Democratic politician of national stature. At first a Unionist, he accepted secession and became a major in the Confederate quartermaster corps. (Courtesy of Richard and Sandra Sherwood von Schilling and Sherwood Scott von Schilling.)

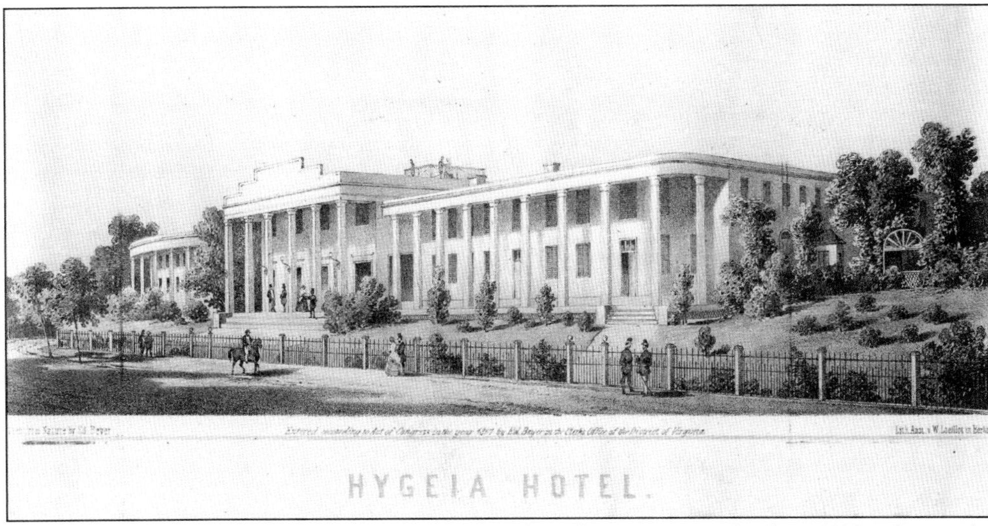

THE HYGEIA HOTEL. Located on Old Point Comfort, the Hygeia was built in 1822 to house the workers erecting nearby Fort Monroe. Soon this elegant hotel began attracting vacationers from across the nation. Among them were Henry Clay and Edmund Ruffin, while Pres. John Tyler and his second bride, Julia Gardiner, honeymooned there. It was demolished during the Civil War. (Lithograph by Ed. Beyer; courtesy of the Library of Congress.)

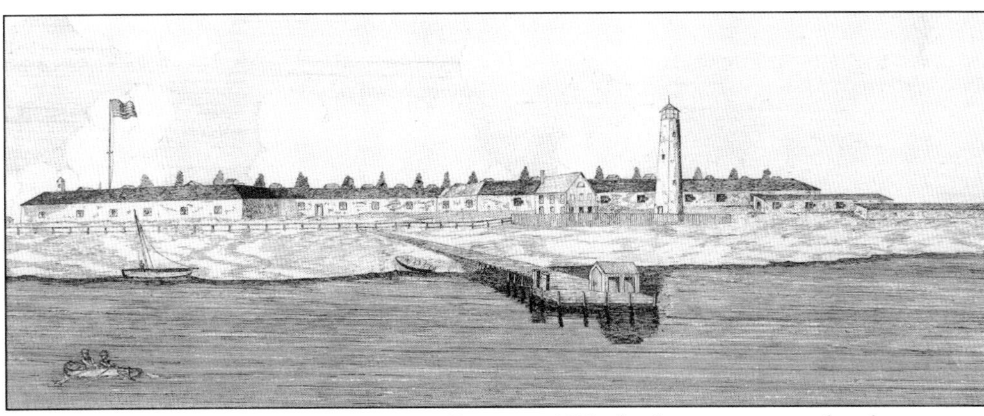

SKETCH OF FORT MONROE, ABOUT 1850. Begun in 1819, this largest seacoast fortification ever erected in the United States was situated on Old Point Comfort to defend Hampton Roads against naval aggression. A distinguished army engineer who had served under Napoleon, Gen. Simon Bernard, designed it. West Point–trained engineer Lt. Robert E. Lee completed the construction in 1834. The lighthouse was built in 1802.

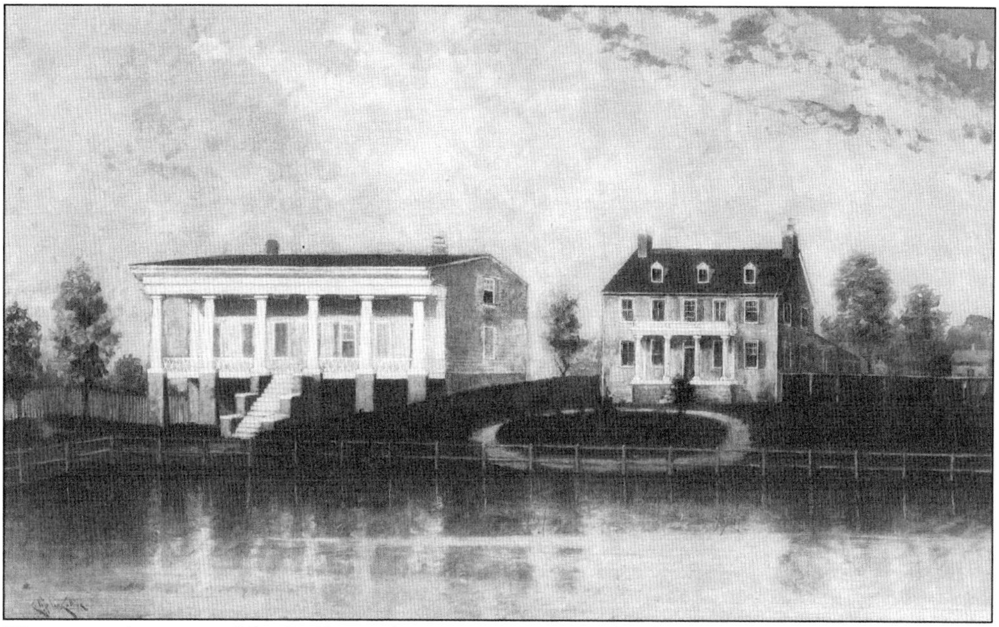

HAMPTON ACADEMY. John B. Cary, a longtime Hampton schoolmaster, built Hampton Academy on Pee Dee Point in 1852. Benjamin West, a student, recalled: "Cary made his a military academy . . . Cary also built quite a large dwelling and kept boarders; the boys slept in the third story of the academy [above right], the girls in his house." (Painting by Charles Myles Collier; courtesy of Robert Mclanahan Smith III.)

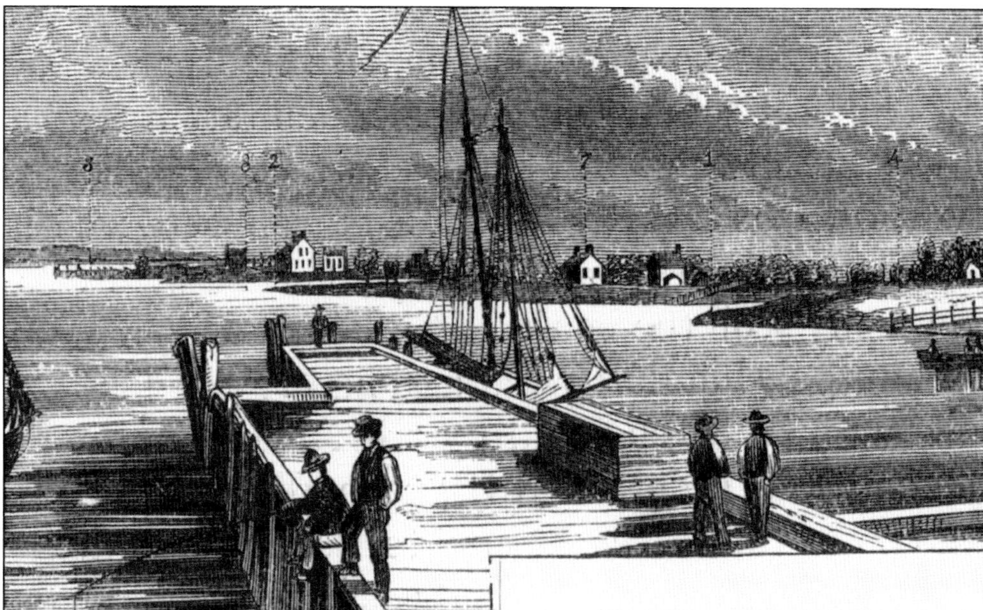

THE KING STREET WHARF, EARLY 1850S. Hampton appeared to the visitor who wrote on this card as a historic, "rather pretty village" on the water's edge. One of its tree-lined streets led to the town wharf. Its houses were brick or white wood, some with stately columns, and were often "flanked by flower gardens in the front and vegetable gardens in the rear." The slave cabins in the back yards reminded him of "shoe shops."

Four

Hampton Burns in the Civil War

The sectional crisis arrived in 1861. Though Unionist sentiment was strong in Hampton, in May, Hampton's citizens ratified Virginia's vote to secede.

A number of Hampton's men, including students at the Hampton Academy, enrolled in the Hampton Grays and the Wythe Rifles, as part of the 32nd Virginia Infantry. The regiment fought in the Peninsula Campaign; at Antietam, where it suffered a staggering 48 percent casualty rate; at Cold Harbor; and at the siege of Petersburg. Hamptonians were important members of the Confederate navy.

Fort Monroe remained in Union hands throughout the conflict. It served as an important symbol of union and a springboard from which expeditions were sent against Confederate seacoast holdings.

Confederate general John B. Magruder ordered Capt. Jefferson C. Phillips's troops to put Hampton to the torch on August 7, 1861, to prevent its occupation by Union troops and to prevent its use as an abode for escaped slaves. The brick husks of several buildings survived.

While many people had already left town, in the dead of night the rest of the white noncombatants were transported to North Carolina, Richmond, or elsewhere. Richmond's citizens established a relief fund for displaced Hamptonians.

In the spring of 1862, the Union's army of the Potomac under Gen. George B. McClellan launched the ill-fated Peninsula Campaign from Fort Monroe in an attempt to reach the Confederate capital at Richmond. The Union army was massive, comparable to the population of America's largest cities.

The murderous, bleak, and exhausting war finally ended in April 1865. Hamptonians returned to the ashes of their town to begin anew. Former Confederates began to rebuild their homes, farms, and businesses.

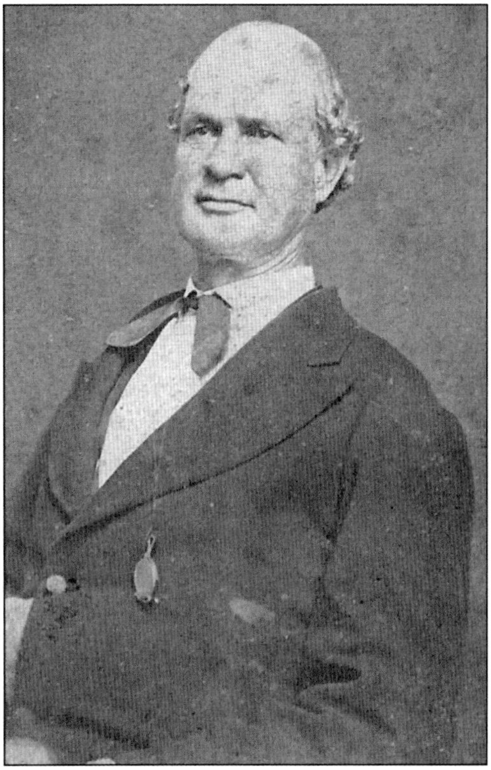

CHARLES KING MALLORY. As Hampton's delegate to the Virginia Secession Convention in April 1861, Mallory represented local sentiment by voting to stay in the Union. But Hampton greeted the news of the firing on Fort Sumter with cannon fire and fireworks, and by the time a sally from Union-held Fort Monroe disrupted the town's secession vote in late May, citizens had changed their minds. They voted 360-6 to ratify secession.

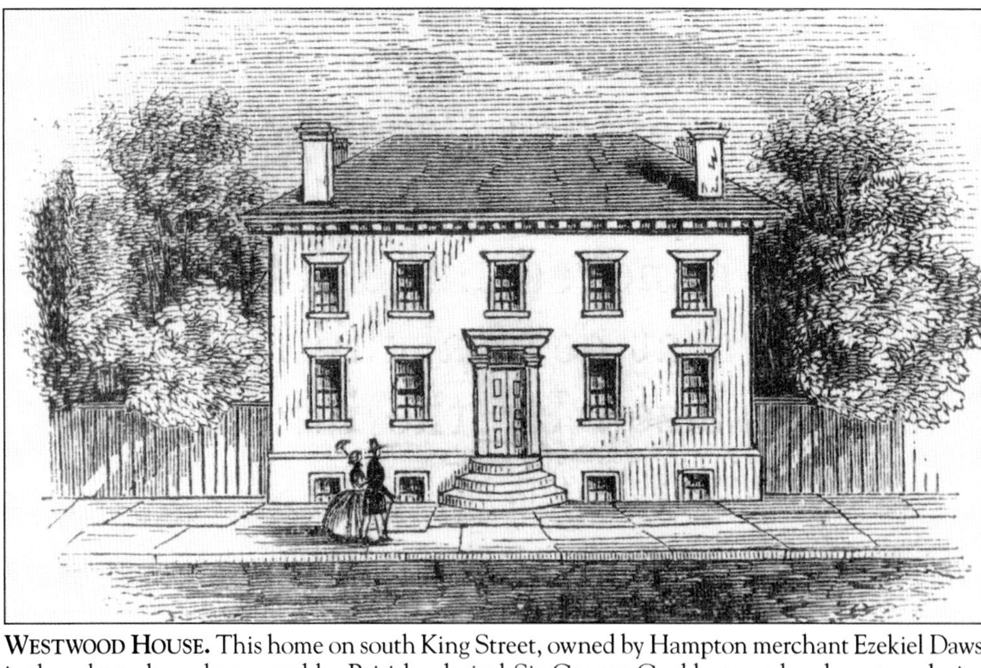

WESTWOOD HOUSE. This home on south King Street, owned by Hampton merchant Ezekiel Daws, is thought to have been used by British admiral Sir George Cockburn as headquarters during the War of 1812. One of Hampton's most stately residences, it was previously owned by Worlich Westwood, who was active in provincial politics, serving in the Virginia House of Burgesses. During the Civil War, it was consumed during Hampton's burning.

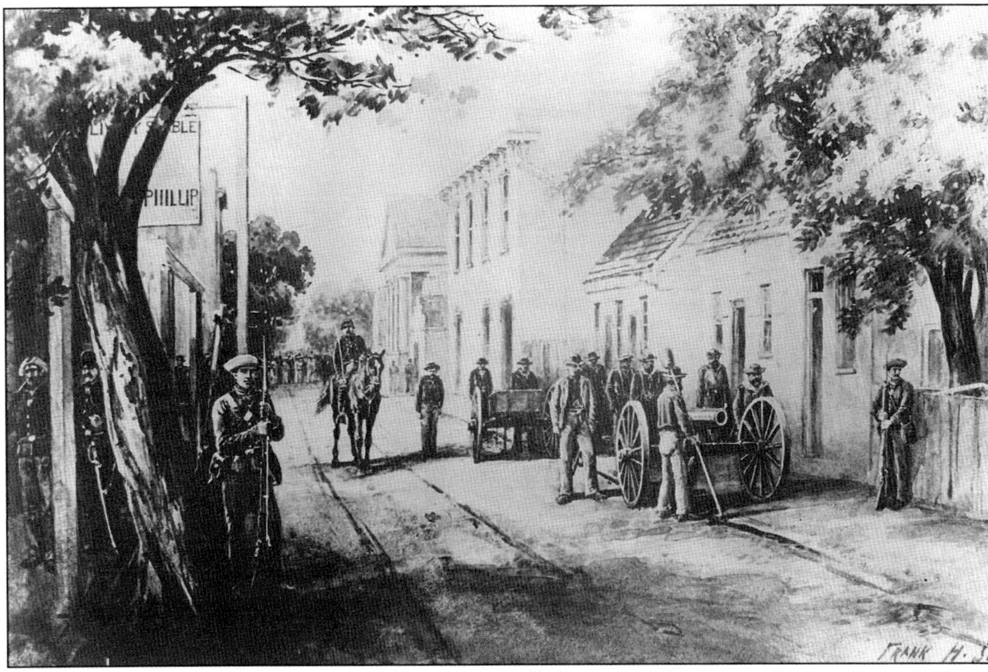

CONFEDERATE TROOPS ADVANCE. This June 1861 drawing, which may be conjectural, shows Southern troops with an artillery piece positioned for action on a "main street" of Hampton, likely King Street. The columned building may be the City Bank. No military contest for Hampton occurred during the Civil War. Note the wagon ruts in the unpaved roadway. (Sketch by Frank H. Schell in *Harper's Weekly*.)

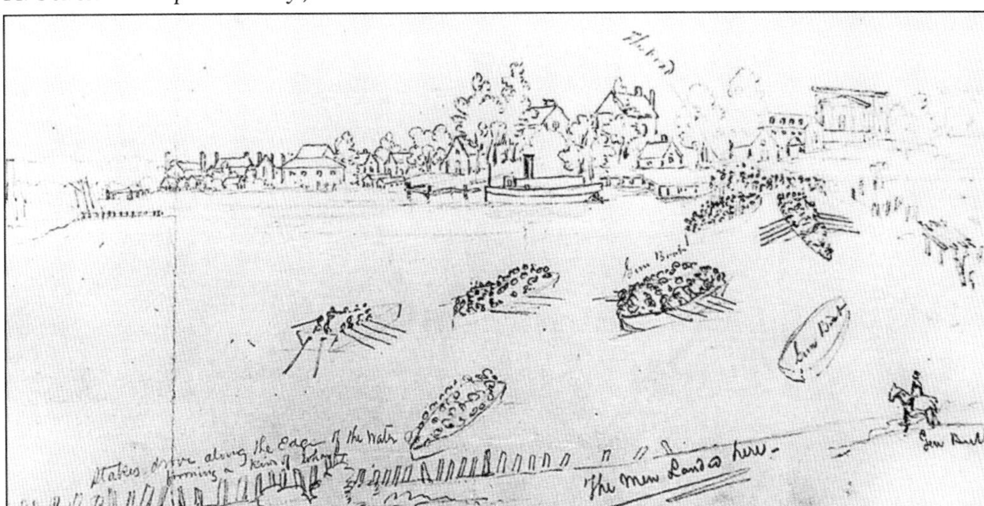

FIRST LAND ENGAGEMENT OF THE CIVIL WAR. The Battle of Big Bethel was fought nearby on June 10, 1861. The outnumbered Confederates under Col. D. H. Hill were victorious, encouraging Southern belief in an early victory. This eyewitness sketch shows Union troops retreating down Queen Street through Hampton and across Hampton River, watched by defeated Gen. Benjamin Butler (lower right). (Courtesy of Chevy Chase Bank.)

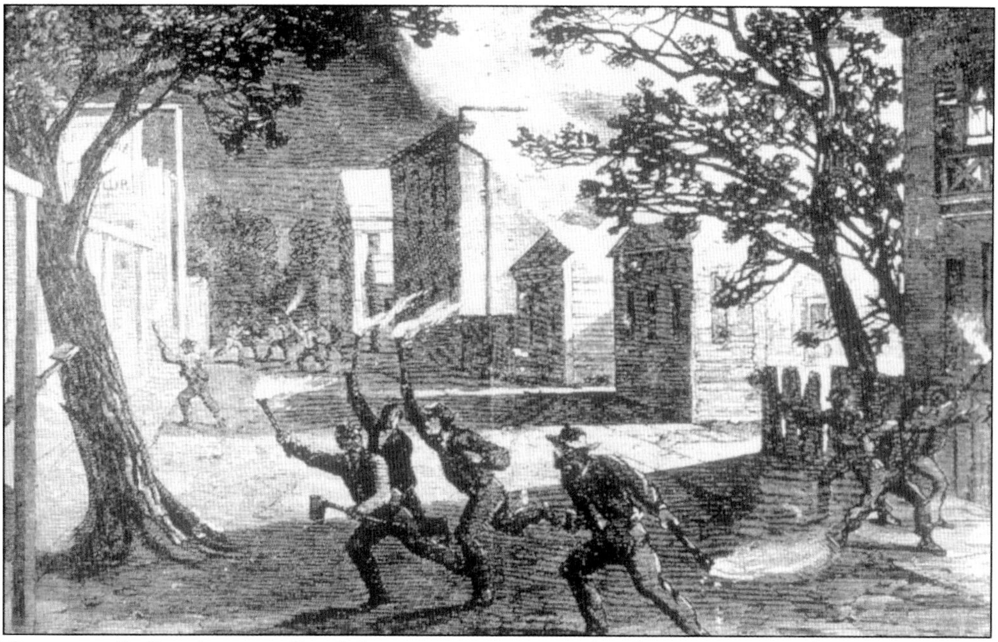

HAMPTON IS SET ABLAZE. Confederate troops converged at the intersection of King and Queen Streets on August 7, 1861, fanning into the four quarters of the town created by the "cross streets" to carry out General Magruder's orders to torch its buildings. Many, including General Butler at Fort Monroe, were surprised at what they judged to be an unnecessary immolation of Hampton. (Sketch in *Harper's Weekly*.)

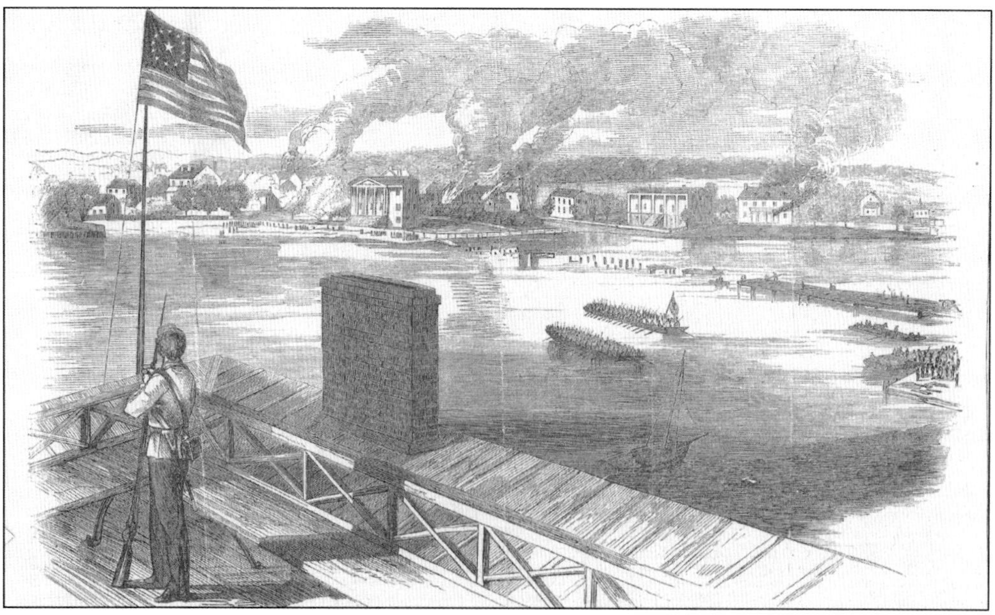

THE BURNING OF HAMPTON. This drawing, published three days after the fire, depicts the town aflame as seen from Villa Margaret's rooftop and gives one of the best ideas of what antebellum Hampton looked like. Cary's Hampton Academy buildings are at center right. The Confederates also destroyed the Queen Street bridge (built in 1822 as a toll bridge) to halt Union progress up the peninsula. (Sketch in *Frank Leslie's*.)

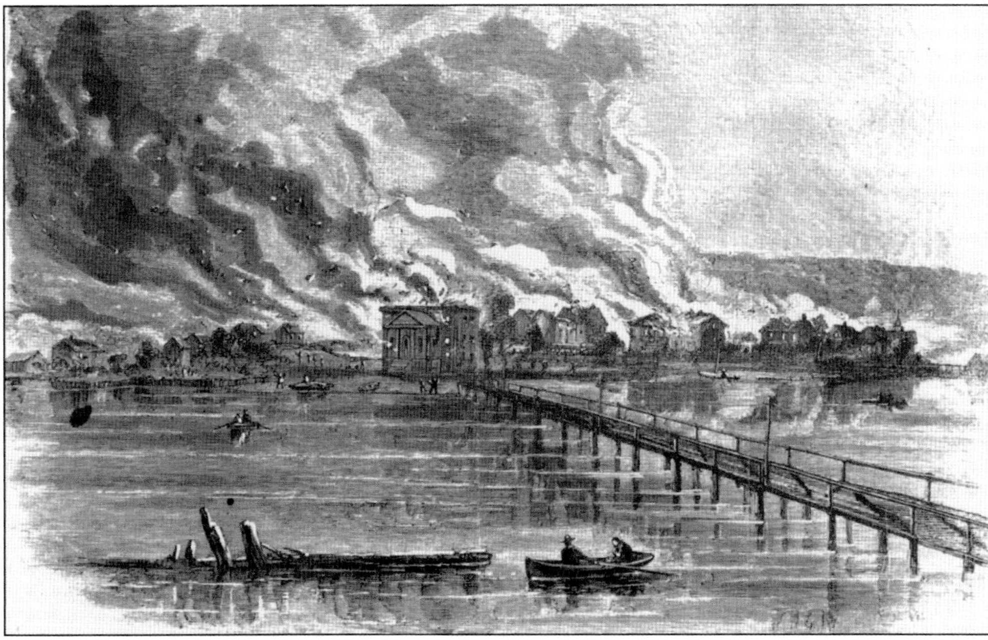

ANOTHER VIEW OF THE CONFLAGRATION. "The houses were entered and fired, and soon the whole town was enveloped in flame casting a bright light over the bay," a Union soldier recalled. Five hundred structures were destroyed, though some survived at least in part. The ruins of many buildings were subsequently ransacked by soldiers and "contrabands" (escaped slaves allowed freedom by General Butler) searching for building materials.

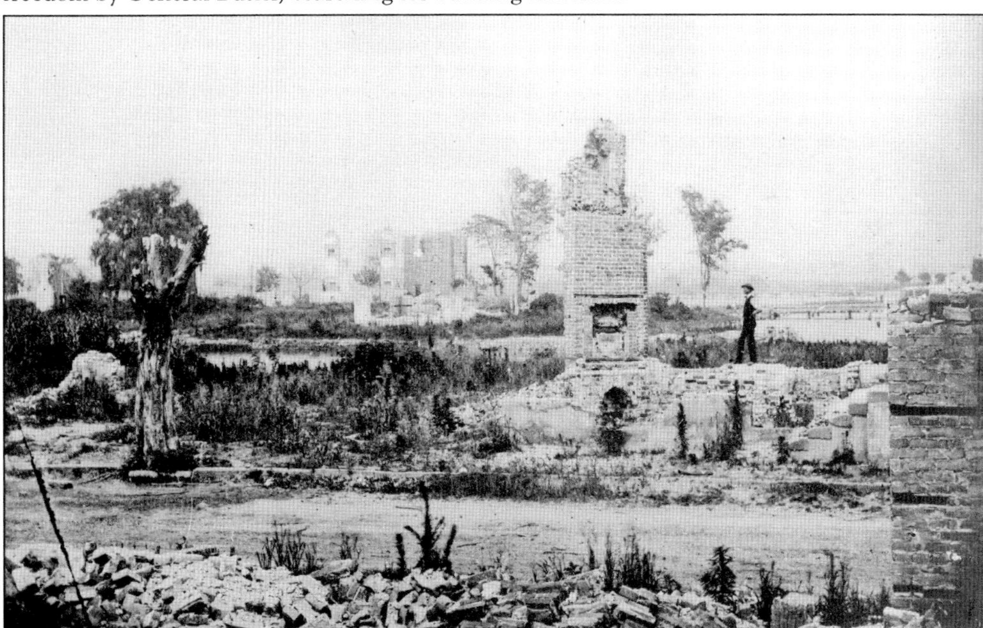

DESOLATION. The photographer himself poses amid the ravages of war. The shady trees along King Street have become a lone stump, the fine houses a jumble of bricks and wrecked chimneys. "I thought of how my little hometown was being made a sacrifice to the grim god of war," said Confederate private Robert S. Hudgins II. (Courtesy of Library of Congress.)

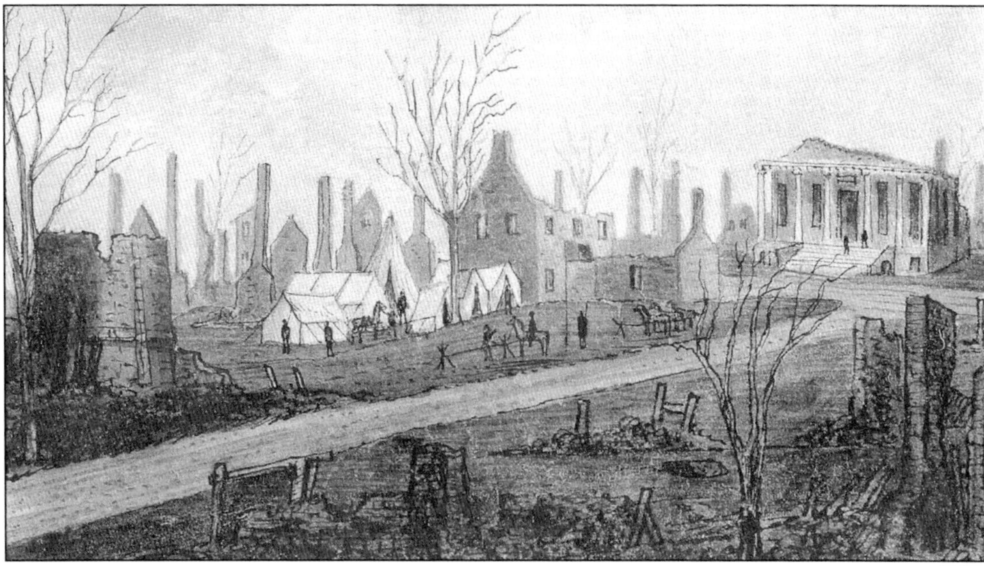

HEINZLEMAN'S HEADQUARTERS. Soldiers' tents nestle next to the ruins of Hampton's courthouse. A Union soldier wrote: "When I thought of the once happy firesides, now made desolate . . . caused by this accursed rebellion I could have wept, but the thought of vengeance, of a retribution, speedy, and as terrible as just, caused each, to clasp his musket with a firmer grasp as we marched on through the deserted streets." (Watercolor by Robert Knox Sneden; courtesy of Virginia Historical Society.)

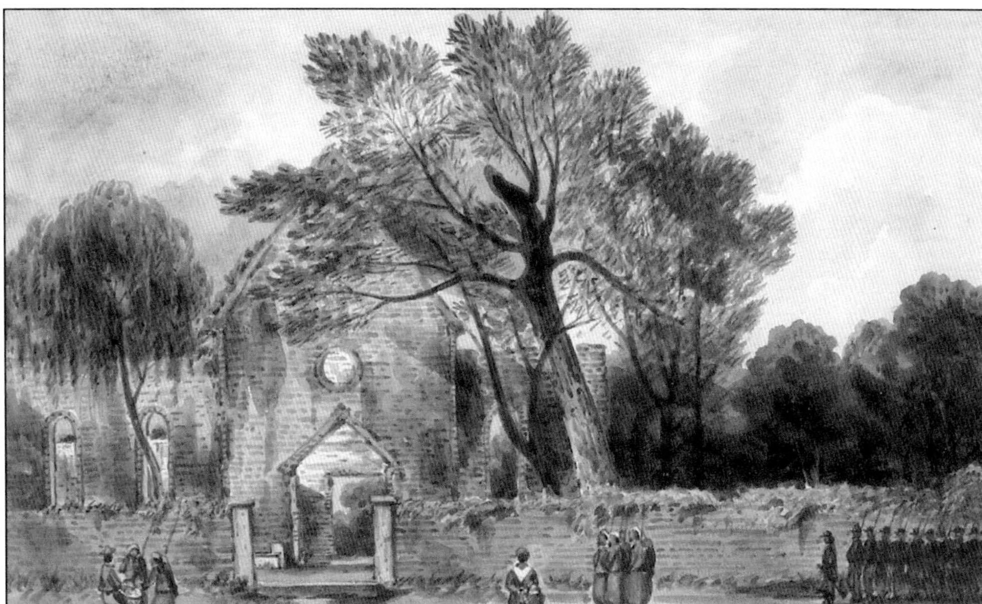

RUINS OF ST. JOHN'S CHURCH. "Suddenly . . . the flaming torches were seen dancing about wildly in all directions, like so many will-o-the-wisps," as an eyewitness Union soldier wrote. Only the walls remained after the fire, as seen in this view drawn by a member of the 5th New York Zouaves following Hampton's burning. It shows members of his regiment and other Union troops, and two contrabands who have produce for sale. (Watercolor by William McLivaine Jr.)

HAMPTON ACADEMY STUDENT, ABOUT 1861. John Davis wears the uniform of the military cadets at Hampton Academy. He was among many young academy students who went into the Confederate army. Davis did not serve long, being mustered out in 1862. At an academy "Old Boys" reunion in July 1888, John A. Curtis told how his artillery company fired at the moon, mistaking it for a "Yankee gunboat coming up the York River."

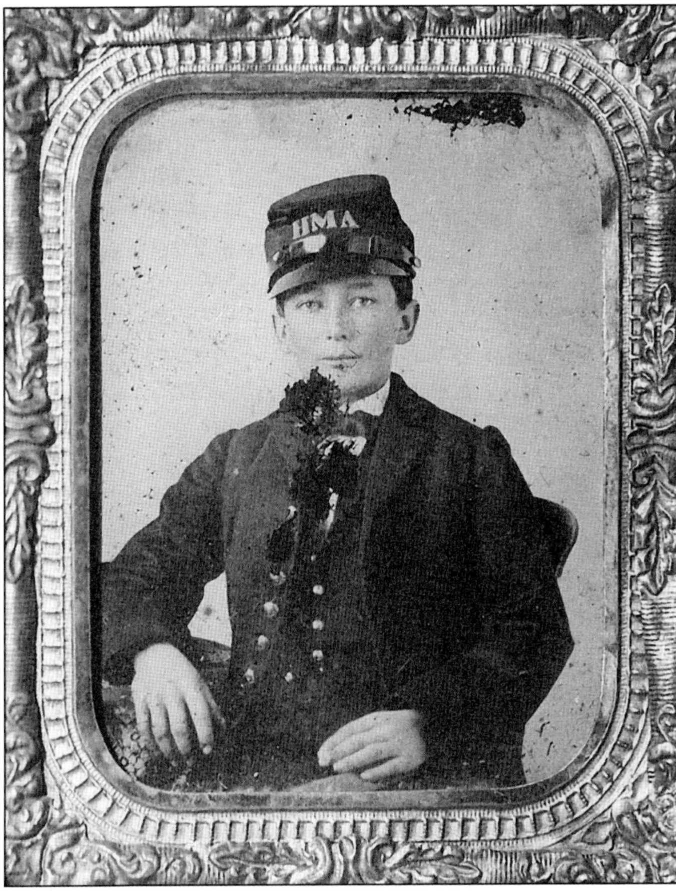

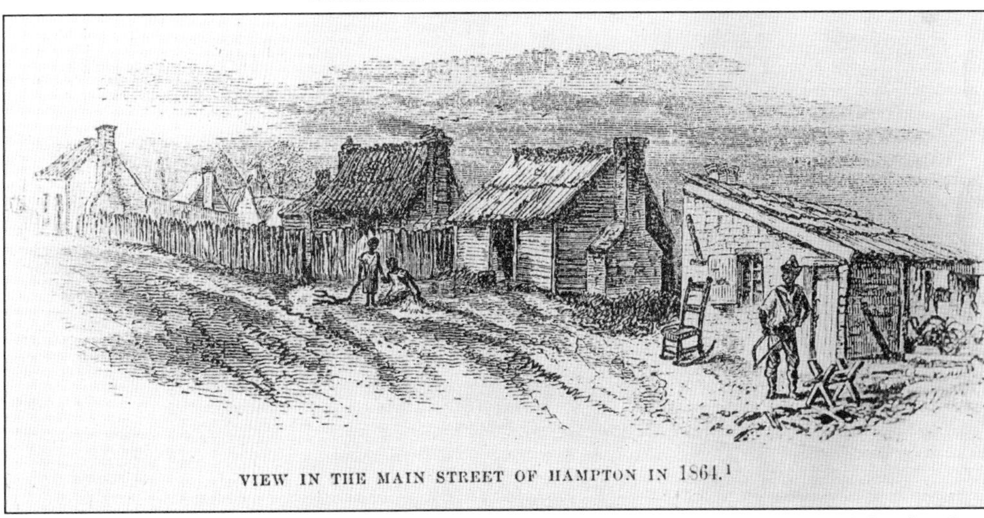

REBUILDING BEGINS. As illustrated in this view of Hampton's "main street" in 1864, the Civil War brought dramatic change to the town. By this time, contrabands had built many homes in the ruins. Following Pres. Abraham Lincoln's assassination, a former Hampton slave recalled, "Every house was white washed and had a black crape hung over the door . . . this was the official military mourning order."

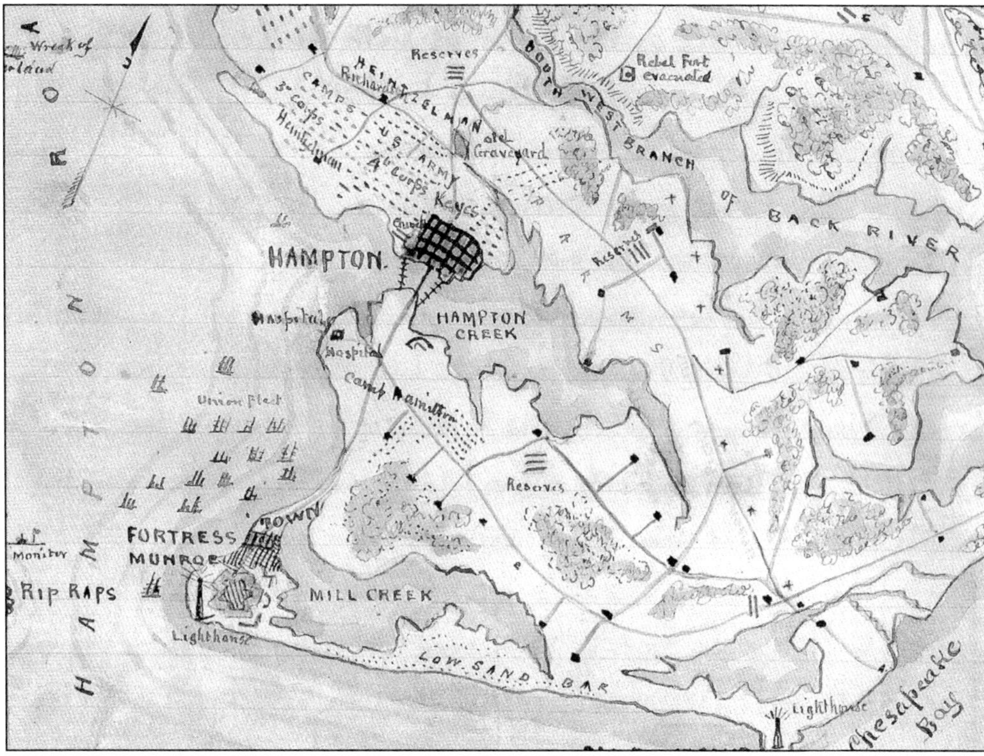

A Union Soldier's Map. The geographic relationship of the town of Hampton to Old Point Comfort and the Union stronghold at Fort Monroe is vividly portrayed here. The map also shows a bridge from King Street to what is now Hampton University, which was burned by the Confederates but re-erected by the Federals to facilitate the flow of traffic. (Watercolor by Robert Knox Sneden; courtesy of Virginia Historical Society.)

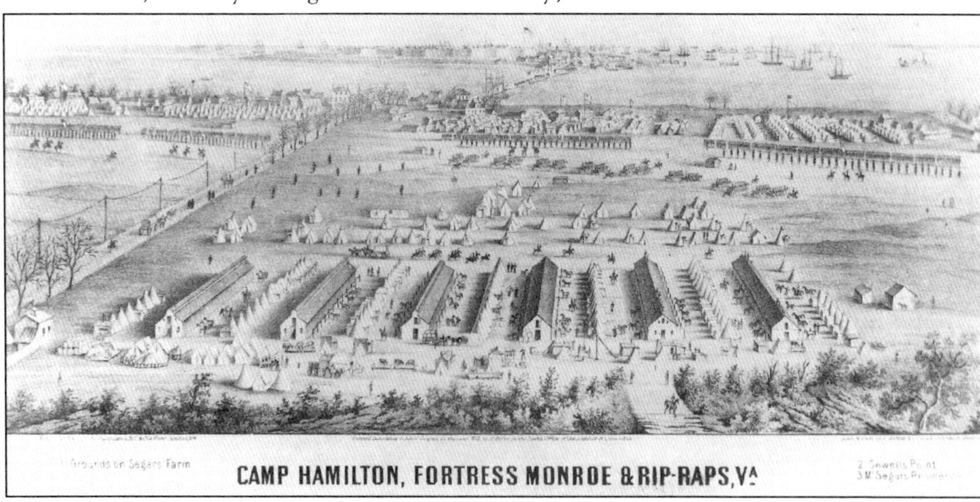

Camp Hamilton. The Union complex in the shadow of Fort Monroe contained more people than the antebellum population of Hampton. The infantry appears to be reviewing a cavalry parade. Sibley tents and horse barns abound. The ships filling the harbor formed part of the flotilla blockading half the Confederacy's Atlantic seaboard. "The white tents at the various regiments . . . were spread out, looking like toys in the distance," a Northern soldier recalled.

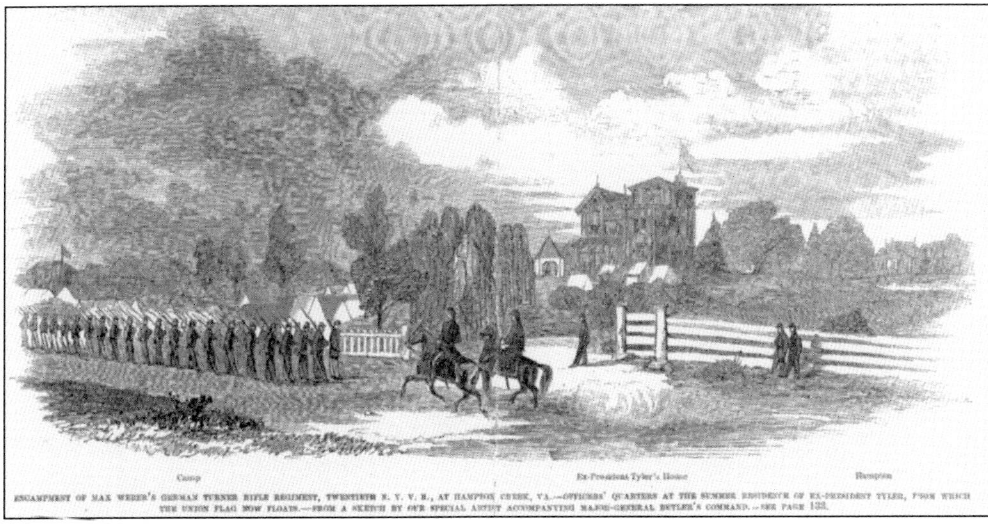

VILLA MARGARET AS UNION POST. Secessionist former president John Tyler's summer home on the east bank of Hampton River was commandeered and ransacked by Union troops in 1861. It became the officers' quarters for more than one Union regiment. It also housed the local office of the Freedmen's Bureau and the ministers and teachers of the American Missionary Society. (Sketch in *Frank Leslie's*.)

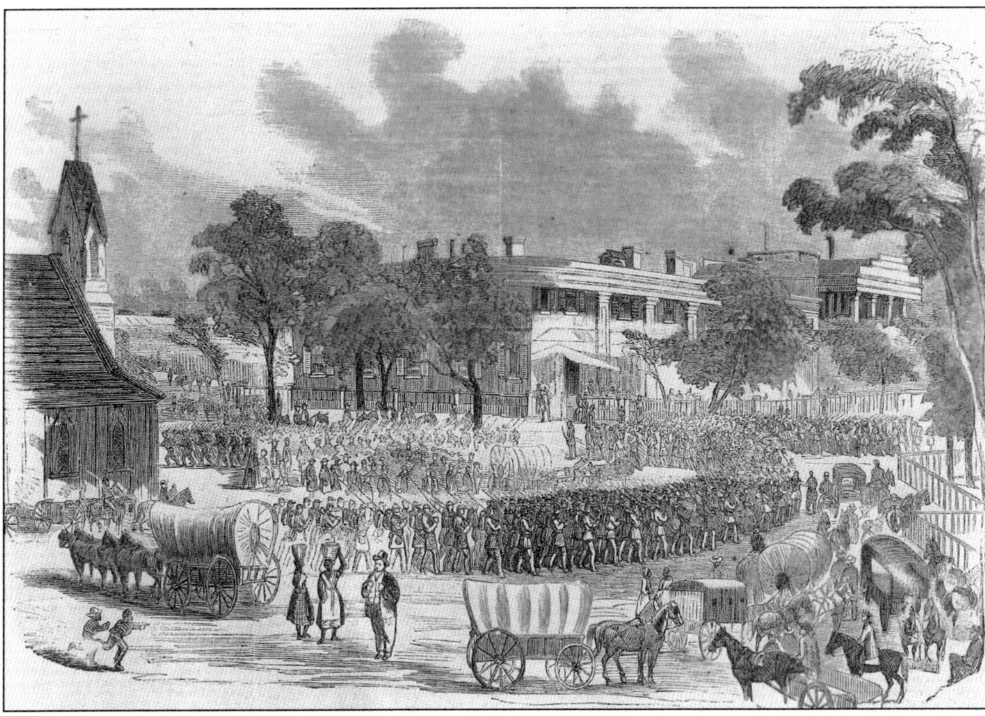

THE PENINSULA CAMPAIGN. Black and white civilians watch thousands of Union troops file past the Hygeia Hotel. The army of the Potomac was massing for its campaign against Richmond, the Confederate capital, which was located about 100 miles distant. A huge, colorful makeshift armada of civilian vessels of all descriptions helped to ferry the soldiers down from Alexandria. (Sketch in *Harper's Weekly*.)

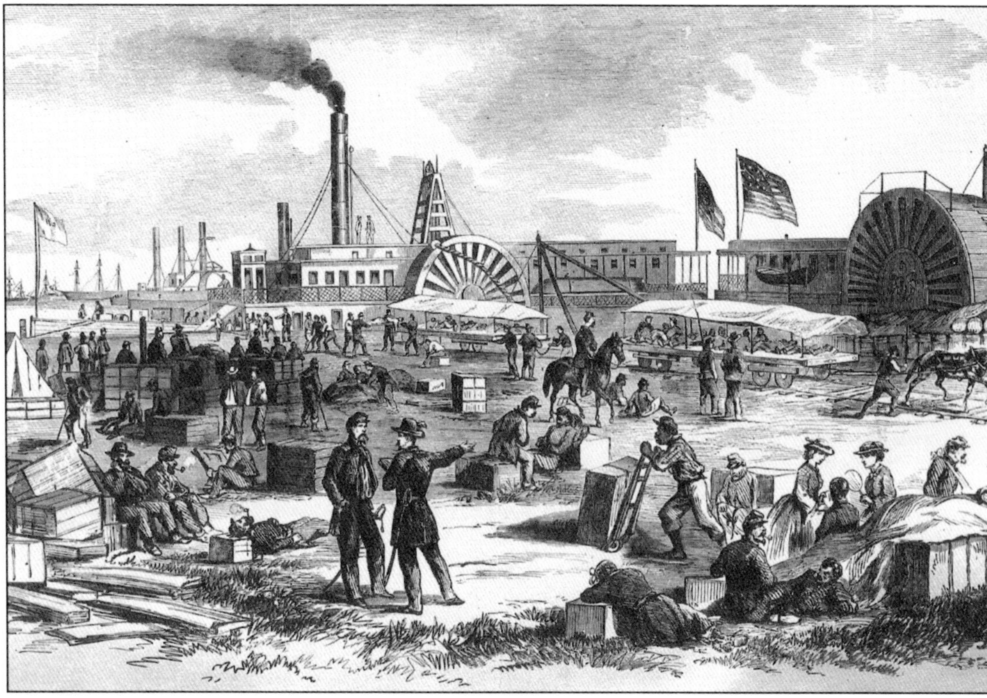

THE WOUNDED. As ships docked at Fort Monroe, transporting casualties from distant battles, the wounded were moved to hospitals on a horse-drawn railway. One of them, hurt near Petersburg, wrote: "I had my arm cut open yesterday . . . they put some stuff in it this morning that stung me . . . but I can stand most anything so long as to set my arm well again." The soldier later died of his wounds. (Sketch in *Harper's Weekly*.)

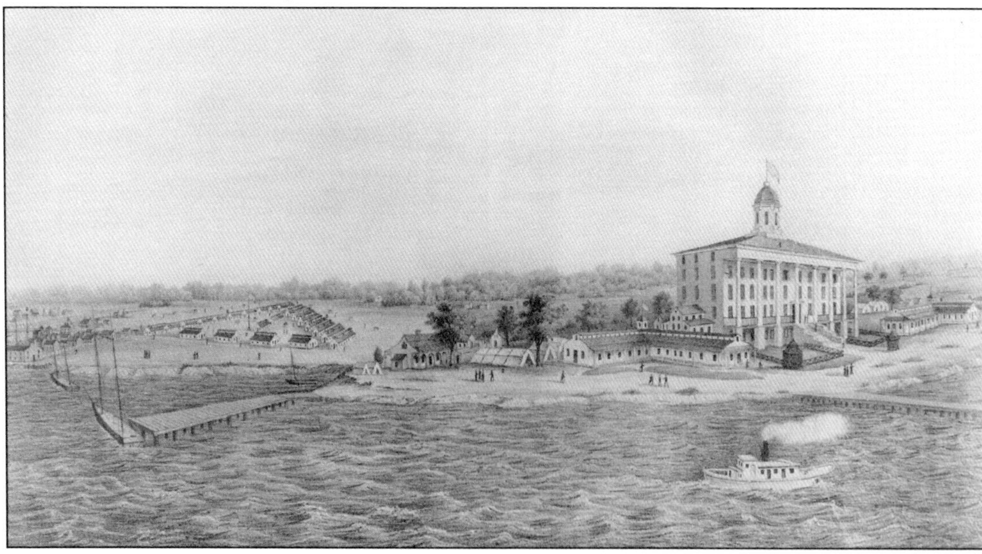

WARTIME MILITARY HOSPITALS. Two hospitals were established for the Union army in Hampton. On this lithograph, the V-shaped Hampton Military Hospital is on the left. It was for enlisted men and was located on "Little Scotland" plantation, occupied by what is now Hampton University. On the right is the Chesapeake Military Hospital for officers. The large building had been the Chesapeake Female Seminary.

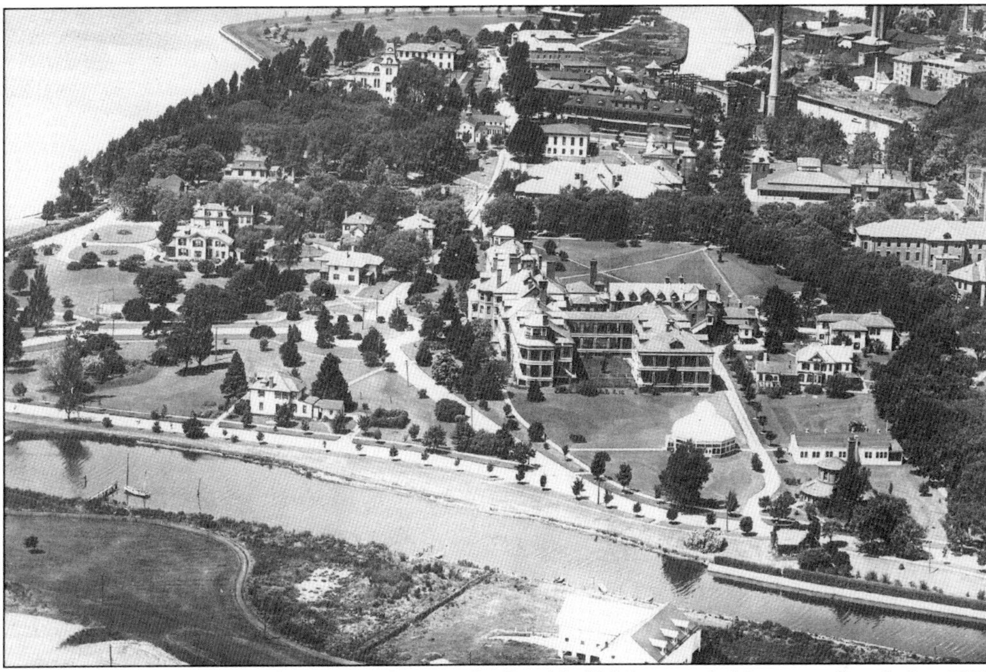

AFTER THE CIVIL WAR. The National Home for Disabled Volunteer Soldiers was founded in 1870 on land acquired by General Butler on the site of the Chesapeake Military Hospital. This 1922 aerial photograph shows how the institution has grown. The soldiers' home offered recreation, music, a library, chapels, and medical care.

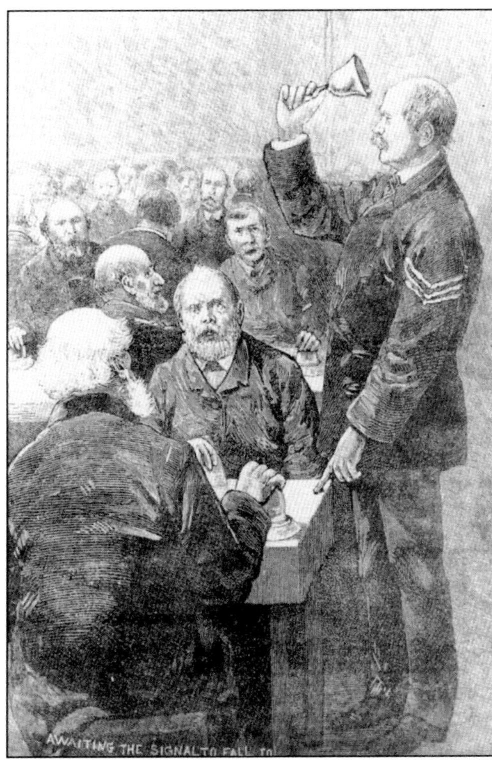

THE SUPPER BELL. Soldiers' home residents take a break from endless reminiscing about the Civil War to sit down to mess. In 1885, the permanent number of residents was between 700 and 800, and it annually administered "to the wants and sufferings of about 1,200 old defenders of the Union. The veterans are well cared for in this quaint, sunny and sleepy place," a newspaper reported. (Sketch in *Frank Leslie's*.)

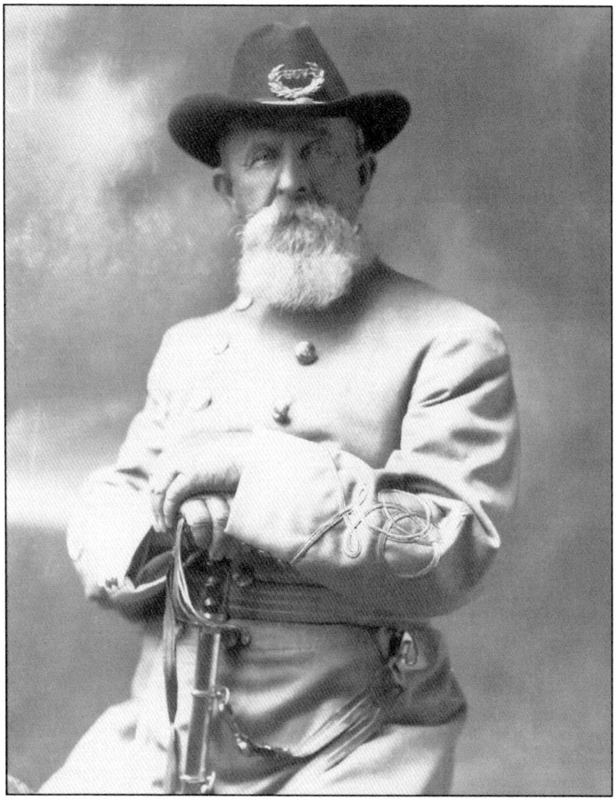

CONFEDERATE VETERAN ROBERT HUDGINS. Hudgins poses in his United Confederate Veterans uniform. His company had been the Old Dominion Dragoons, and he participated in the burning of Hampton, about which he wrote a valuable pamphlet in 1931. Hampton's Confederates long remembered the war when, as Hudgins recalled, "brother fought against brother, and father against son." Many Hampton Confederates joined the Robert E. Lee Camp No. 3 veterans' organization.

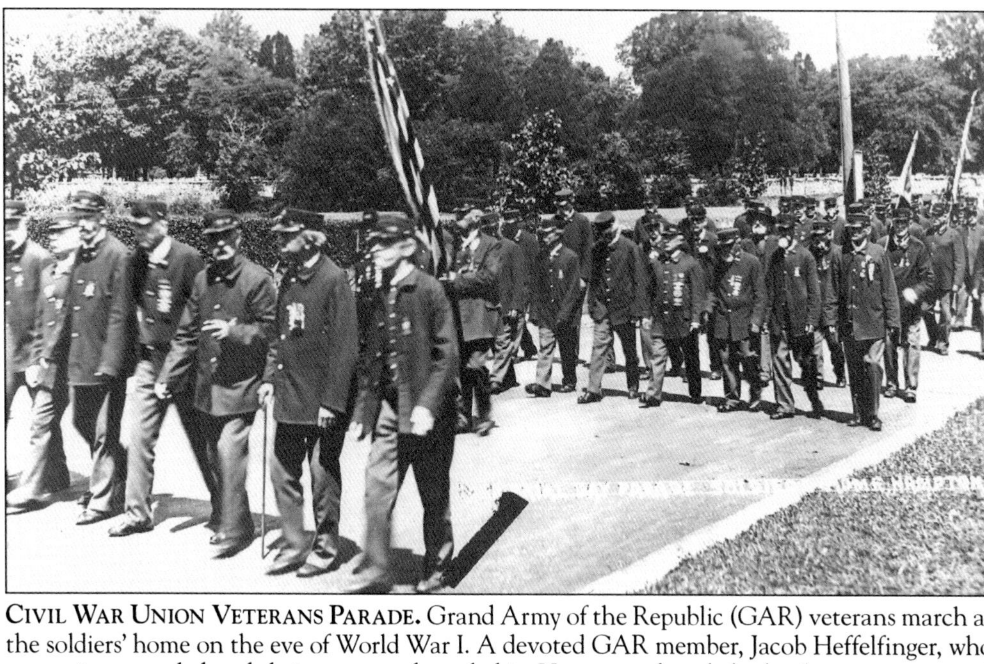

CIVIL WAR UNION VETERANS PARADE. Grand Army of the Republic (GAR) veterans march at the soldiers' home on the eve of World War I. A devoted GAR member, Jacob Heffelfinger, who was twice wounded and thrice captured, settled in Hampton, founded a lumber company vital to rebuilding the town, and was a member of St. John's vestry. Having shared the hardships of a bloody war, Confederate and Union veterans were surprisingly amicable.

Five

The Generation of First Freedom

America's enslaved persons hated slavery and wanted their freedom. When three brave, local enslaved men fled to Fort Monroe, General Butler on May 24, 1861, declared them "contraband of war," thus not returnable to their masters under the Fugitive Slave Act. Word quickly spread. Multitudes escaped to "Freedom's Fort," with about 7,000 African Americans in "contraband" camps by 1863. Many of the former slaves joined the Union army or navy, or otherwise aided the Union cause.

One contraband camp was located in, and to the west of, the ruins of Hampton. The people named the streets of their community Union, Grant, and Lincoln, names that persist to this day.

After the Civil War, Hampton became an important center of the American Missionary Society, which attempted to demonstrate that freedmen could live independently. Six schools were established to offer a basic education. The most important of these was in the ruins of the county courthouse. Hundreds of students attended these schools.

Gen. Samuel Chapman Armstrong, local superintendent of the Freedmen's Bureau, was convinced that education was the real path to freedom for former slaves. At his urging, the American Missionary Society purchased land on the east bank of Hampton River and built an institution of higher education. Armstrong became the first principal of Hampton Normal and Agricultural Institute, which taught thousands of blacks and many Native Americans. It opened in 1868.

Another dream of the former slaves was to become farmers or householders upon their own land. The failure of the First Reconstruction meant they had to purchase land. Capital was scarce, especially with racial tensions at an all-time high, and funding was essentially unavailable to African Americans from local banks. Their savior was the Peoples Savings and Loan Company, located on north King Street.

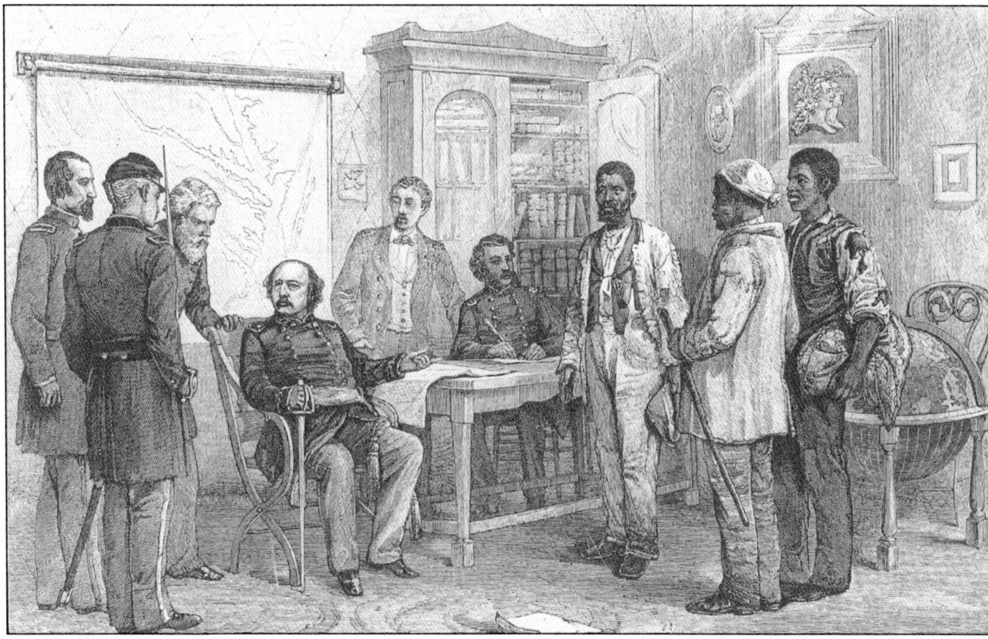

THE FIRST EMANCIPATION. Sanctuary at Fort Monroe is here granted to contrabands Frank Baker, Shepard Mallory, and James Townsend. The three, slaves of Charles King Mallory, had been erecting Confederate defenses at Sewell's Point in Norfolk. Those batteries of guns menaced Union shipping in Hampton Roads. General Butler, a Massachusetts politician, lawyer, and abolitionist, was motivated both by principle and by political necessity. Other Union commanders quickly followed his lead.

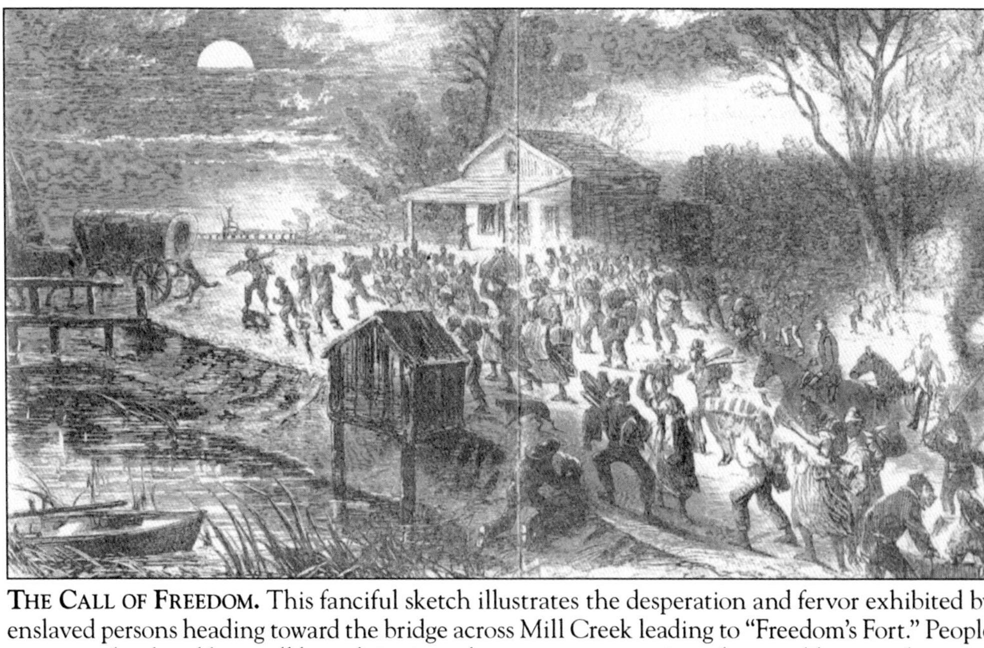

THE CALL OF FREEDOM. This fanciful sketch illustrates the desperation and fervor exhibited by enslaved persons heading toward the bridge across Mill Creek leading to "Freedom's Fort." People came overland and by small boat, bringing what meager possessions they could carry, plus some animals. A Massachusetts soldier noted, "Slaves are brought in here by guard hourly." (Sketch in *Harper's Weekly*.)

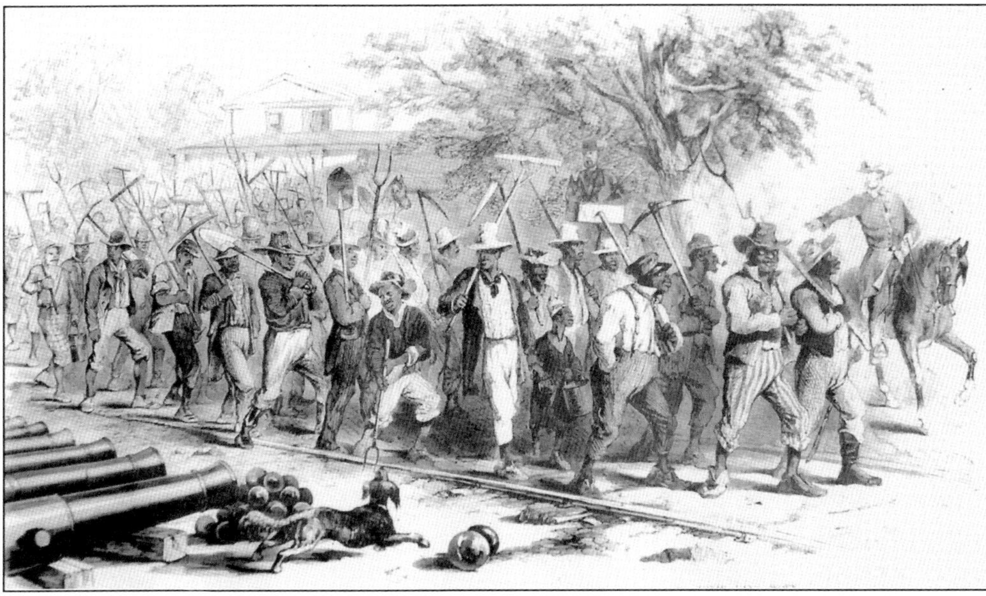

Freedom Meant Work. To most Union soldiers, the escaped slaves were a nuisance and a burden. Most Northerners shared Southerners' views of the innate inferiority of blacks. It was dangerous for contrabands to farm away from Union lines, so General Butler put them to work around the Union positions. Tasks emphasized manual labor with wages paid in kind at first. Freedom now meant wage labor.

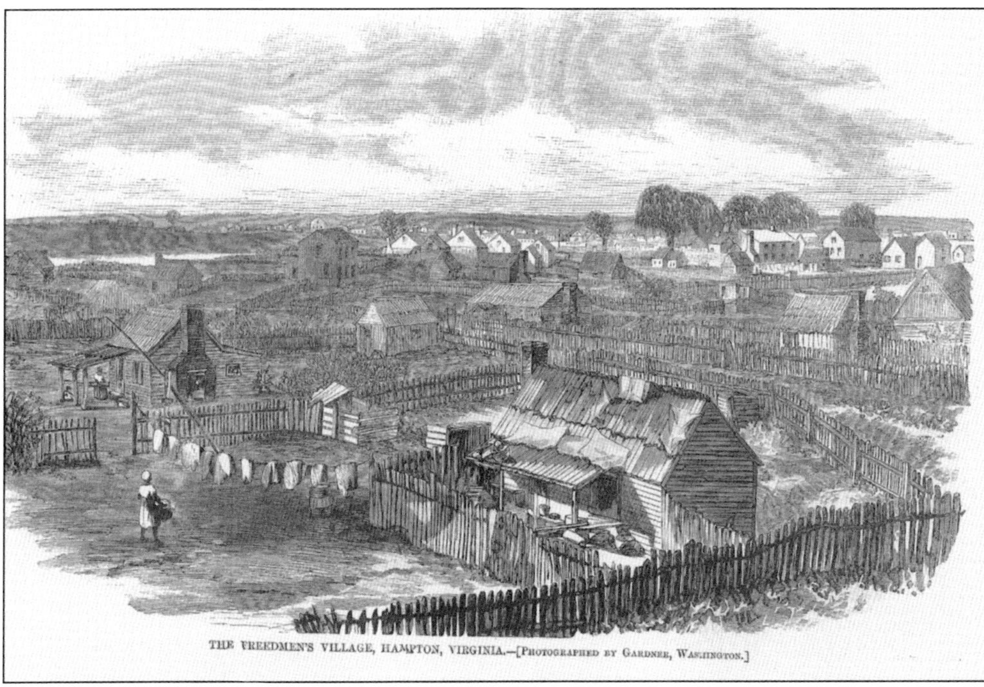

THE FREEDMEN'S VILLAGE, HAMPTON, VIRGINIA.—[Photographed by Gardner, Washington.]

Freedmen's Village. This sketch, made from an 1865 photograph, shows the contraband camp westward of the ruins of Hampton. These houses were built of discarded "slabs," the first cuts made from logs at a sawmill. To this day, the area of the "Grand Contraband Camp" is overwhelmingly African American, and descent from contrabands is remembered. (Sketch in *Harper's Weekly*.)

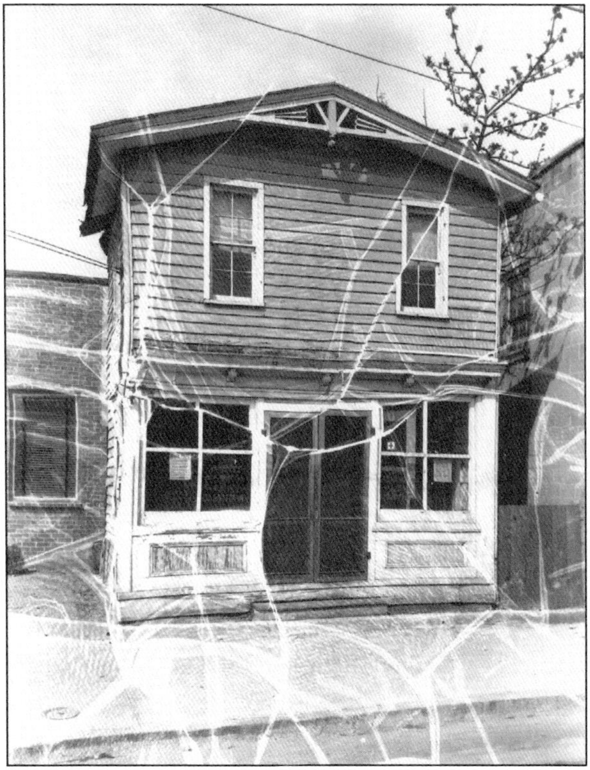

BUILDINGS WITH LOANS. Perhaps the most important institution in the emerging black community was the People's Building and Loan Association, founded in 1886. Though some retained their land and others saved their wages, hundreds of blacks were only able to purchase their homes with its aid. They were finally able to realize the American dream of buying a little piece of land of their own.

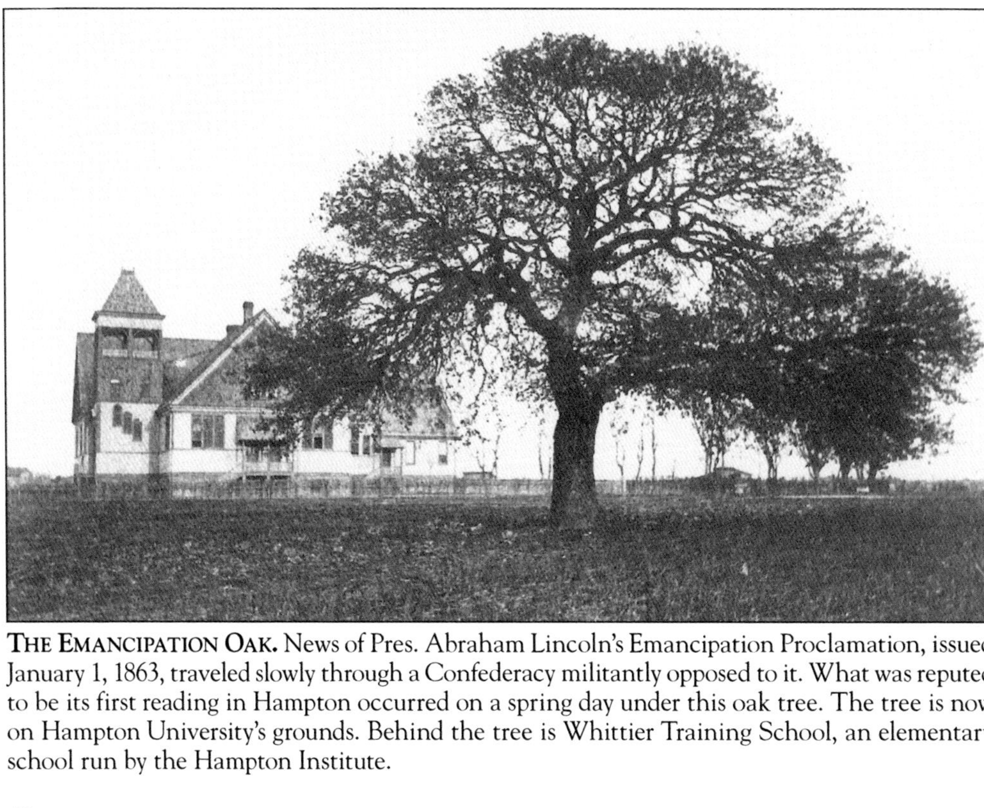

THE EMANCIPATION OAK. News of Pres. Abraham Lincoln's Emancipation Proclamation, issued January 1, 1863, traveled slowly through a Confederacy militantly opposed to it. What was reputed to be its first reading in Hampton occurred on a spring day under this oak tree. The tree is now on Hampton University's grounds. Behind the tree is Whittier Training School, an elementary school run by the Hampton Institute.

EDUCATION FOR BLACKS, SLAVE AND FREE. Mary K. Peake was a freeborn black. She exemplified Hampton's illegal but existing tradition of educating slaves to read and write before the Civil War. In 1861, she opened a school for 50 pupils, both children and adults. Others continued freedom education for blacks after her untimely death from consumption in 1862. (Courtesy of Hampton University.)

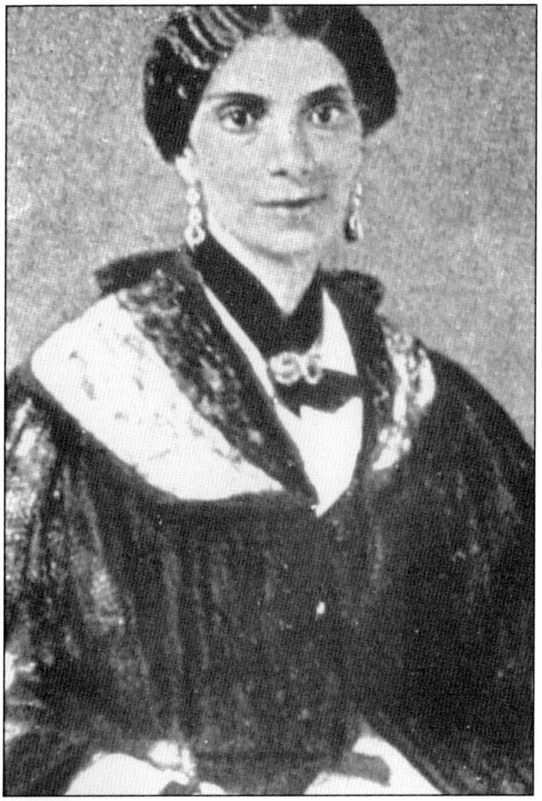

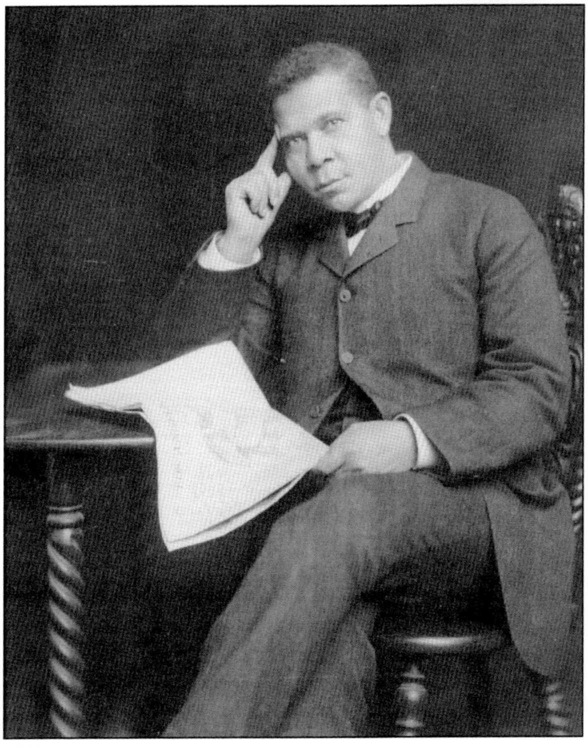

NOTABLE HAMPTON INSTITUTE GRADUATES. Booker T. Washington, who walked from West Virginia to enroll, graduated to become a teacher there. Later he was the first president of the Tuskegee Normal and Industrial Institute in Alabama. Catherine Fields (not pictured), from Hanover County, Virginia, graduated and became a teacher at Lincoln School, the black elementary school in Hampton. Both kinds of teaching efforts were crucial for the African American community.

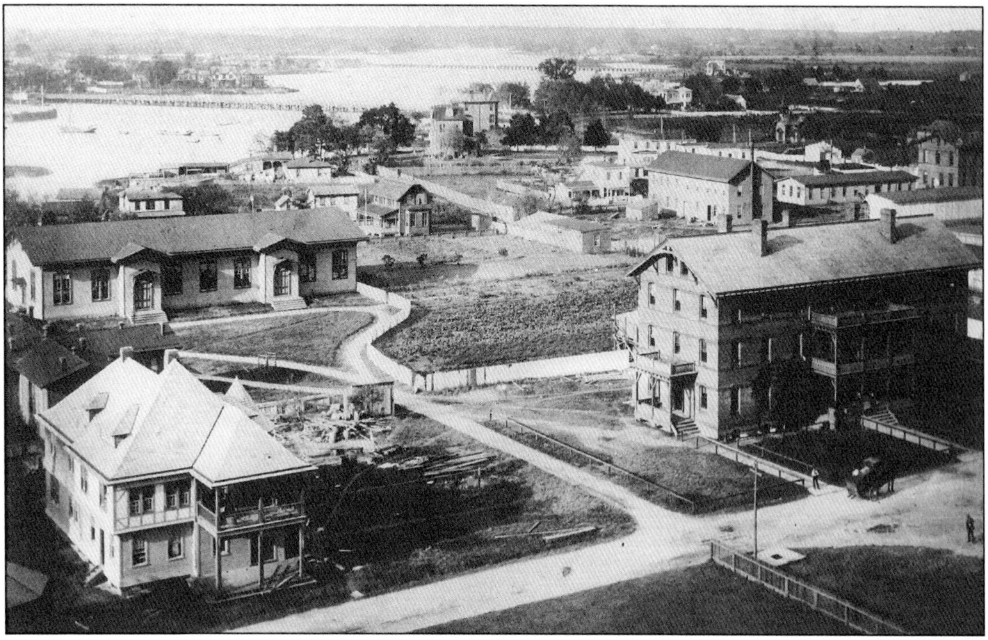

HAMPTON INSTITUTE. By the time of this 1892 photograph, the Hampton Normal and Agricultural Institute—present-day Hampton University—was well established. Its buildings are in the foreground with the town of Hampton in the distance. Its students made their supplies purchases downtown, while Hampton residents got leatherwork, furniture, and other household items repaired at the institute. Much of Hampton's furniture and many Hampton homes were built by Hampton Institute carpenters.

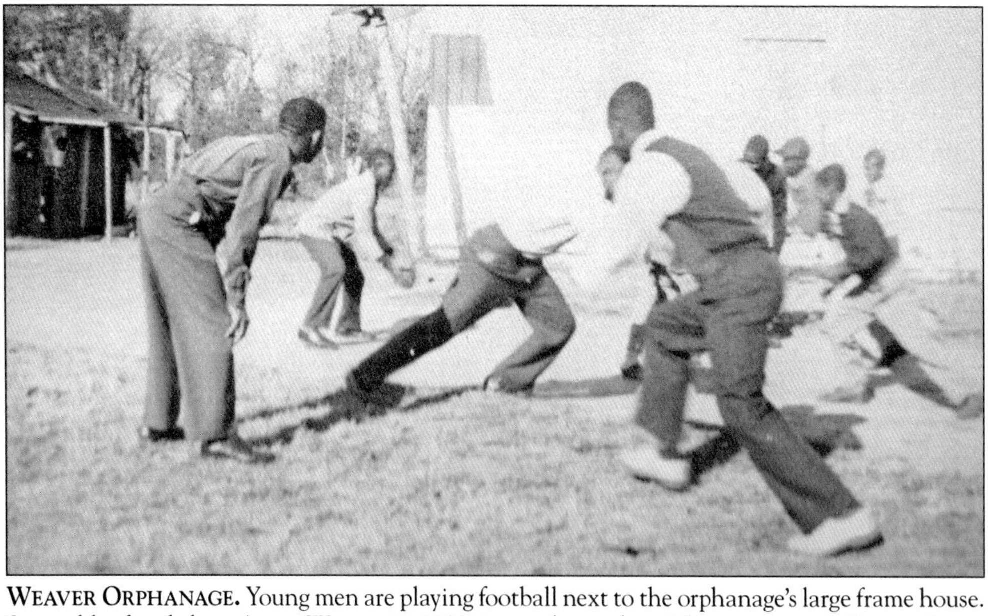

WEAVER ORPHANAGE. Young men are playing football next to the orphanage's large frame house. Started by freed slave Anna Weaver in 1904, it was located on 15 acres on west Queen Street beyond today's St. Cyprian's Church. It housed a maximum of 20 people. The Weaver Home was supported from boarding fees paid by relatives, the sale of agricultural produce, and community gifts. Weaver reared and educated more than 400 orphans.

Six

HAMPTON BECOMES "CRABTOWN"

From anyone's standpoint, Hampton was a miserable place when its citizens began to rebuild it in 1865. However, seafood and entrepreneurial ingenuity gave Hampton a new life and identity. Two men born elsewhere were the key to the growth of seafood, and others followed suit in that industry and, perhaps inspired by their example, moved in other ways to stimulate Hampton's development.

Irish-born Bostonian James McMenamin in 1879 perfected a practical method of preserving crabmeat in cans, which allowed this delicate product to be shipped throughout the country. He built a large plant on Hampton River where hundreds of workers steamed, picked, and canned crabs that had been brought to the factory. McMenamin had a sizeable fleet of boats. Others established crab factories in Hampton also, and the town justly became known as "Crabtown."

New York City gave Hampton James Sands Darling, who settled here after the Civil War. Founded in 1882, his firm bought, shucked, canned, and shipped large quantities of oysters. Darling soon became the king of the oyster business. His company was said to be the largest producer in the world, his oysters were shipped nationwide, and his four-story pile of oyster shells dominated the downtown Hampton landscape for more than half a century.

Blacks had a long-established tradition as watermen. Many were independent entrepreneurs, such as Hampton Institute graduate John Mallory Phillips, whose vessels had exclusive rights to certain oyster grounds and who had his own seafood business.

Ironically, the tragic fire of 1884, which destroyed about a quarter of the town, cleared the way for grander new construction. Hampton now came of age and was duly incorporated as a city in 1887.

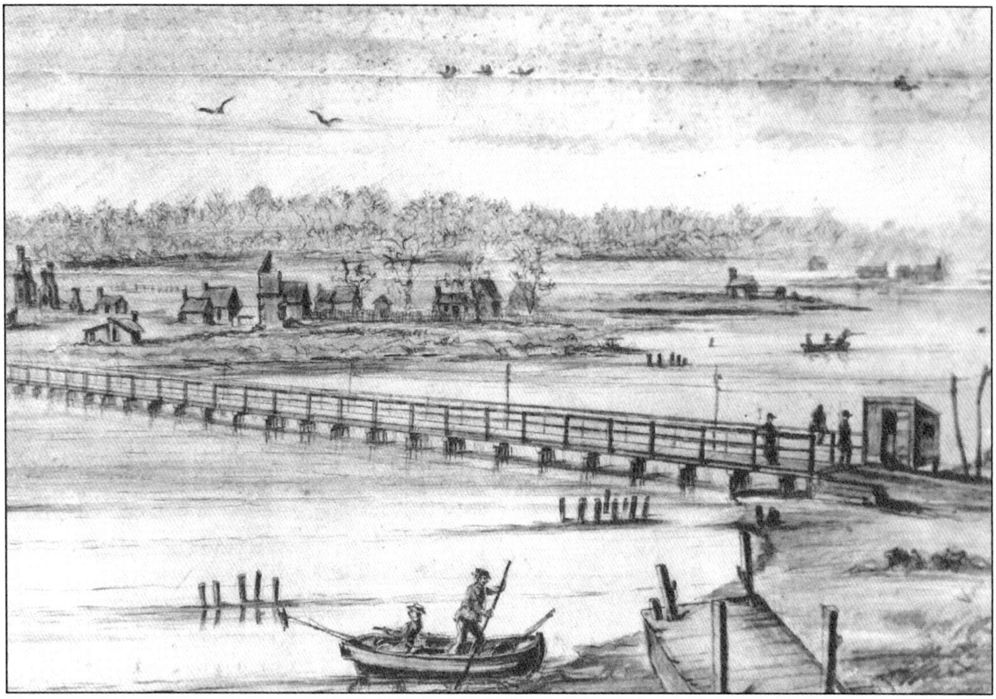

HAMPTON'S PEE DEE POINT. It looked like this when the Civil War ended. A few men are fishing from boats, but the ruin of Cary's Hampton Academy (left center) amid "a straggling collection of small wooden houses and shanties," as an observer noted, shows how much returning residents had to do. Unpaved streets were mud bogs in winter and were sources of choking dust in the summer. In the turmoil of rebuilding, a number of taverns soon appeared.

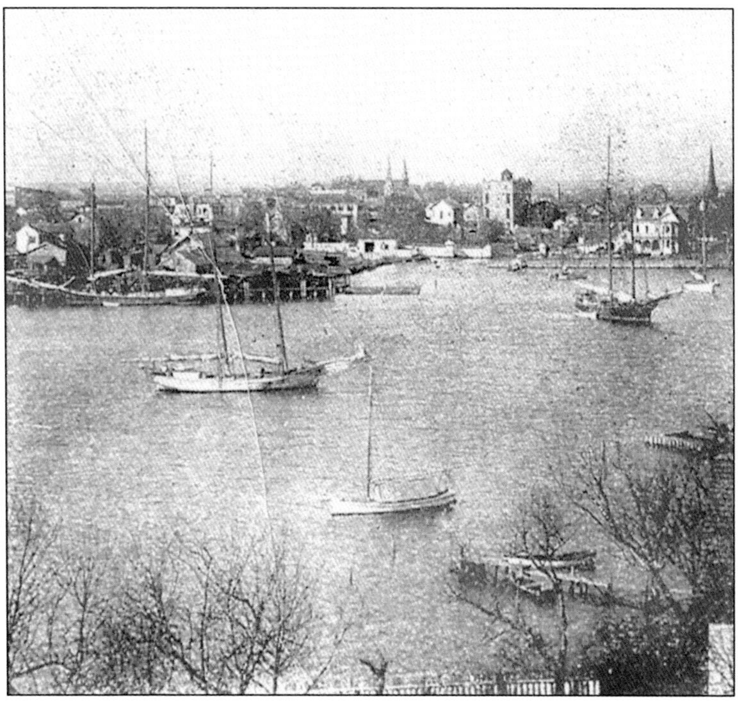

HAMPTON'S WATERFRONT, ABOUT 1900. Progress has been made. Two large boats ride at anchor. Another large boat is moored at the south end of King Street next to Jacob Heffelfinger's lumberyard. The still-standing Masonic Temple (tall building) was completed in 1888, and the former spire of the First Methodist Church near it (center right) helps define a new and growing Queen Street.

DARLING AND OYSTERS. Northerners spearheaded the development of the crab and oyster industries as the seafood trade rebuilt Hampton. This is James Sands Darling, oyster entrepreneur extraordinaire, who started out in lumber and fishing, then founded his oyster business in 1882. In 1938, one hundred thousand barrels of crabs, 50,000 gallons of oysters, and 30,000 bushels of unshucked oysters were shipped from Hampton. Darling's descendants still benefit Hampton.

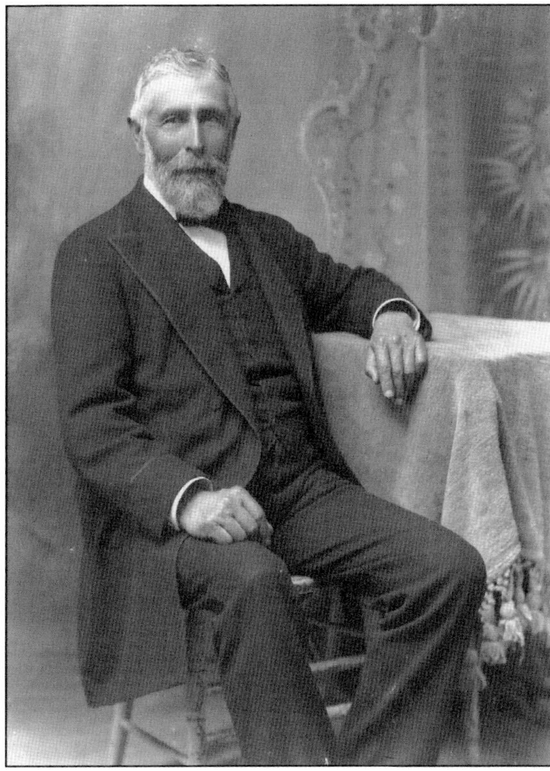

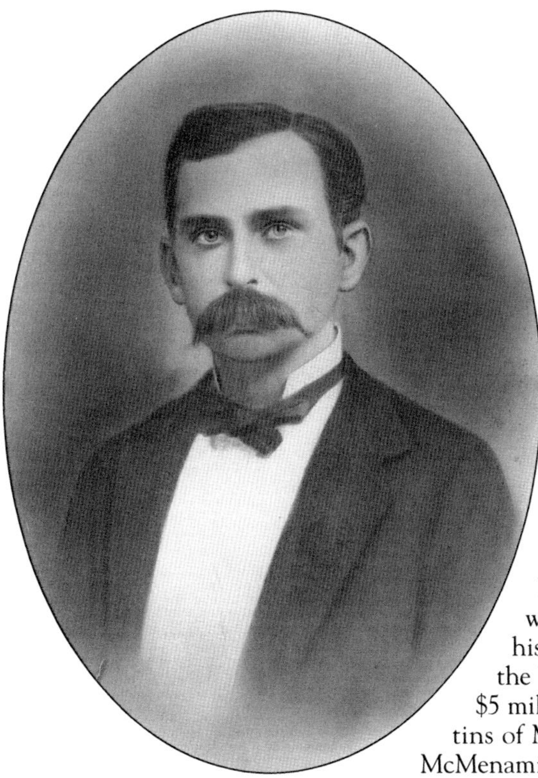

MCMENAMIN AND CRABS. James McMenamin, driven from Ireland by the potato famine, spent eight years developing his method of canning crabmeat. His process won prizes in Berlin, London, and Paris, and his plant came to cover 20,000 square feet. At the height of his business, McMenamin grossed $5 million per year. In 1909, Robert Peary carried tins of McMenamin crabmeat to the North Pole. McMenamin put the "crab" in Crabtown.

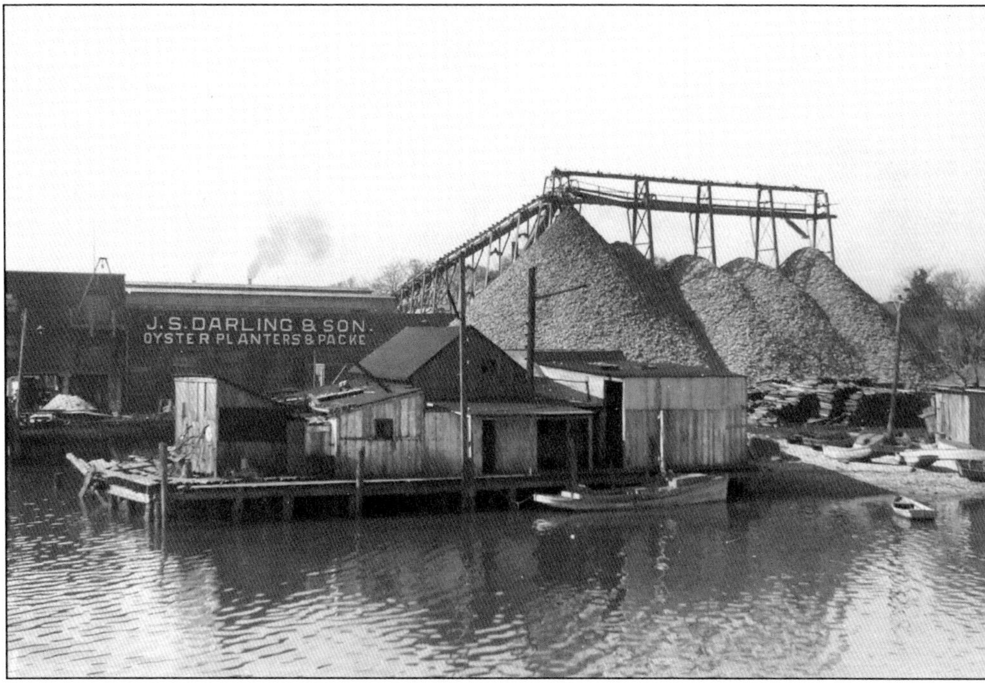

HAMPTON'S PYRAMIDS. One of the most memorable features of downtown Hampton was its four-story mountain of oyster shells at James Sands Darling's plant. Visible from a distance, it was featured in *National Geographic* in 1916. The shells were not wasted, being shipped back to the waters of the Chesapeake to provide beds for new oysters and being crushed for sidewalks and road paving. (Courtesy of Sargeant Memorial Room, Norfolk Public Library.)

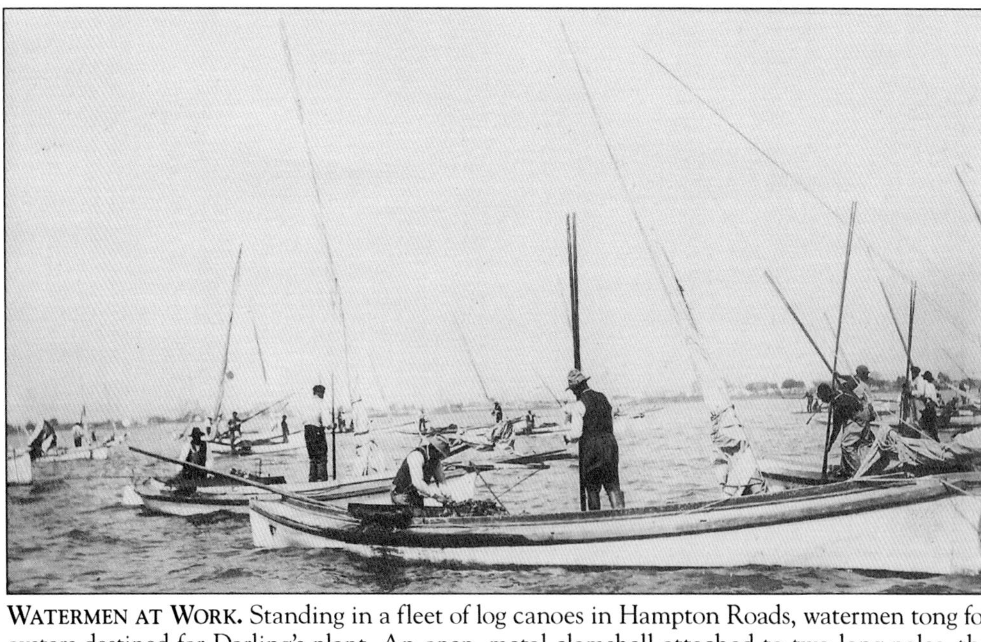

WATERMEN AT WORK. Standing in a fleet of log canoes in Hampton Roads, watermen tong for oysters destined for Darling's plant. An open, metal clamshell attached to two long poles, the tongs were lowered, closed, and then raised up with their harvest. Oyster grounds were private, leased from the state. Later oysters were dredged up with a large metal scoop.

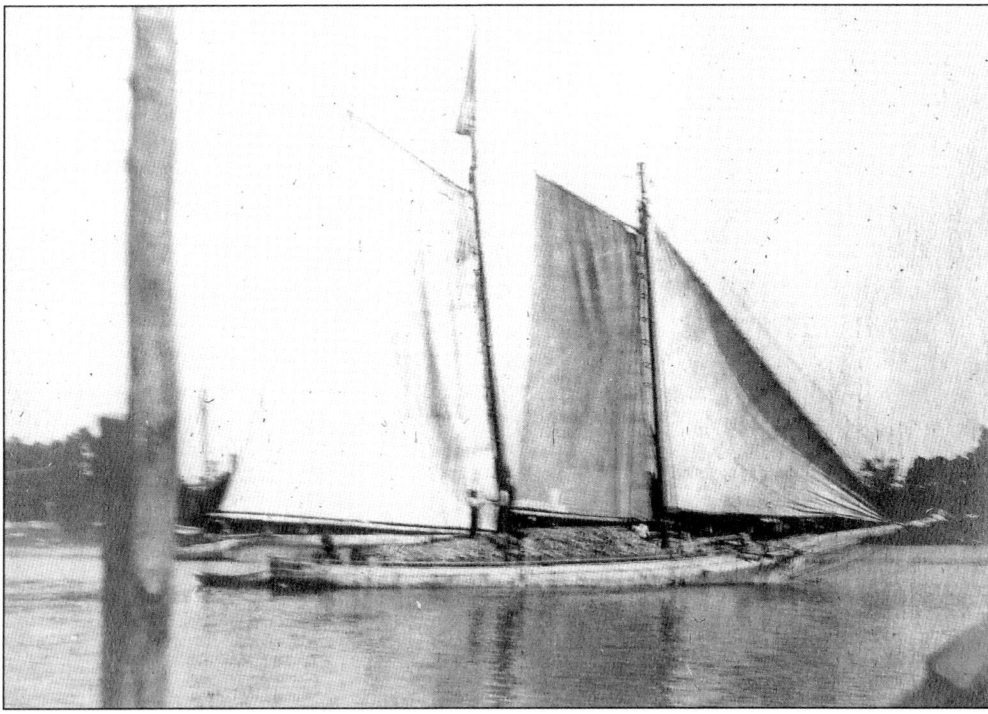

Bringing Oysters to the Plant. Loaded to the gunwales, a "buy boat" sails up Hampton River, making for Darling's plant. These oysters probably would have been purchased from independent contractors working their own grounds in Hampton Roads or Chesapeake Bay. The crew of the large boat appears to be four men.

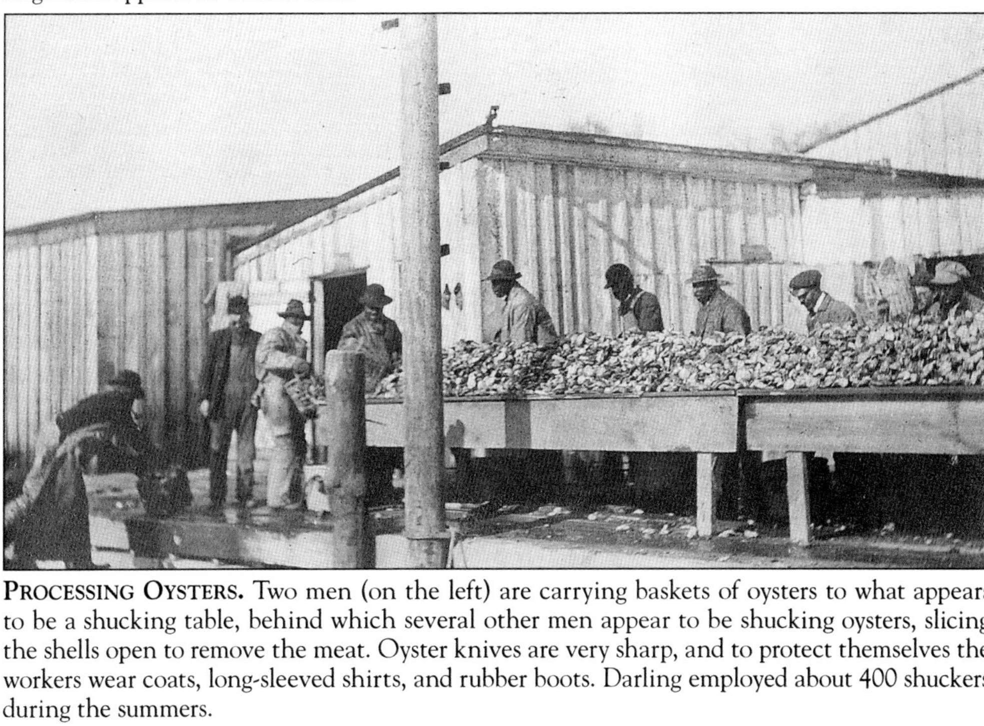

Processing Oysters. Two men (on the left) are carrying baskets of oysters to what appears to be a shucking table, behind which several other men appear to be shucking oysters, slicing the shells open to remove the meat. Oyster knives are very sharp, and to protect themselves the workers wear coats, long-sleeved shirts, and rubber boots. Darling employed about 400 shuckers during the summers.

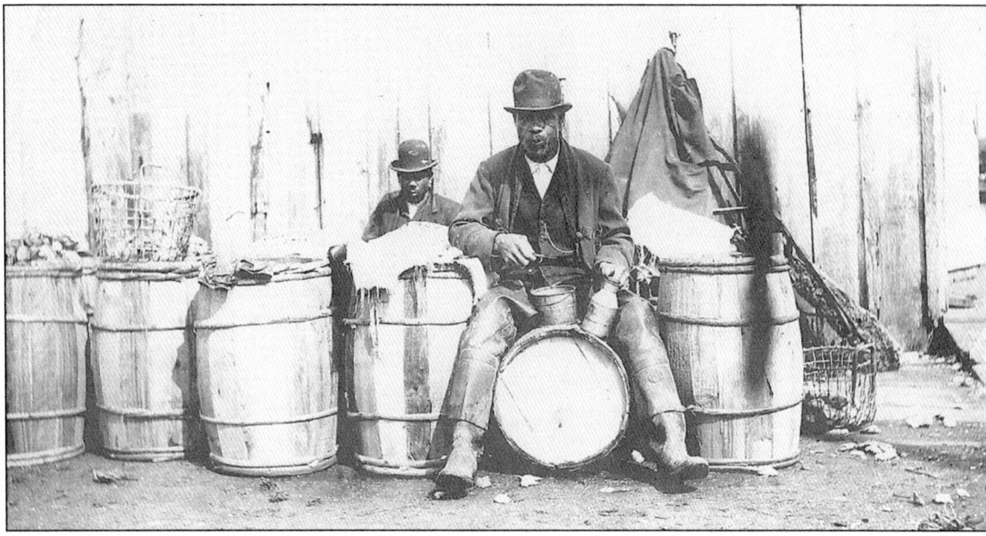

OYSTERMAN'S LUNCH BREAK. An anonymous oysterman at Darling's takes time out from shucking to eat his lunch astride a tumbled oyster barrel. Note his protective rubber boots and trousers, his watch chain and oyster-spattered derby, the shucking knife in his right hand, and an "agate" drink can in his left. Oyster knives were usually highly prized, were personal to the shucker, and lasted a long time.

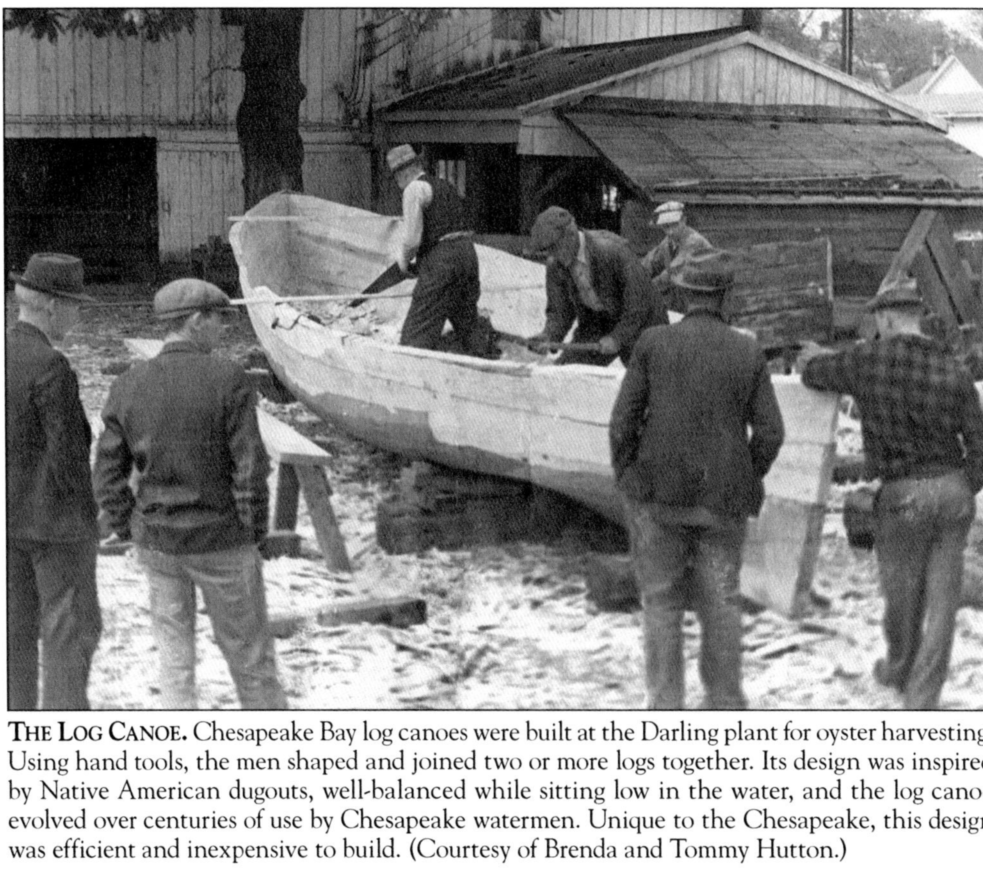

THE LOG CANOE. Chesapeake Bay log canoes were built at the Darling plant for oyster harvesting. Using hand tools, the men shaped and joined two or more logs together. Its design was inspired by Native American dugouts, well-balanced while sitting low in the water, and the log canoe evolved over centuries of use by Chesapeake watermen. Unique to the Chesapeake, this design was efficient and inexpensive to build. (Courtesy of Brenda and Tommy Hutton.)

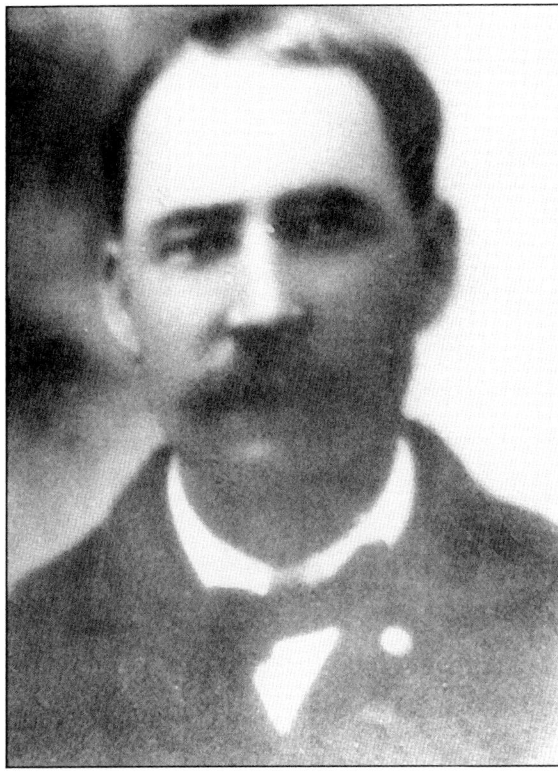

JOHN MALLORY PHILLIPS. Many Hampton blacks were not tied to the land but had a long-established tradition as watermen (crabbers, oystermen, and fishermen). During the Civil War, contraband watermen sold their catch to soldiers at Fort Monroe. John Mallory Phillips and others later started their own seafood businesses. Phillips had a fleet of seven boats and sold his catch northward. The family-owned business prospered for about a century.

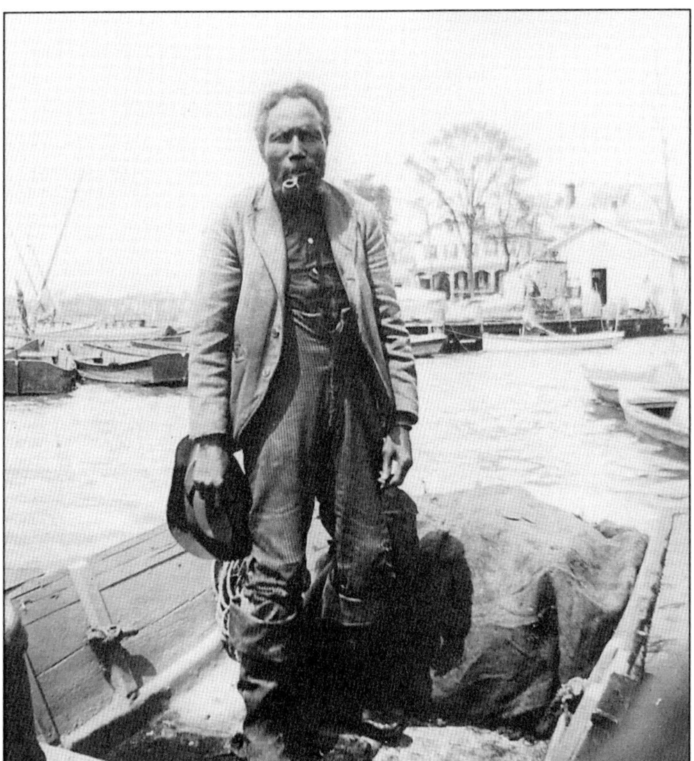

TAYLOR ARMISTEAD. In this photograph, taken about 1930, waterman Taylor Armistead, born into slavery, poses with pipe in mouth in his bateau on the Hampton waterfront. He was 85 years old. Working on both plant-owned and self-owned boats gave blacks a degree of economic autonomy unusual in the South at this time. Armistead resided downtown on Wine Street in a cluster of modest dwellings inhabited by blacks.

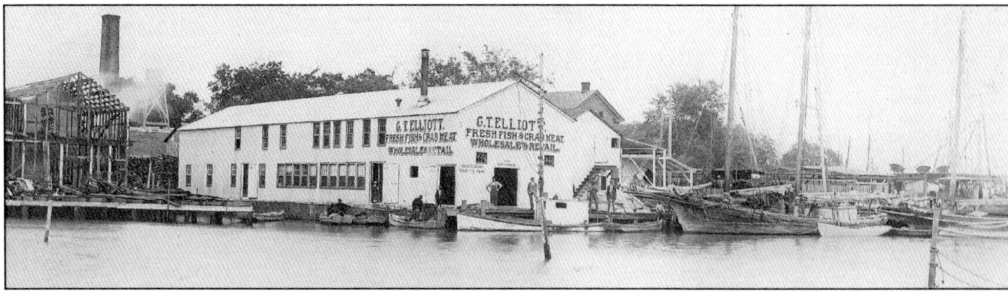

ELLIOTT SEAFOOD. G. T. Elliott, Inc., sold all sorts of seafood, including clams and fish. It employed 75 to 100 people in the plant and on its boats. In 1915, it advertised "perfect cold storage facilities" and that it sold directly to "fashionable hotels." It was the Hampton agent for New York City's Fulton Market. Four small crabbing skiffs are docked in front with barrels of crabs.

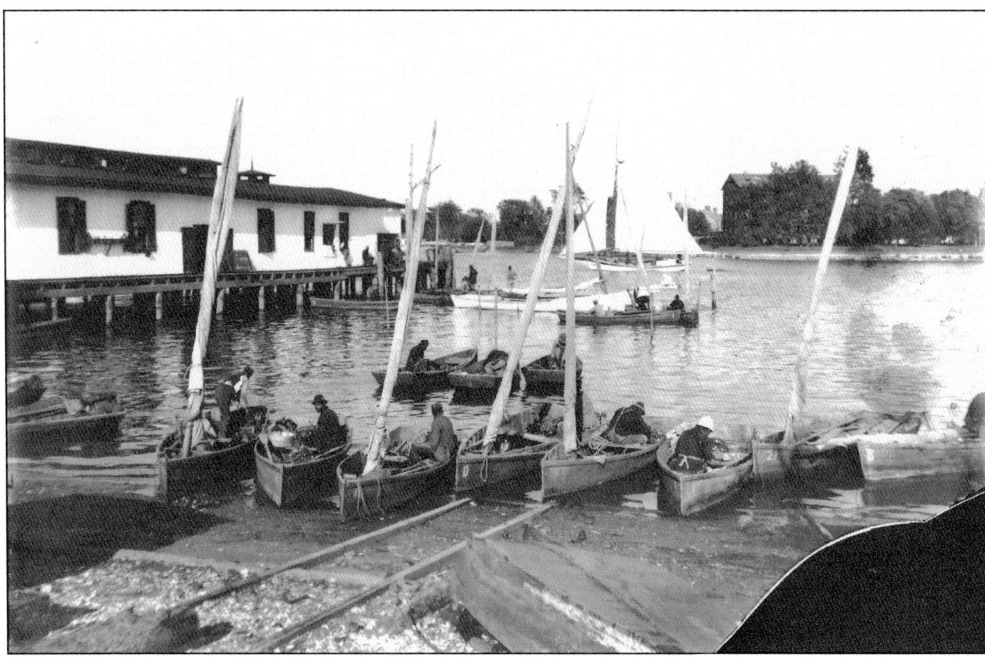

CRAB BOATS GETTING READY. McMenamin's crab fleet is resting in front of his crab factory. According to McMenamin, "It's a pretty sight off old Hampton Roads when, at the purple of the coming morning, sixty boats spread wing for the fishing grounds. Dawn has hardly winked at the day before the crab-catchers are out in the blue waters of the bay." (Courtesy of John R. Wilt.)

RUNNING TROT LINES. This 1900 photograph shows a McMenamin waterman attempting to scoop up a crab that has dropped from his trotline. Crabbers dredged for crabs in the winter and used trotlines in the summer. Trotlines could be as long as 1,500 feet, dangling crab bait (visible here) every foot or so.

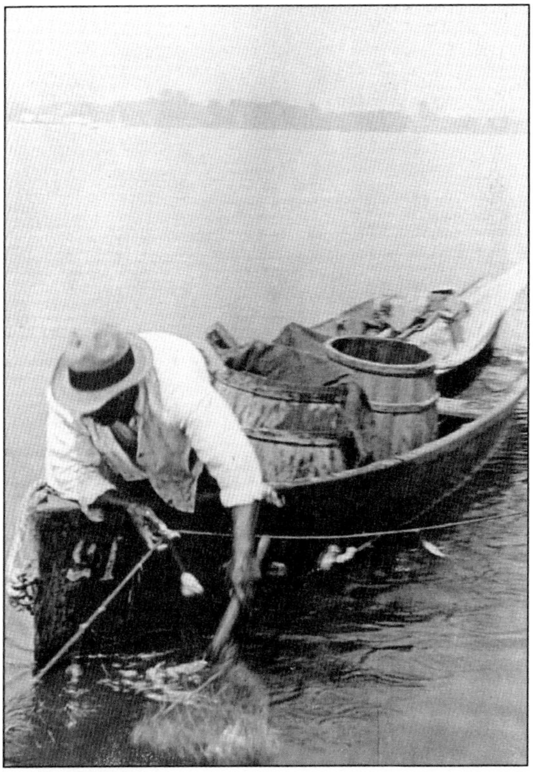

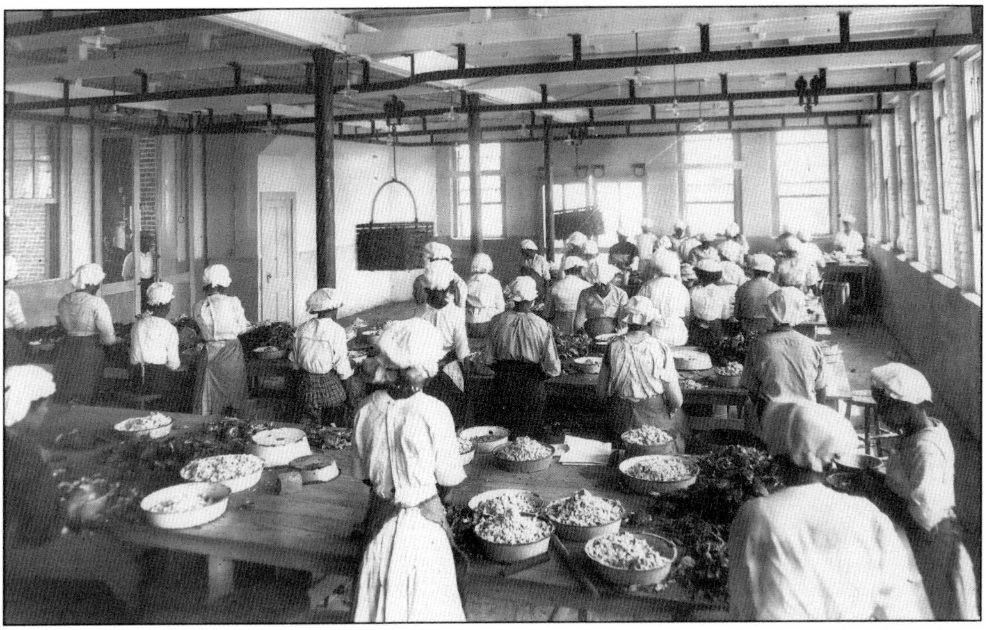

WOMEN AT WORK. Women clad in immaculate white caps and sleeves are meticulously picking crabmeat for the Samuel S. Coston Company, whose building is still today at the foot of Bridge Street. Crabs came to each worker from the overhead basket, and the meat was put in the porcelain-veneered metal bowls. Three hundred bushels of crabs were processed daily. Coston sold crabmeat as far away as Chicago, Illinois, Omaha, Nebraska, and Salt Lake City, Utah.

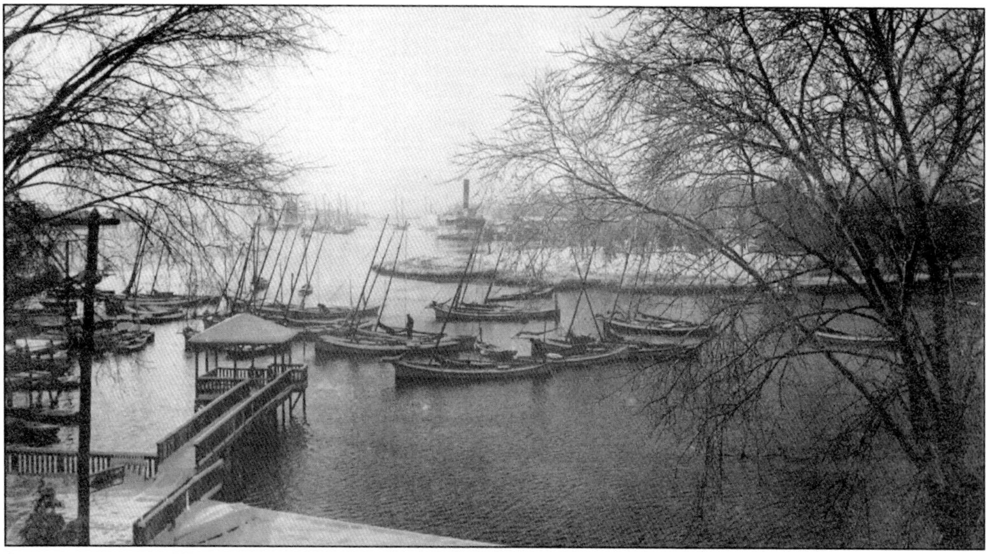

STEAMSHIP IN HAMPTON RIVER. A steamship, having arrived from Norfolk in this 1905 photograph, is docked at the McMenamin crab factory to take on cargo, with a forest of thin-masted log canoes between it and the photographer. Before the present bridge-tunnels connected the two shores of Hampton Roads, steamships (and later automobile ferries) provided Hampton shoppers, visitors, and businessmen regular access to Norfolk.

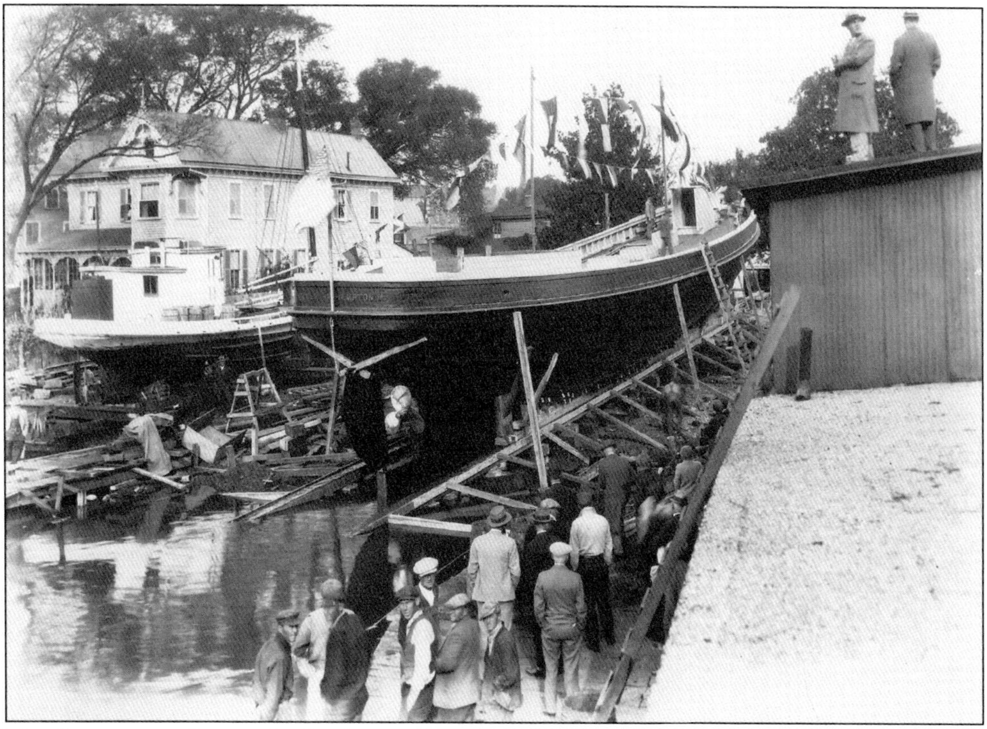

THE BUSINESS OF BOATS. Seafood meant boats, and watermen's boats were often built in Hampton. This 1926 photograph shows the launching of the *Malolo*, owned by M. C. Armstrong, at the tiny Darling shipyard. Captioned by Herbert Milholen, the *Malolo* later sank. Note the attending crowd—perhaps boat builders, perhaps watermen—some of whom are facing the camera.

Seven

Hampton's Heyday

Seafood brought prosperity. Banks, stores, and hotels sprang up along King and Queen Streets. Electricity and the telephone made their appearances. The clang of trolley cars long preceded the automobile horn as a measure of Hampton's bustle, and the whistle of steam railroad engines began to be heard, adding to the traditional noise of wagons and ships. Echoes of Hampton's antebellum tourist trade also were felt as regular summer excursion trains brought throngs of vacationers to Buckroe Beach.

Segregation created and regulated enclaves for African American businesses, such as Taylor's Grocery and many other small firms. The Bay Shore Hotel opened in 1897 to offer black citizens a place on the water for bathing and recreation.

Much of Hampton's development was spearheaded by J. S. Darling's son Frank and his business associates, among whom were Nelson S. Groome, H. R. Booker, and Harry H. Holt. The Bank of Hampton, and then two other banks, opened at the corner of King and Queen Streets. A second Hygeia Hotel was built on Point Comfort, and soon the 554-room Chamberlin Hotel appeared next to it. It was a victim of fire in 1920 but was rebuilt in 1928 by Darling and his associates.

Hampton's economic stability became even more well anchored when, in 1916, Holt and other leaders with connections in Washington, D.C., convinced the government to locate both its first military airbase and its aeronautical laboratory, the National Advisory Committee on Aeronautics (NACA), in the town. The base was named Langley Field after aviation pioneer Samuel P. Langley. The influx of scientists, engineers, military personnel, and workers brought unprecedented growth and prosperity.

By the 1920s, Hampton was booming again. King and Queen Streets remained the heart of downtown, a gathering place to enjoy drugstores, moving picture theaters, and window-shopping. Neighborhoods grew along the streetcar lines connecting Hampton to Newport News—whose great shipyard and coal terminal provided work for many Hamptonians.

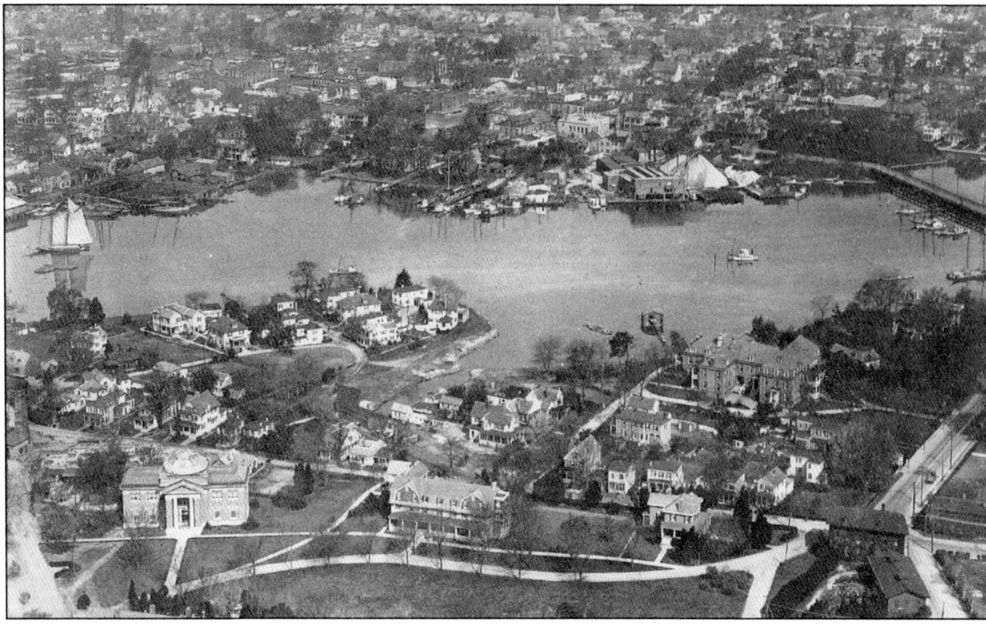

DOWNTOWN HAMPTON AND HAMPTON INSTITUTE, 1918. Many benefits flowed to Hampton from Langley Field, including the airmen's penchant for aerial photography. This panorama along Hampton River shows a growing town. Landmarks, starting in the photograph's upper center and proceeding clockwise, include the post office, the giant Darling oyster pile, the old Queen Street bridge, the old Dixie Hospital, the Hampton Institute, and a full-rigged ship under sail.

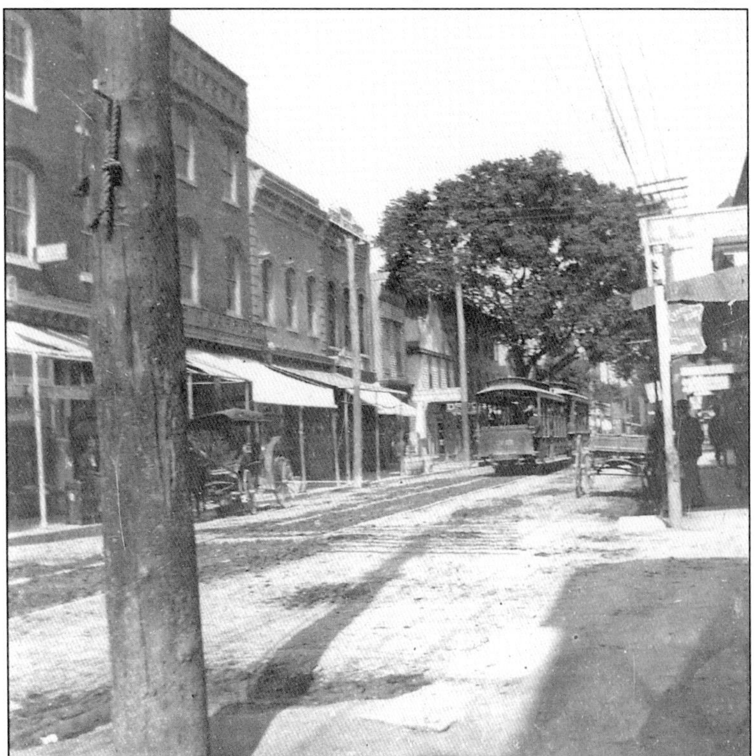

THE CENTER OF HAMPTON, ABOUT 1895. The trolley car runs along an unpaved east Queen Street. A buckboard wagon is parked just beyond the King Street intersection on the right, while a covered buggy sits on the left in front of Daniel Morrow's dry-goods store. Awnings and a leafy tree provided pedestrians a haphazard pattern of shade, but the dust must have been daunting.

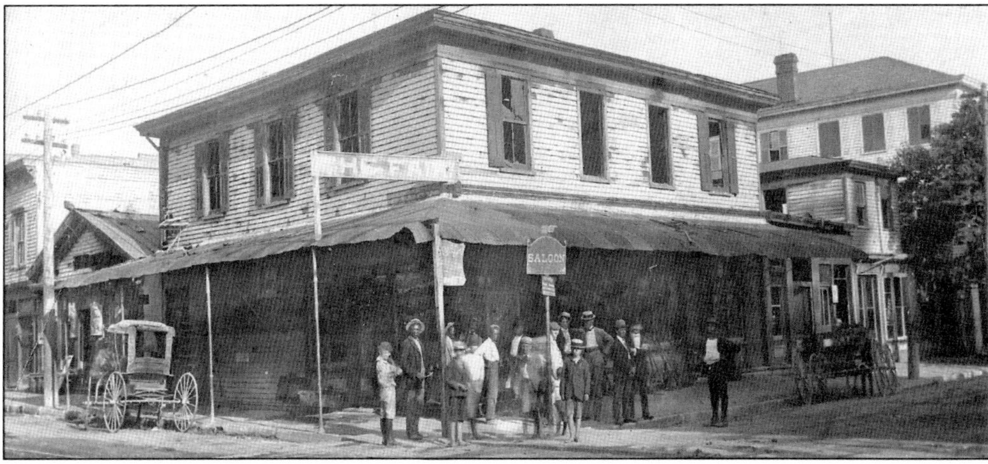

CONVIVIALITY AND SALOONS. A remarkably integrated group of men and boys poses in the heat of summer on the corner of King and Queen Streets in front of the abandoned saloon called "The Fair" around 1895. Fire damage to the saloon is evident, and the remnant of an older, more casual Hampton was soon torn down. The tall building on the right is the Barnes Hotel, one of the town's three hostelries.

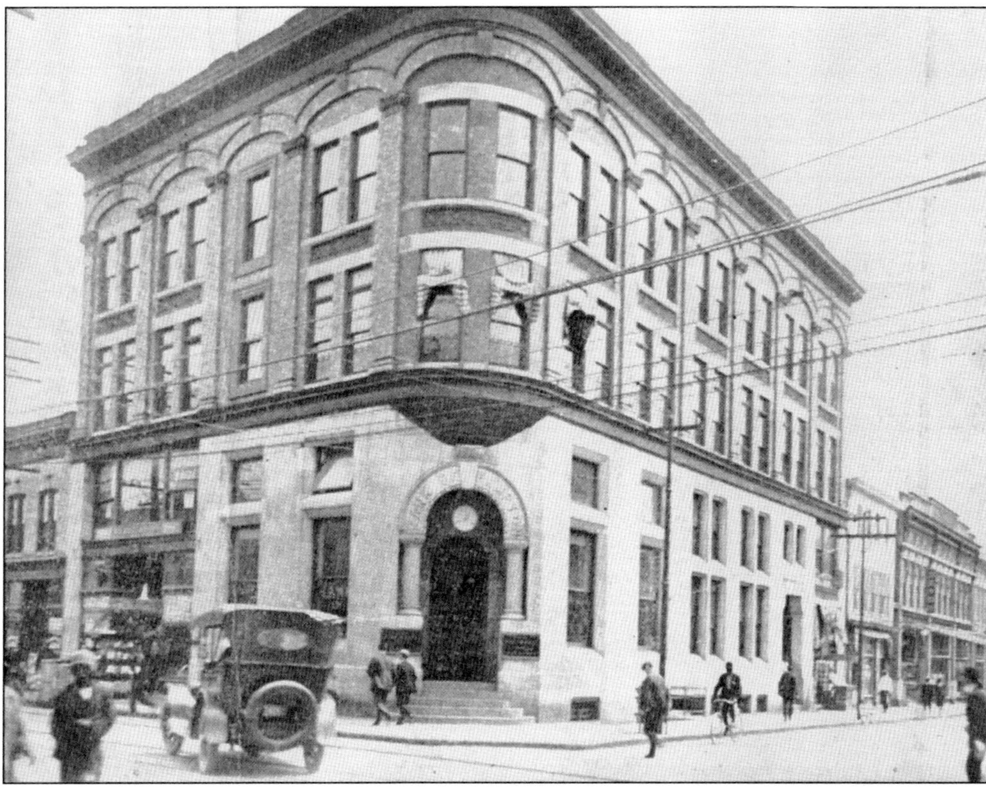

BANKING MEANS PROSPERITY. In 1901, the magnificent new Bank of Hampton building replaced The Fair to dominate the corner of King and Queen Streets. The streets are paved, and automobiles have superseded horse-drawn vehicles in this photograph from the 1920s. A 1903 bank reorganization brought oyster entrepreneur Frank W. Darling and his associates Henry L. Schmelz and Nelson W. Groome into management, stabilizing the bank for a quarter of a century.

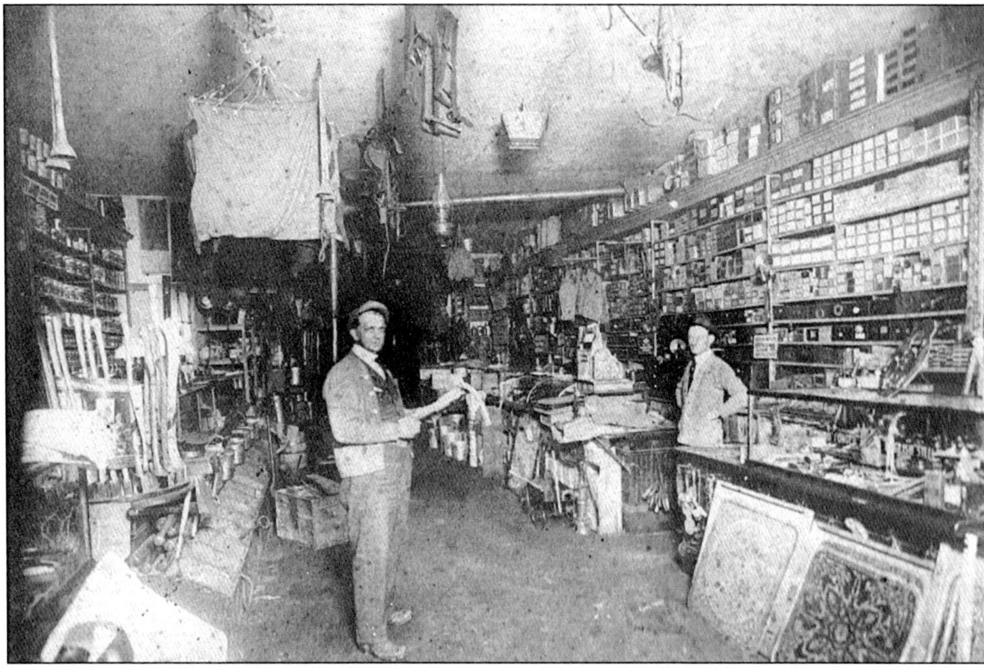

HAMPTON'S HARDWARE TRADITION. The cluttered shelves and aisles of W. T. Patrick and Son's hardware store on west Queen Street have changed little since this photograph was taken around 1910. Farmers and city folk have been able to obtain almost everything they need here since 1895. The store was moved to its present location in 1907, where Patricks still wait on customers. (Courtesy of W. T. Patrick and Son.)

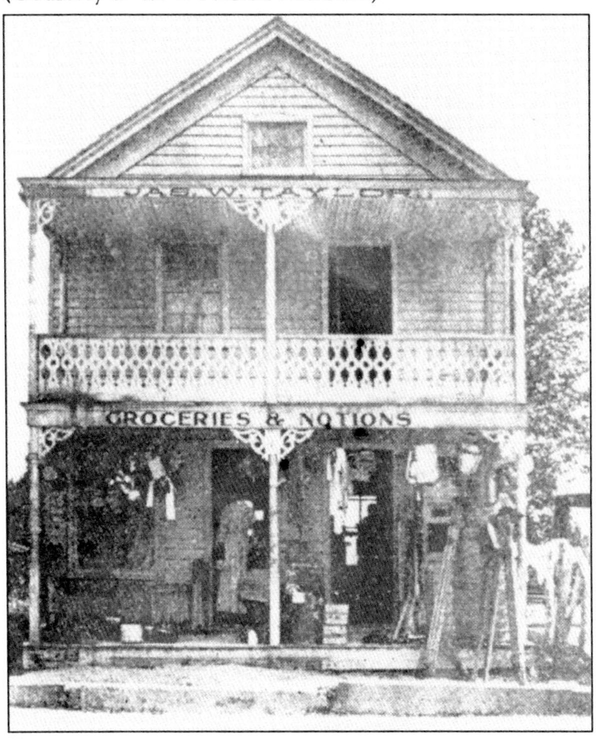

ENTREPRENEURSHIP IN HAMPTON "EXTENDED." James W. Taylor, a black barber recently arrived from Washington D.C., stands in 1907 silhouetted in the right-hand door of the grocery store he owned on west Queen Street. Taylor also cut hair in an adjacent location and probably lived upstairs. So-called by whites who resented black freedom, Hampton's "extension" filled the area previously covered by the Grand Contraband Camp.

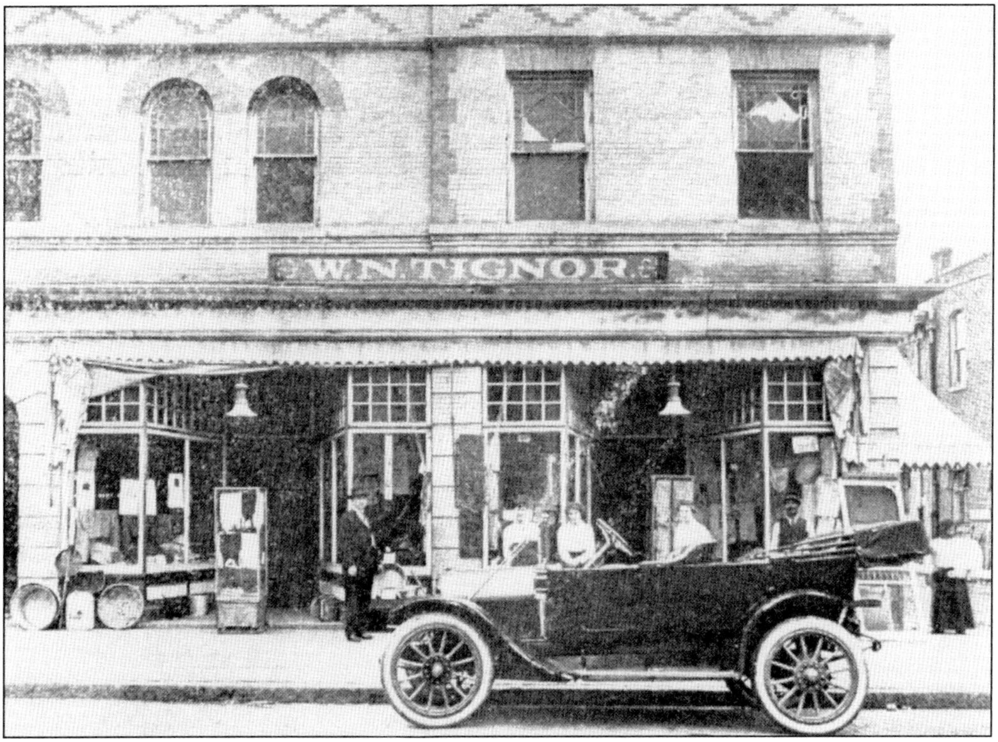

NOTIONS. W. N. Tignor opened his notions store at 47 East Queen Street soon after 1900. This 1920s photograph shows how he has expanded into 45 East Queen Street and the store has become an early department store. The "five and dime" movement of nationwide chain stores and the Great Depression would later drive him from business. The striking brick mosaic pattern of decoration later disappeared from American downtown architecture.

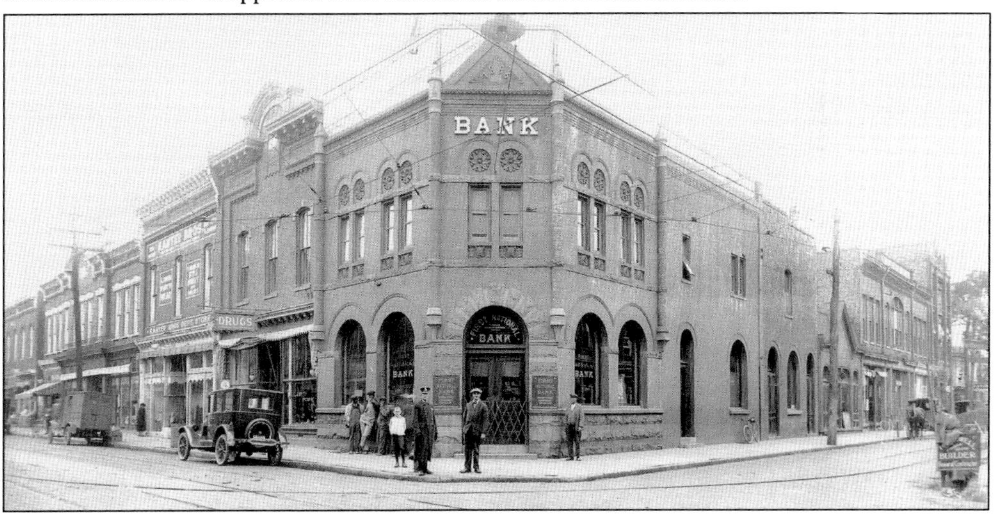

A STUNNING CITYSCAPE. The photographer uses an imposing policeman and other bystanders gazing at the camera to draw us into the angles and shapes of a city block, framed by rooflines, trolley wires, and tracks. The angled front of the First National Bank was matched by the Bank of Hampton building across the King and Queen Streets intersection to form what Hampton historian Sis Evans called "a sense of place and importance."

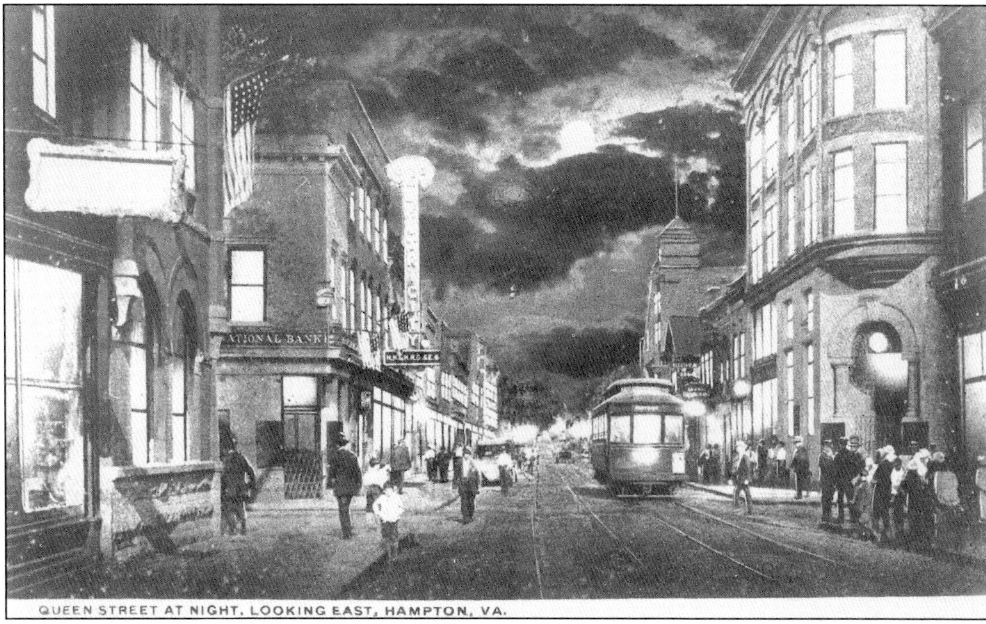

LIVELY HAMPTON, ABOUT 1925. All three Hampton banks on their respective corners can be seen in this vivid, busy nighttime image of the intersection of King and Queen Streets. Automobiles and the trolley have their headlamps lit. At left center is the illuminated sign of the local gas, electricity, and trolley company—a private utility. Cheap electricity, a mark of modernity, has set Hampton ablaze.

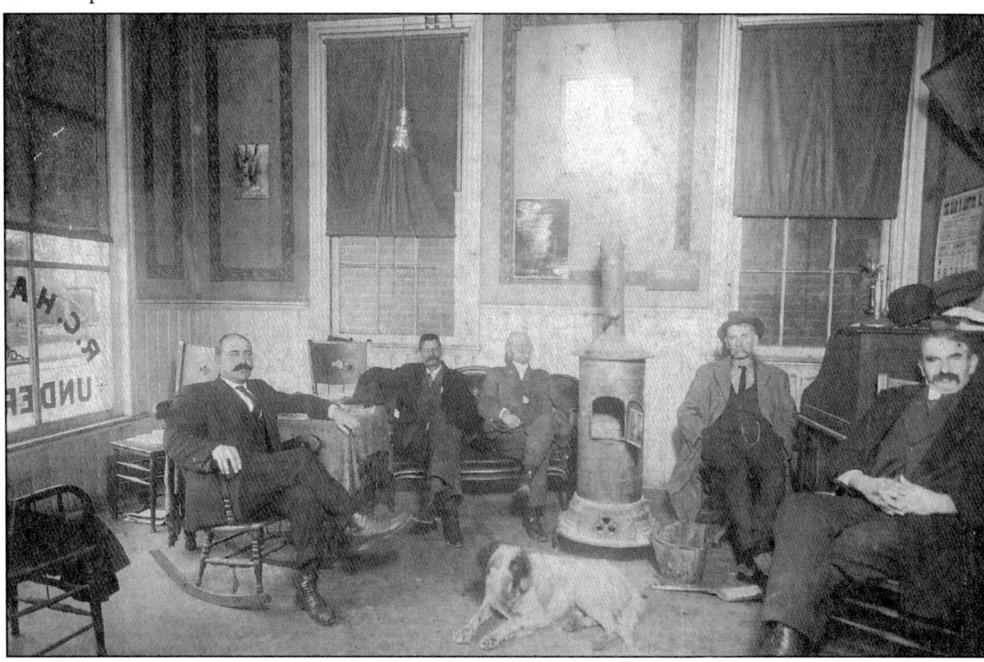

THE FUNERAL DIRECTORS. Sitting around a pot-bellied stove, five nicely dressed gentlemen and a beautiful English setter pose for the photographer in their undertaker's parlor. The owner, R. C. Hall, sits on the sofa in the left-center next to the stove, while his son Arthur is in the rocking chair. Then, as now, funeral direction was a family business.

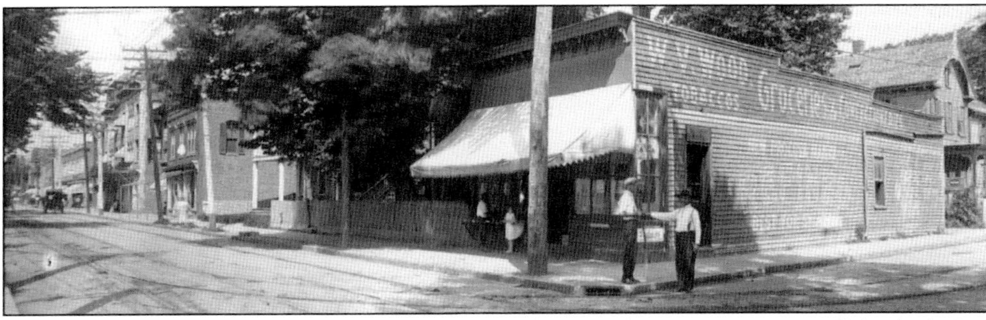

A Spring Morning, about 1900. Girard Chambers Sr., longtime surveyor of Elizabeth City County, stands in Locust Street near its intersection with east Queen Street handing a surveying pole to his tall, young assistant outside Walter V. Wood's grocery store (established in 1882). The horse-and-buggy up Queen Street is parked outside the partially awning-covered windows of the Augusta Hotel. The huge shade trees soon disappeared from downtown.

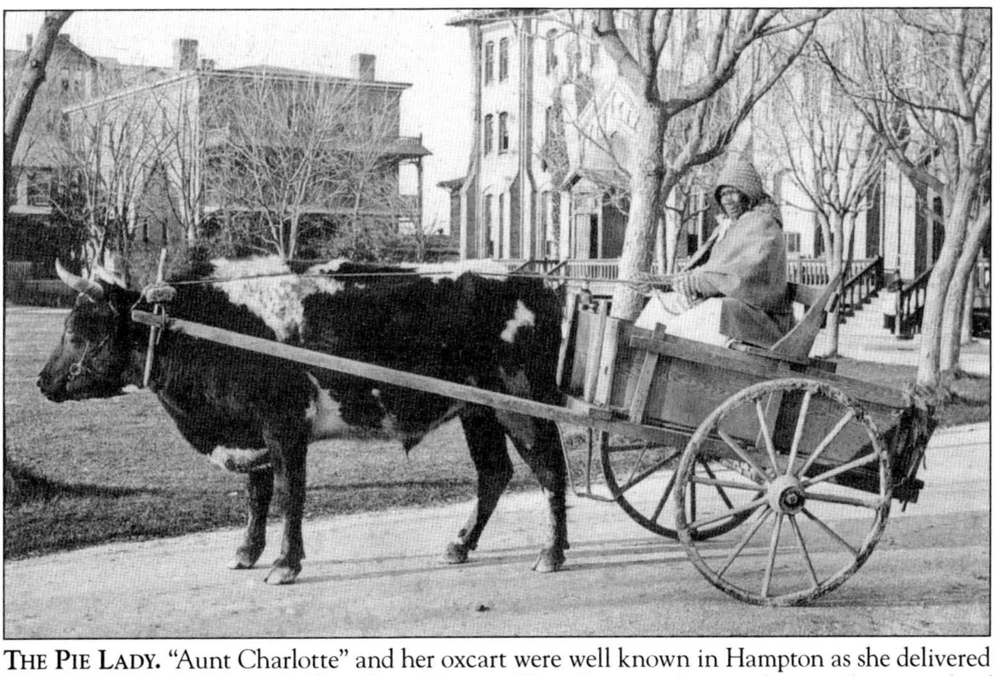

The Pie Lady. "Aunt Charlotte" and her oxcart were well known in Hampton as she delivered pies to her customers, especially at Fort Monroe. This photograph was taken on the grounds of Hampton Institute. Independent entrepreneurs like Aunt Charlotte purveyed many necessities and delicacies from wagons, carts, and (later) small trucks until well after World War II—including the ice cream man.

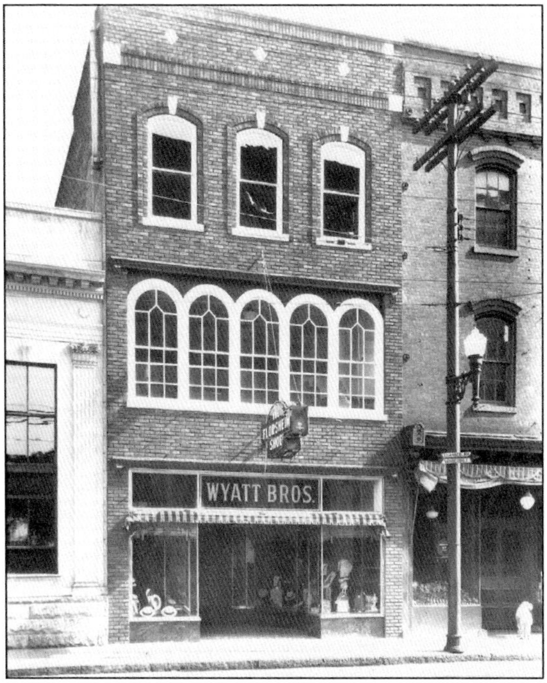

HAMPTON'S OLDEST COMMERCIAL BUILDINGS. This building and the brick building next door were built in 1872. Wyatt Brothers, the iconic men's clothing store, was located here from 1930 to 1969. It previously housed Lemuel H. Sclater's drugstore and H. R. Booker's hardware store. It has since 1969 contained law offices, first those of Sclater descendants E. S. and David Montague, and now the firm of S. Frear Hawkins, Thomas A. Burcher, and Robert A. Boester.

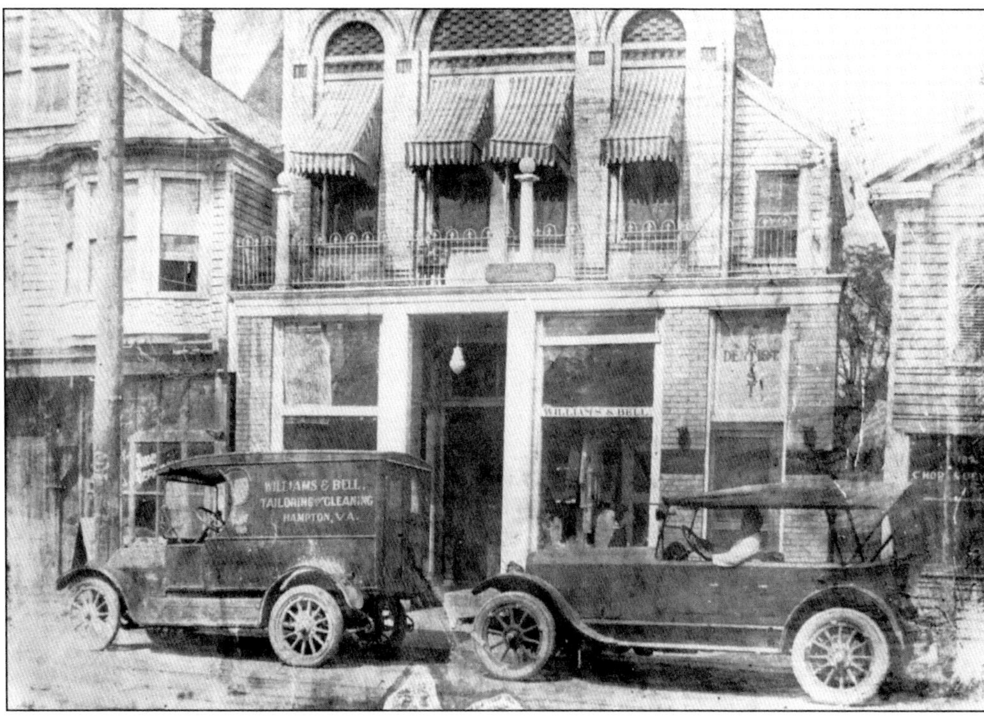

THE DIFFICULTIES OF BUSINESS. Around 1920, Jacob Williams, a black tailor, partnered with William Bell in a laundry venture in the building of the defunct black-run Galilean Fisherman's Bank. However, Bell soon disappeared from the business scene, and Williams became an employee of Wyatt Brothers, apparently never to own his own enterprise again. Note Lee Hong's eating house next door. (Courtesy of Virginiana Room, Hampton Public Library.)

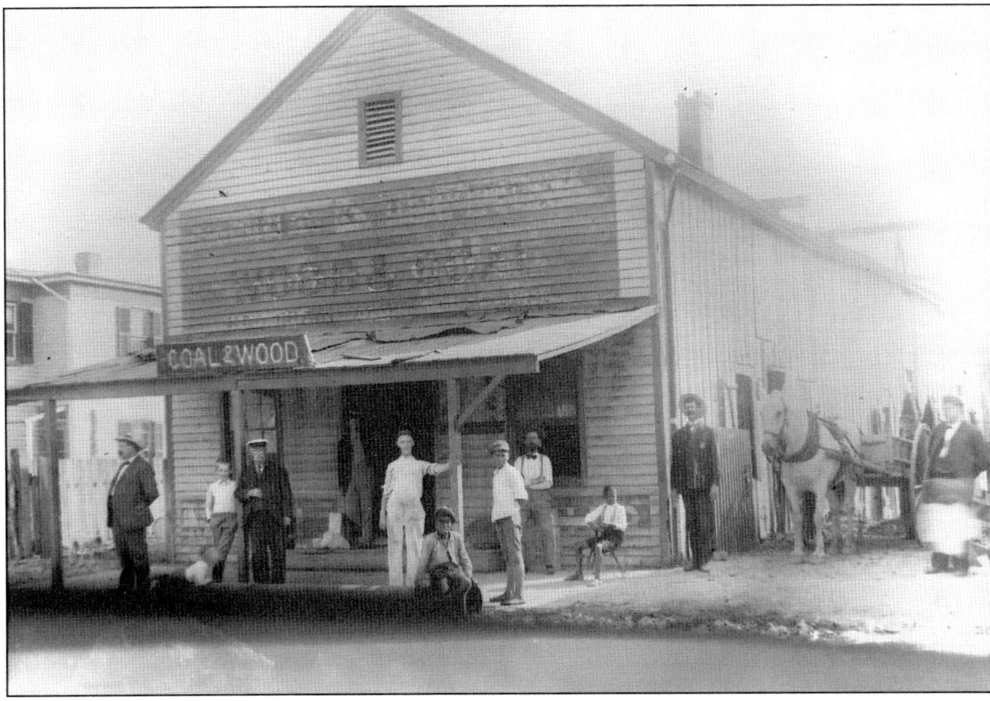

TENNIS'S STORE. The photographer has carefully posed an array of Hamptonians young and old outside Richard B. Tennis's wood, coal, and feed store on Armistead Avenue at the edge of downtown about 1898. The sign is fading, and the place would soon house a grocery. The cart-hitched horse patiently awaits his load. Agriculture was as important as seafood to the local economy.

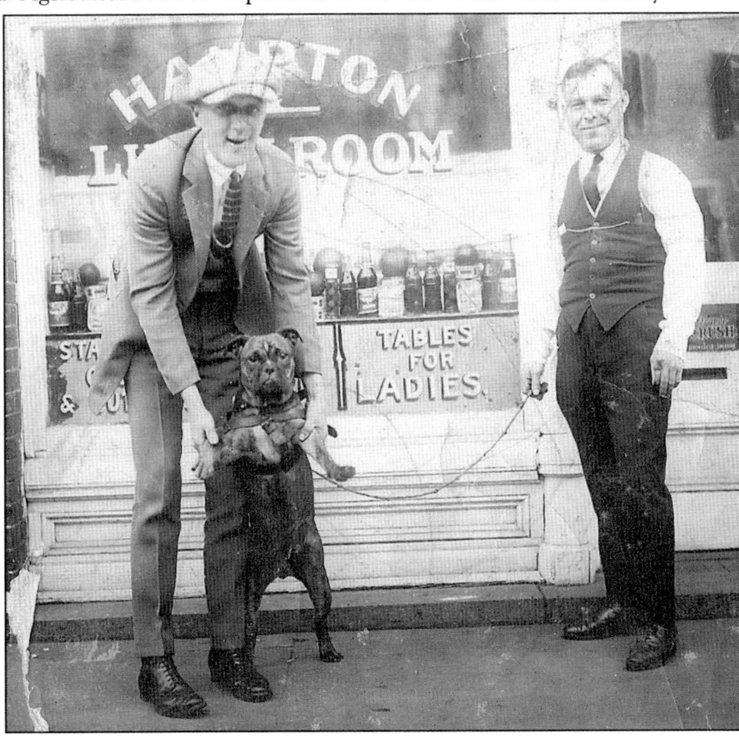

THE HAMPTON LUNCH ROOM. People dined out much less frequently in this period than they do today. Nevertheless small eateries, such as the one shown in this 1923 photograph, were places of conviviality and businessmen's lunches. The Hampton Lunch Room was on north King Street and had a short existence. As the window sign shows, it was still difficult for women to eat in public places unescorted.

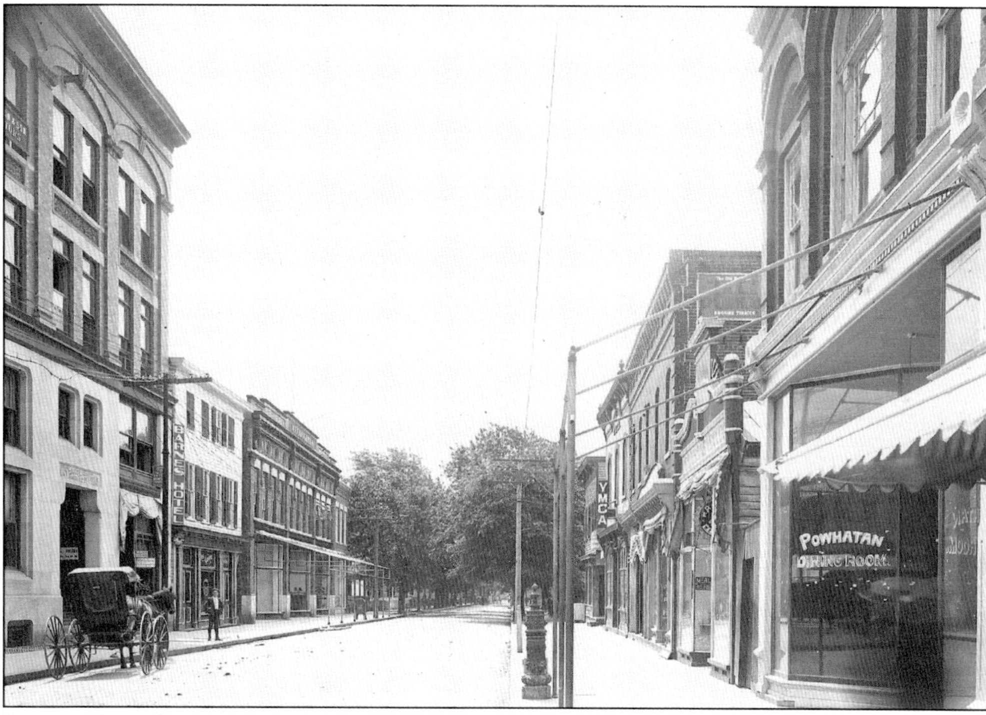

SOUTH KING STREET BUSINESSES. Leafy shade envelops the wharf and seafood end of King Street in this photograph from about 1905. The YMCA would soon become the Elks' Lodge. Across the street are the Kecoughtan Building and the Barnes Hotel. After losing to John L. Sullivan in an 1888 prize fight, Jake Kilrain hid out for two months at the Barnes, a stag hotel with a bar and dining room.

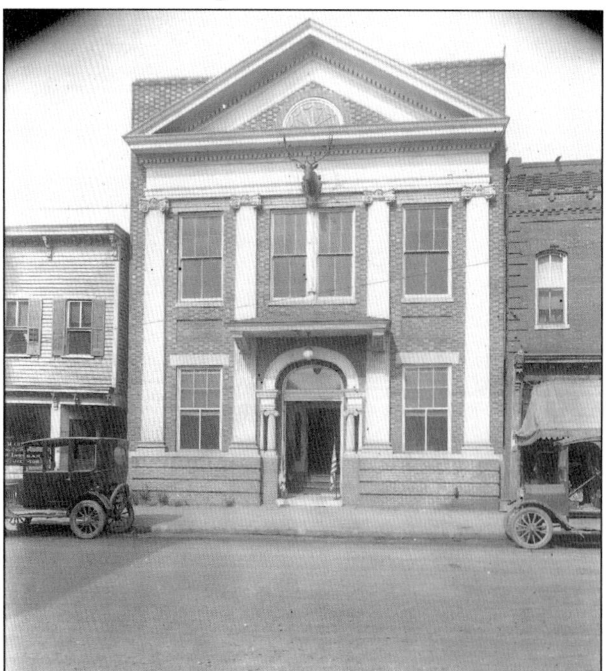

CIVIC CLUBS. The Elks have purchased the YMCA for a meeting hall and, later, a residence hall. Springing up simultaneously with other secret societies, such as college fraternities, civic clubs like the Elks, the Eagles, the Red Men, and the Odd Fellows gave men a night out each week, a means of acquaintance, a sense of clandestine pomp and ceremony, and projects with which to improve their community.

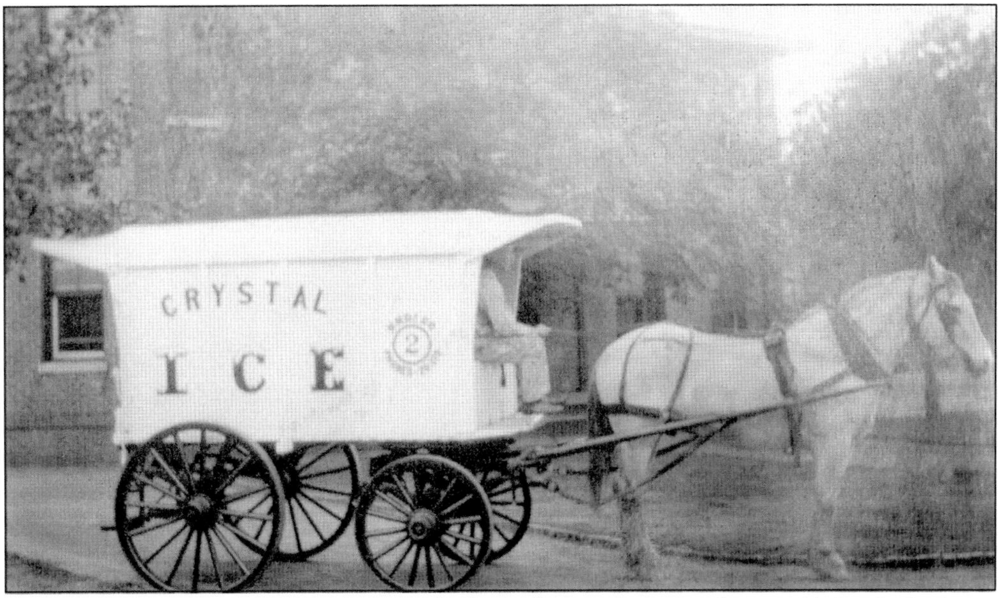

BEFORE REFRIGERATORS. Seafood spawned other industries. Ice was indispensable for the freshness of the harvest from the sea. It was delivered daily. Home iceboxes also used the products of the Crystal Ice Company, a subsidiary of the private utility company, located on Sunset Creek. A delivery wagon is shown here. A cardboard or wooden "ice today" sign would be placed in a front window when ice was needed.

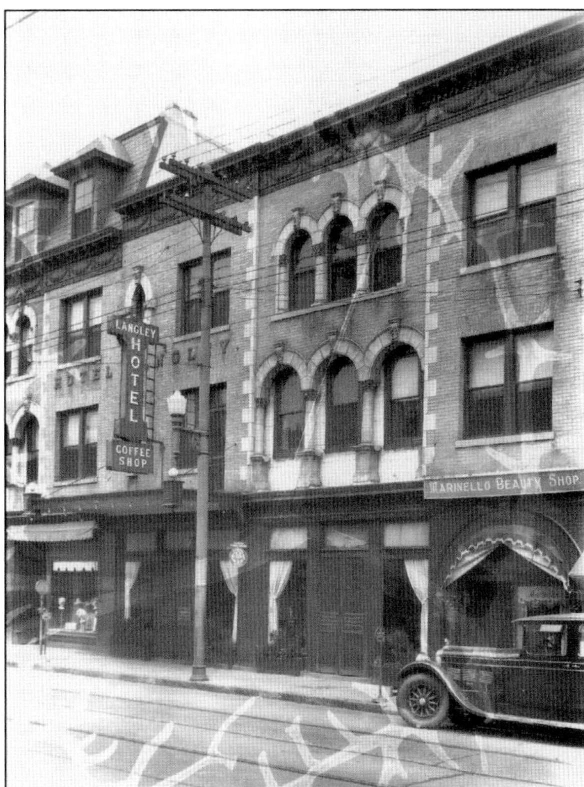

THE LANGLEY HOTEL. After the advent of Langley Field, the best downtown hotel, the Augusta on east Queen Street, was remodeled and renamed the Langley, as shown in this 1935 photograph. Various stores always took space on the ground floor. Note the beauty shop and the ladies' millinery. Note also that AAA recommendations existed even then.

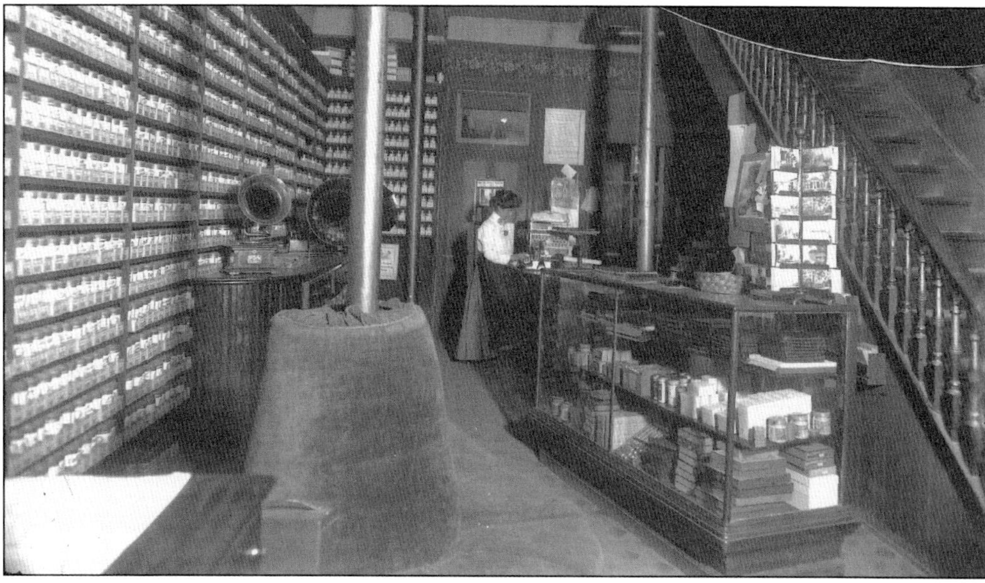

A LOCAL PHOTOGRAPHY STORE. This is the first-floor interior of C. Ethelbert Cheyne's photography business, where film, Kodak cameras, developing chemicals, and postcards were sold. One had to climb to the second floor to have one's picture made by Hampton's master photographer. Note the Victor Victrola record player on the counter; Cheyne also sold Edison Phonograph Cylinders (records) and record players.

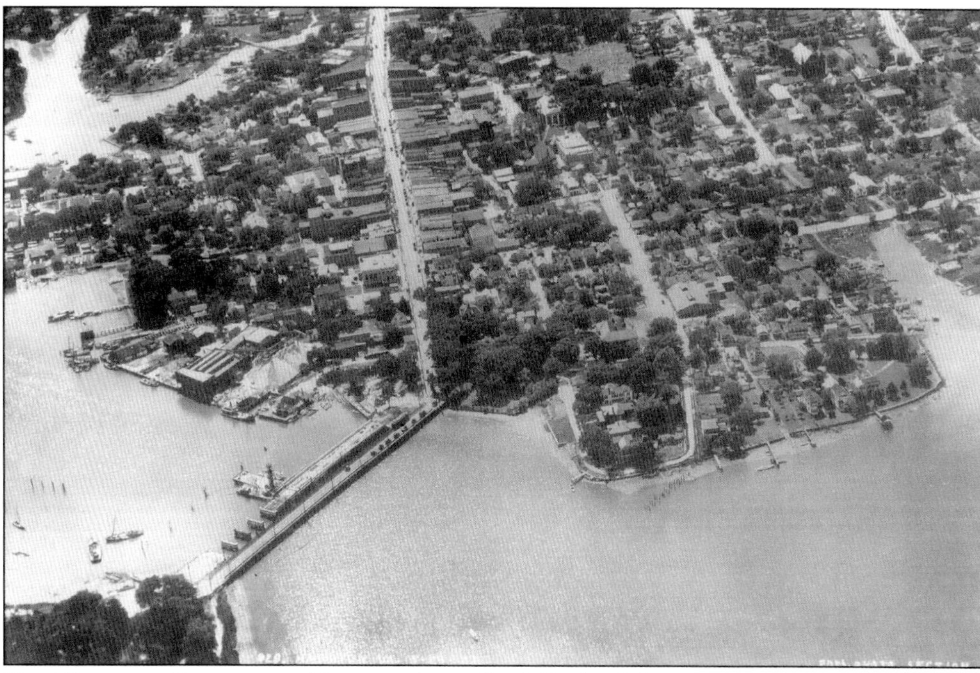

THE HEART OF CRABTOWN. Marine railways flank Darling's large oyster enterprise and several smaller seafood businesses on Custom House Point (lower left). Nearby, in this 1922 photograph, the Queen Street bridge is being replaced. To the right, the Syms-Eaton Academy sits on Pee Dee Point. The white-columned courthouse is in the center. There is no Bridge Street at upper left, but the old footbridge from Acorn Point to downtown can be seen.

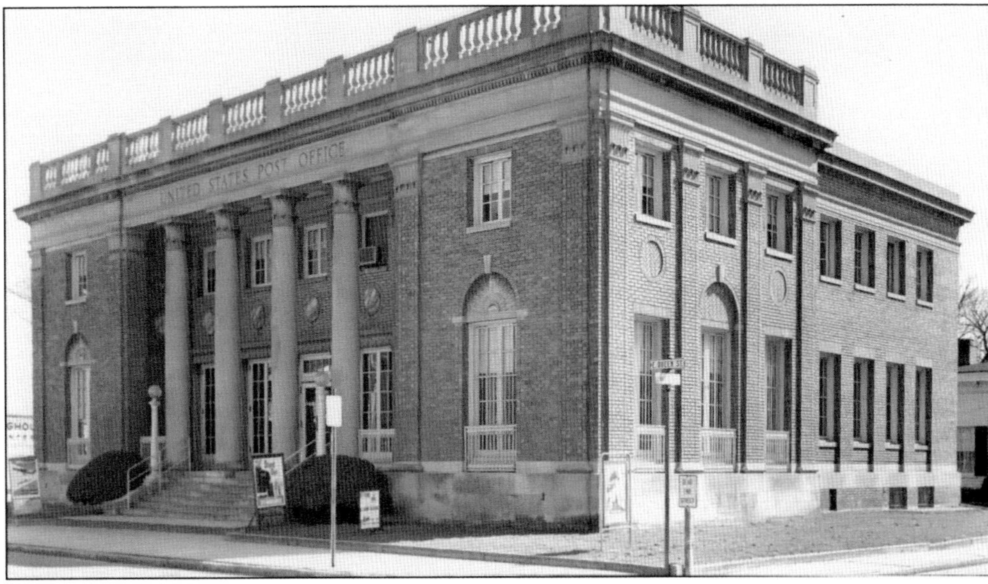

POST OFFICE. Hampton's post office was constructed in 1914. According to Hampton historian Sis Evans, "When John M. Willis was postmaster in 1836, he carried the mail in his big cream colored plug hat, delivering it as he met people on the street. In 1885, when Mattie K. Chisman was postmistress, the office was on north King," then on east Queen Street, and finally on south King Street—always in private buildings.

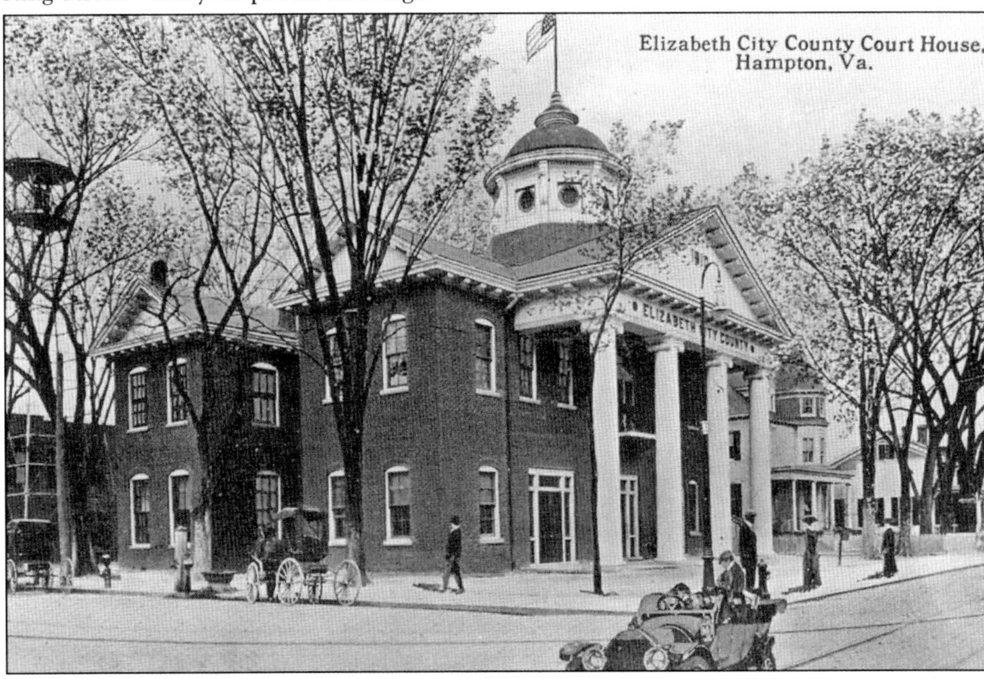

ELIZABETH CITY COUNTY COURTHOUSE. The courthouse has served the Hampton Circuit Court since 1952 when, through consolidation into Hampton, the county disappeared. The present building was constructed in 1876 using the walls of the previous courthouse, which had been consumed by fire in 1861 and had been built in 1714. Thus, George Wythe practiced law in this location.

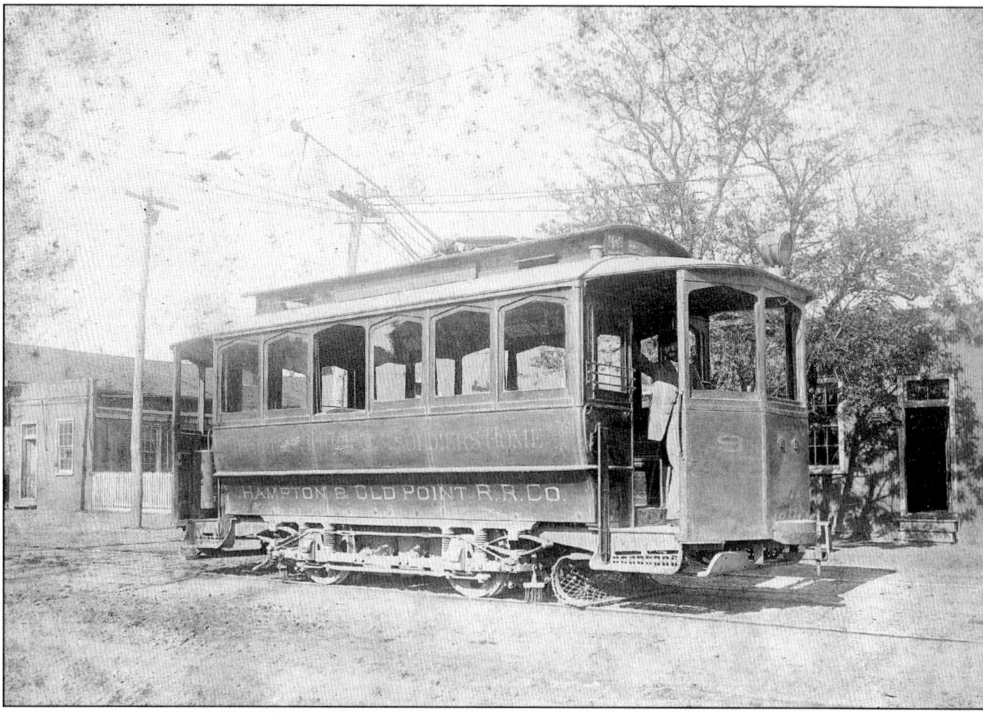

TROLLEY CAR NO. 9. Trolley tracks crossed Hampton long before the coming of the automobile, linking the town to Newport News, Old Point Comfort, Phoebus, and the popular beach resort of Buckroe. Several competing trolley companies were consolidated by the Darlings into the local utility company. The trolleys disappeared after a disastrous accident on Queen Street in 1946.

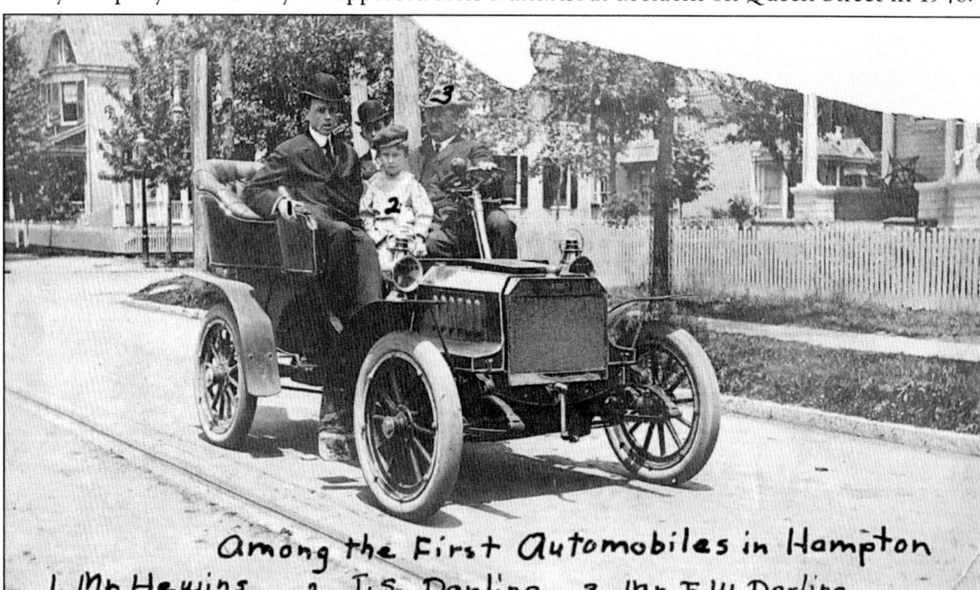

THE 20TH CENTURY MEANT AUTOMOBILES. Frank W. Darling sits at the wheel of one of the first automobiles in Hampton accompanied by Charles Hewins, J. S. Darling II, and an unidentified young man in a photograph taken about 1905. The hand-cranked starter, in front, could break a man's arm, while rutted, rocky wagon tracks made even the shortest trip an adventure.

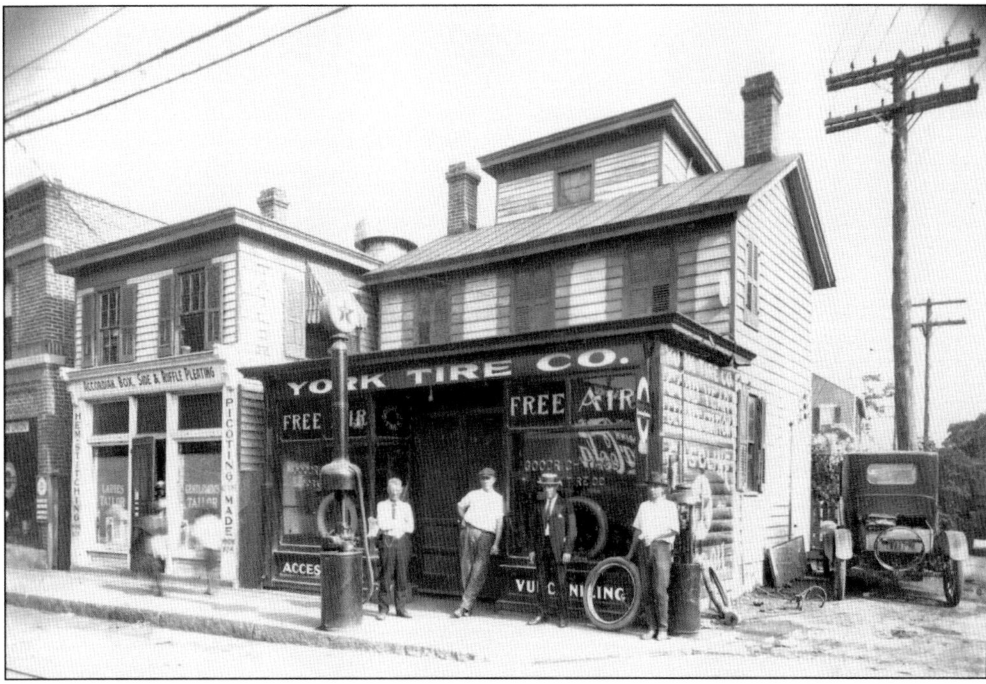

AUTOMOBILES NEED GAS AND TIRES. Thomas J. White's York Tire Company, located at 142 East Queen Street, catered to the novel needs of the automobile age. In the early 1920s, it was the only listed tire dealership in town. The gas pump, the air dispenser, and the station itself have clearly been wedged into the existing landscape. Note the tailor shop next door.

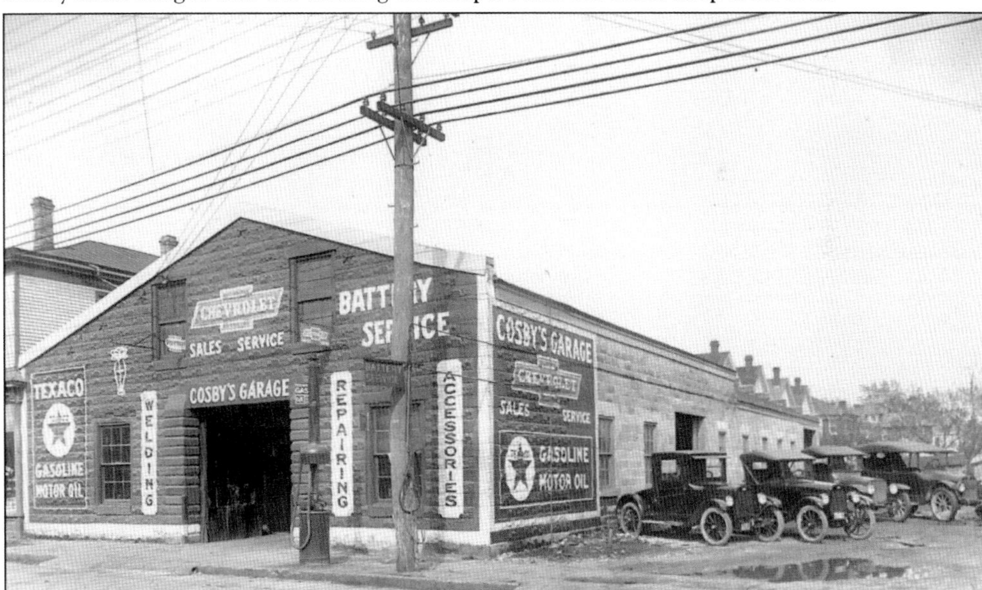

COSBY'S GARAGE. O. Garland Cosby was a master mechanic on the trolley line. By 1916, he had become the owner of Cosby's Garage at 115 Armistead Avenue, where he repaired automobiles. Then, by 1925, he was the Chevrolet dealer in Hampton. The Texaco gasoline pump on the street is still an early type.

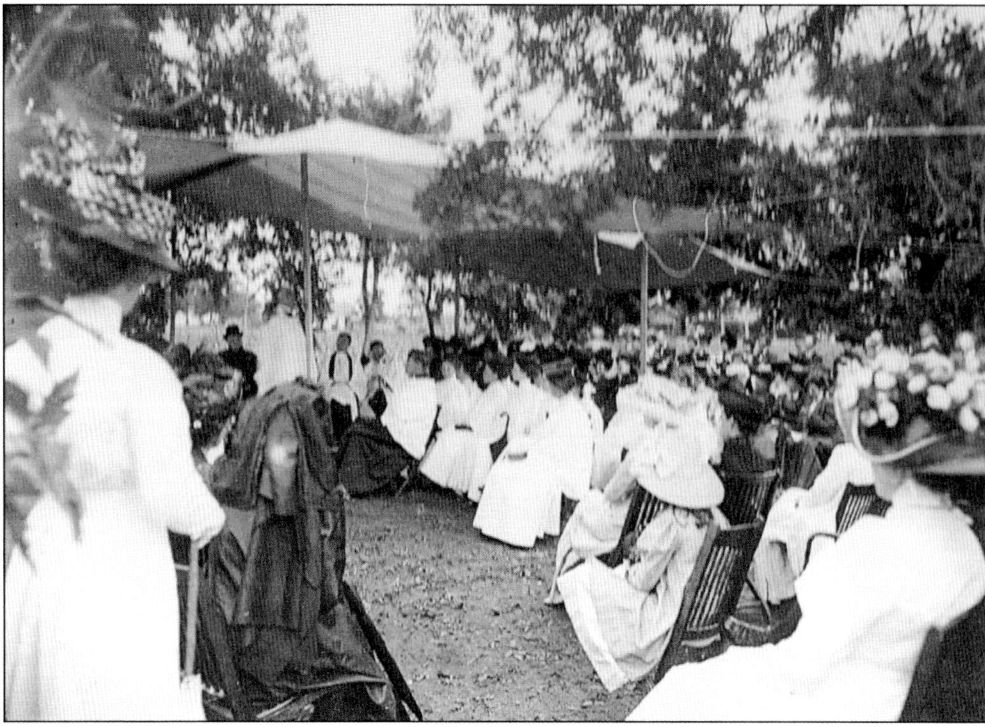

St. John's Church. Services are being held about 1910 in the open at the then recently rediscovered second site of the oldest continuous Episcopal parish in North America. The present church building, dating from 1728, is on the fourth site. The second site was expertly excavated under the direction of Eleanor Holt.

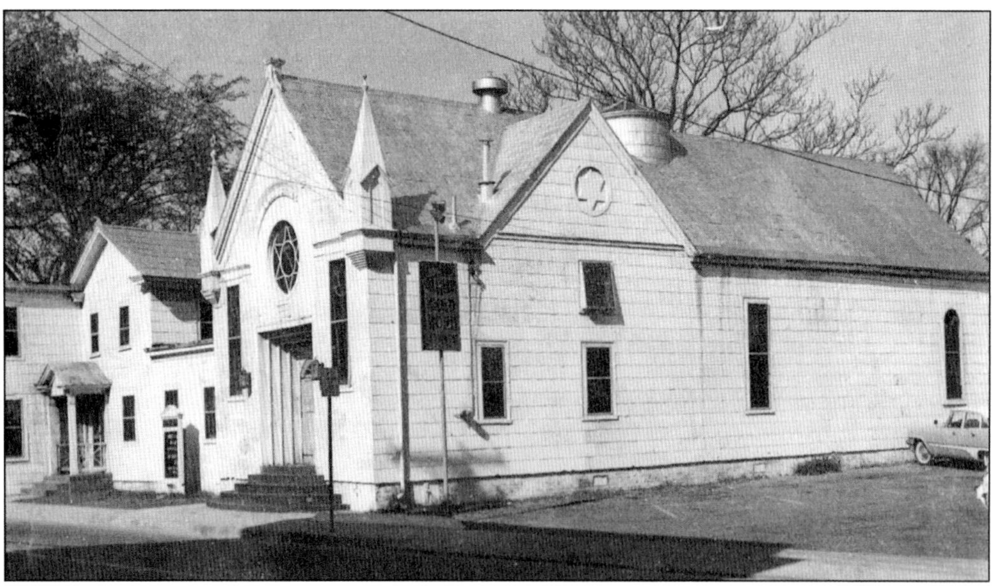

Hampton's Jewish Community. This long and narrow Synagogue was built on a 25-foot lot on Locust Street (now Eaton Street) in 1908. The congregation later added the educational buildings to the west, as seen in this photograph from the 1950s. In 1959, the structures and lots were sold to the Unitarian Fellowship of the Peninsula.

QUEEN STREET BAPTIST CHURCH. Organized in the ruined courthouse in 1865, the Second Baptist Church (as it was originally) is a "monument to faith and fortitude," according to Hampton historian Sis Evans. Its African American congregation moved into this building on west Queen Street in 1906. A new steeple was added in 1977, replacing the one shown here.

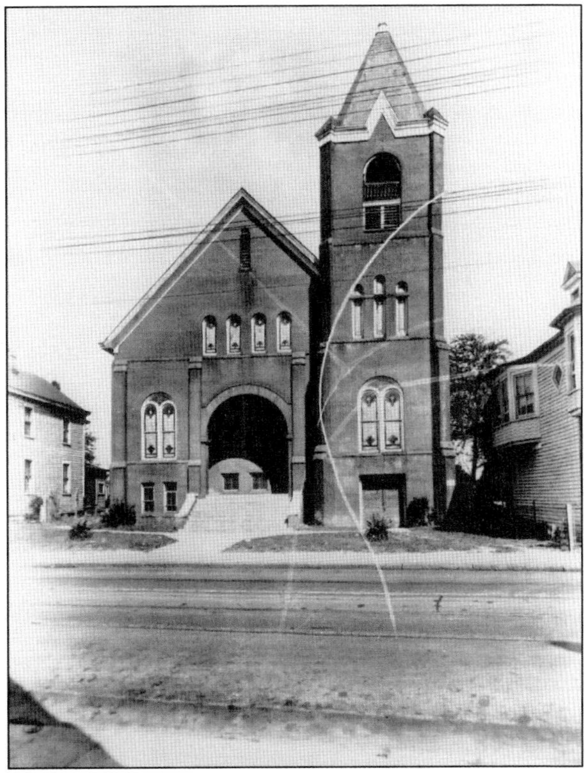

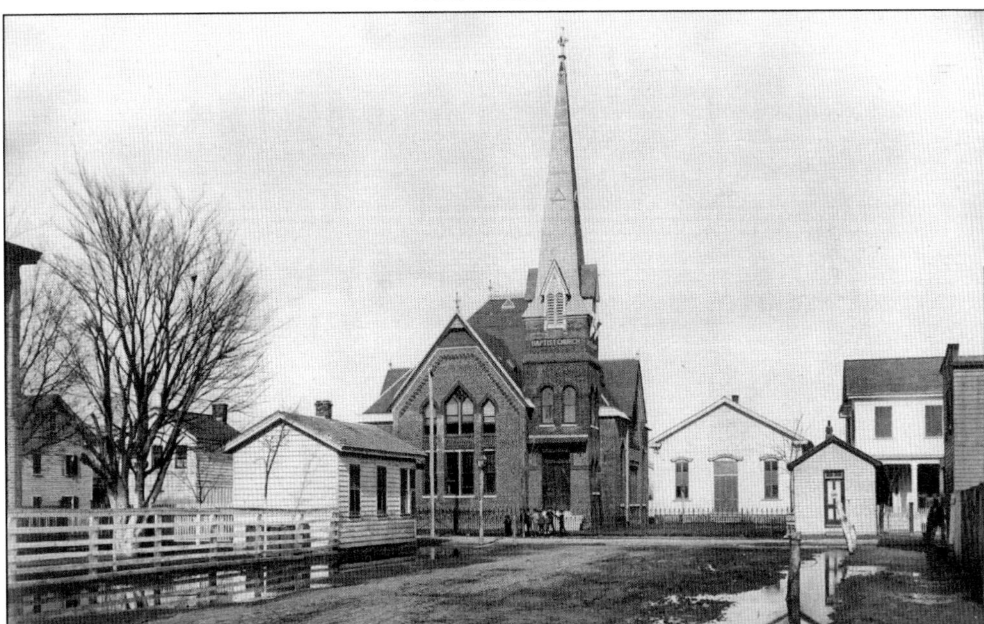

HAMPTON BAPTIST CHURCH. The tallest steeple in town marks this church, formerly known as First Baptist Church, on north King Street near the courthouse, just barely visible at the left edge of this 1899 photograph. The steeple was blown over in a freak storm in 1999 and has been replaced.

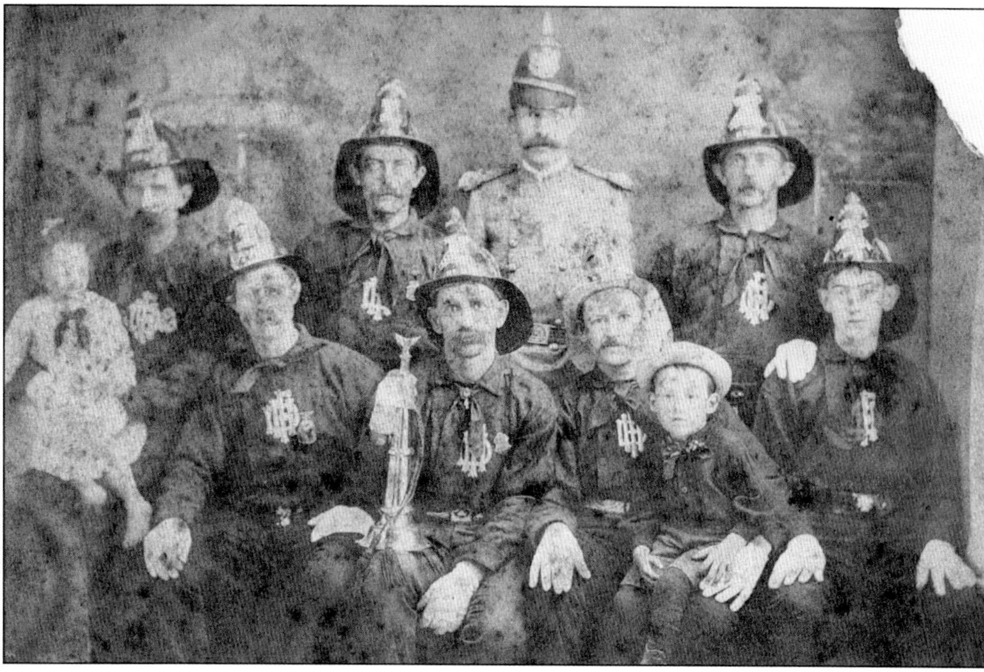

FIRE PROTECTION. Due to the lack of a Hampton fire brigade, the great 1884 fire had to be handled by equipment and men from the Hampton Institute, the old soldiers' home, and Fort Monroe. Citizens then hastily established a volunteer fire company. The first Hampton firefighters, shown here (with two of their children), came from all walks of life. In 1887, the city contributed funds for equipment and a fire station.

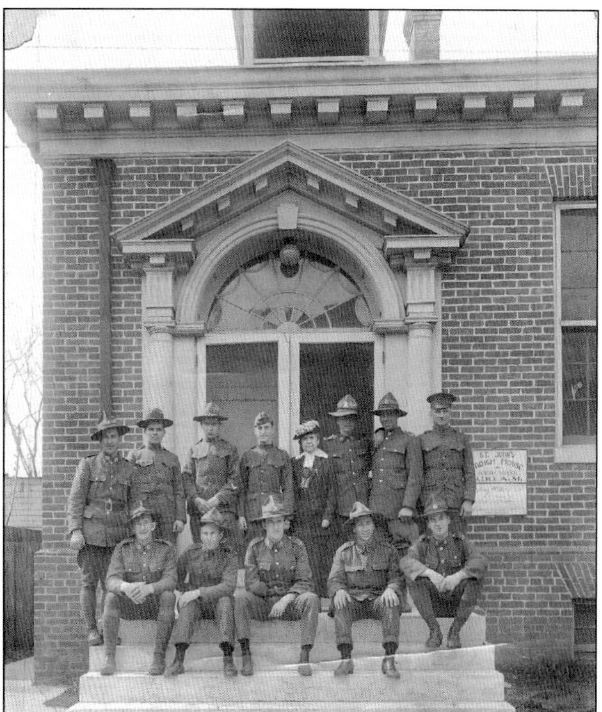

THE GREAT WAR. Grace Norris, a longtime supervisory employee and officer of St. John's Church, stands on the steps of the Parish House with 12 World War I soldiers, at least two of whom are amputees. The men had probably recently returned from the 15-month stay of American forces at the front in Europe.

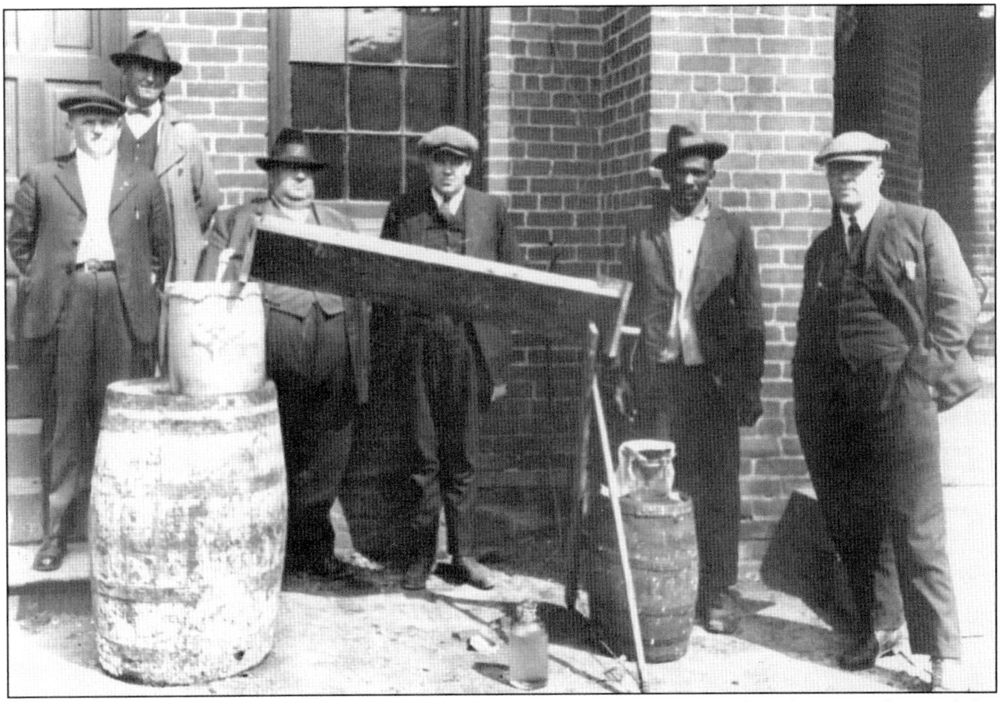

A Prohibition Bust. A captured rough-hewn bootlegger's still is displayed here in front of the old county jail. A bottle of pure but illegal hootch sits on the ground under the still. Longtime county sheriff Charles Curtis is at the right, and the other men are likely his deputies. Nothing caused the police more trouble than enforcing Prohibition.

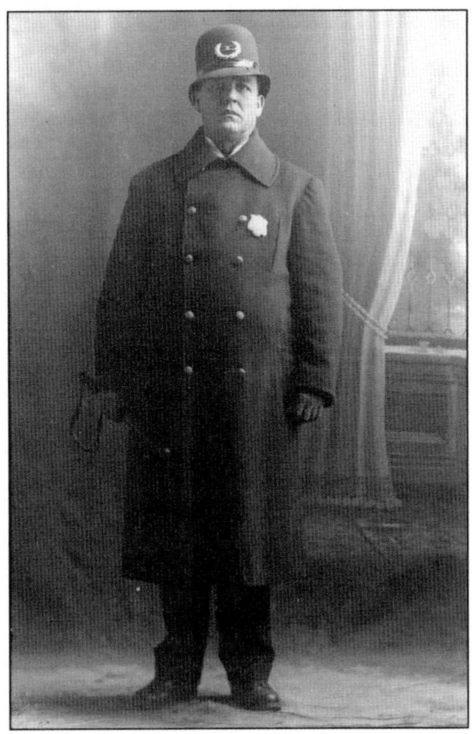

Hampton Policeman. This officer, standing in a house with billy club in hand, is unidentified. One of his 1920s police contemporaries was John Wesley Cunningham. Perhaps a victim of downsizing because of the Great Depression, Cunningham was a carpenter, a house painter, a soft drink bottler, and a truck driver during the 1930s.

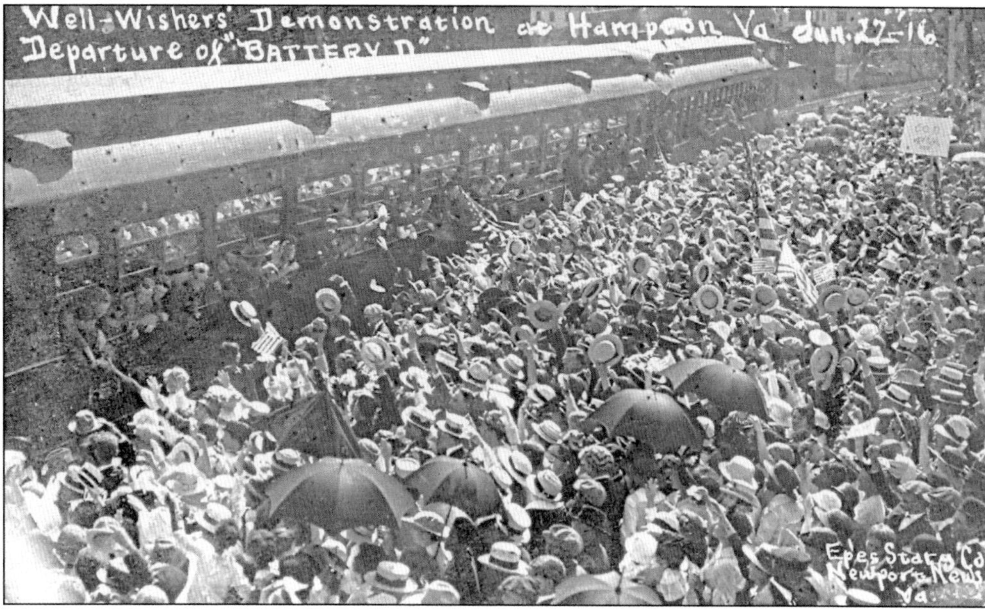

THE MEXICAN OPERATION. Pres. Woodrow Wilson dispatched U.S. troops to Mexico in 1916 to deal with the bandit Pancho Villa. Here hundreds of Hamptonians send "their boys" off with much cheering and good wishes as Hampton's Battery D gets on a troop train on June 27. Battery D was a unit of the 111th Artillery.

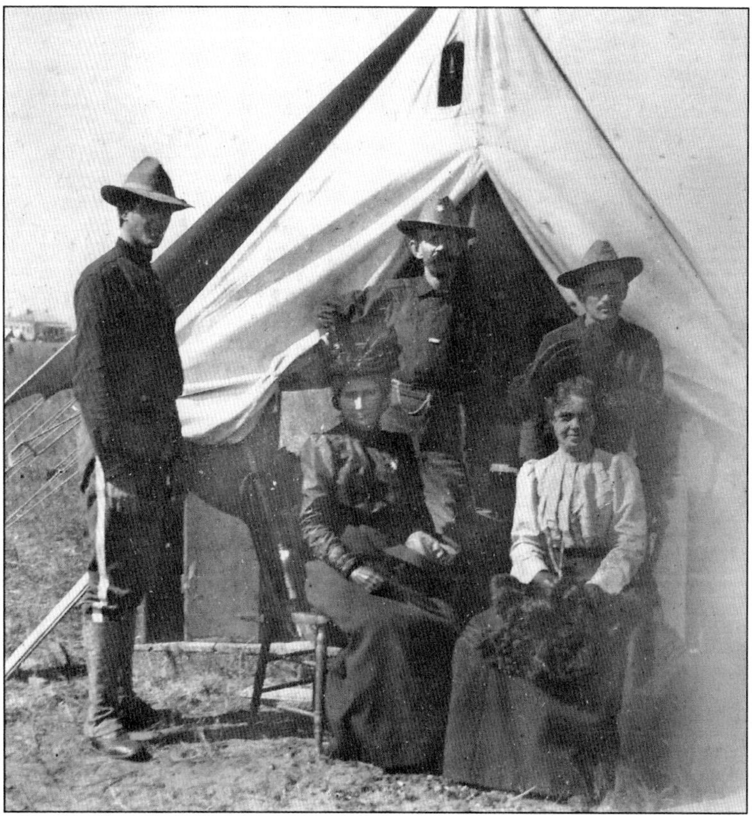

EN ROUTE TO WAR. Three members of Hampton's Battery D (left to right), Sgt. Thornton Jones, Tip Hope, and George Booker, pose in front of an army tent in 1898 in Savannah, Georgia, where they were training for the Spanish-American War. They have been joined by Mrs. Booker (possibly on right) and an unidentified lady. The soldiers were about to sail for Cuba, but they arrived after the war had ended.

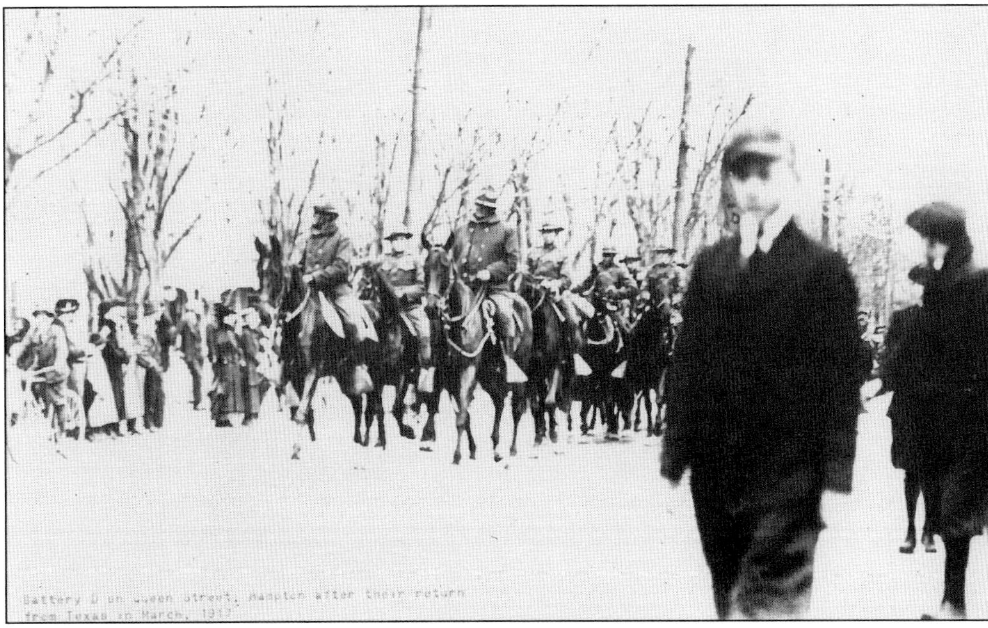

COMING HOME. Accompanied by children, Battery D's troops are being welcomed home by Hamptonians in March 1917. They had gotten as far as Leon Springs, Texas, when the punitive expedition against Pancho Villa was terminated. Battery D was ever a bridesmaid, never a bride, in its wartime mobilizations.

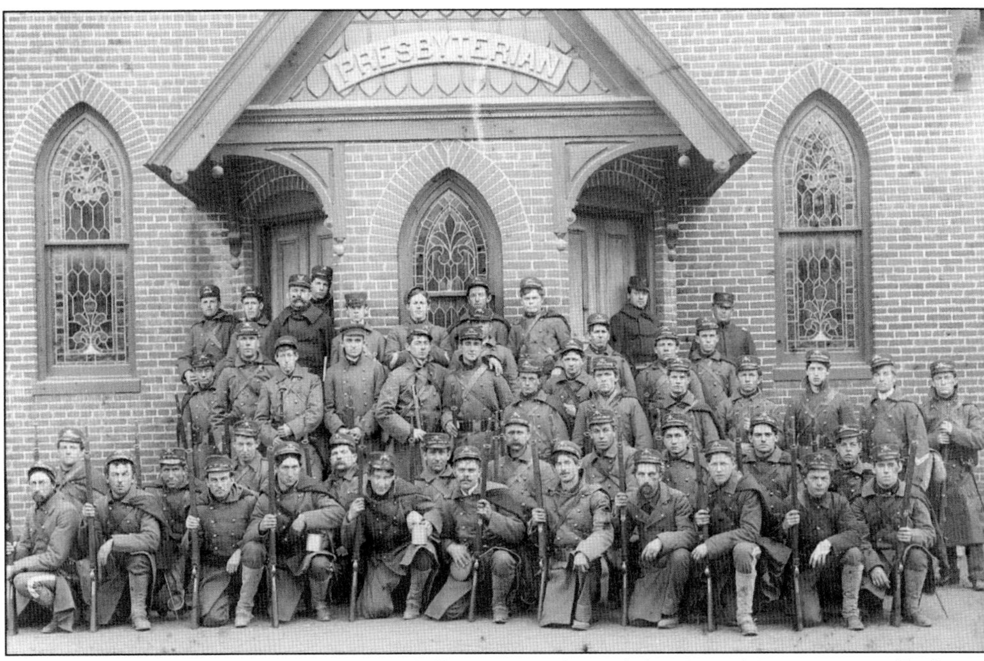

DOMESTIC PEACEKEEPING. Unrest of a different sort plagued the United States internally during the period from 1870 to 1925—strife between workers organizing into industrial unions and management determined to be non-union. This photograph shows the men of Battery D in front of the First Presbyterian Church on west Queen Street readying to travel to Norfolk in 1900 to put down a streetcar workers' strike. The unit's officers are in the darker uniforms.

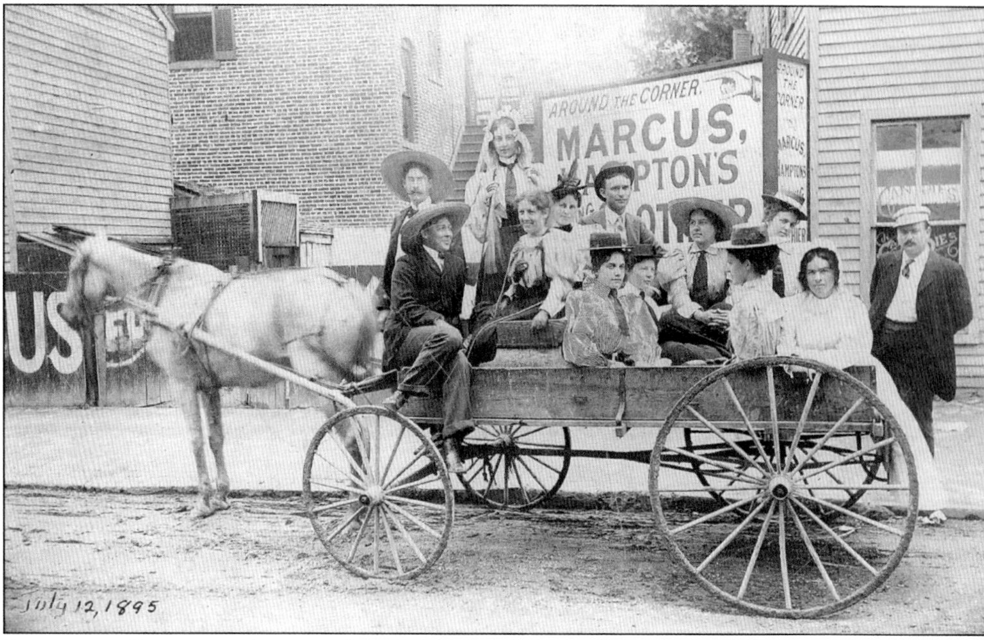

BOUND FOR BUCKROE. A group of young Hamptonians is about to set off for an outing at Buckroe on July 12, 1895. Included are (from left to right): Selwyn Bickford, John Ross, Susie Jones, Jennie Vaughan, Eliza Tabb, Howard Saunders, Fannie Barnes, Mary Blackmore, Bessie Love, Annie Chisman (in profile), Mary Lee, Nancy Jones, and the buckboard's owner, Livingston Whiting.

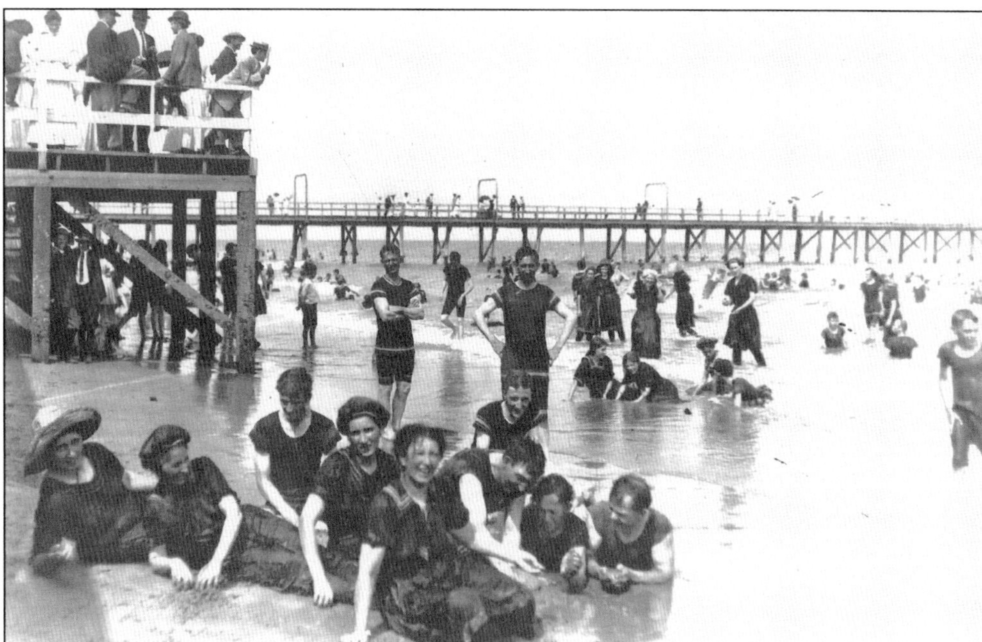

A DAY AT THE BEACH. People wore more clothing than now when they went bathing in the sea, as these happy young people are doing in 1910 at Buckroe Beach. Even the onlookers are dressed to the nines. On the shores of the Chesapeake Bay, looking off toward the Atlantic Ocean 15 miles to the east, Buckroe has been a popular resort at least since 1883.

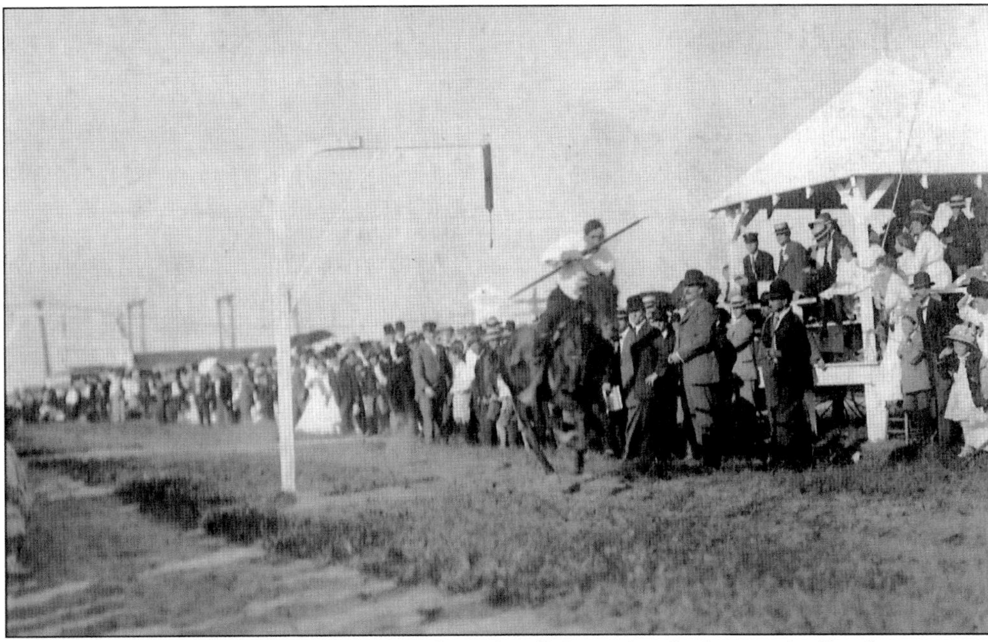

A HIGH SOCIETY AFFAIR. A large number of well-dressed onlookers and officials are gazing intently as Frank Sinclair, at full gallop, has apparently just maneuvered his wooden spear so as to take a brass ring from the clothespin dangling by a cord from the suspension pole. Called "jousting," this event took place in 1908 probably at a field to the north of Hampton. Sinclair came in second.

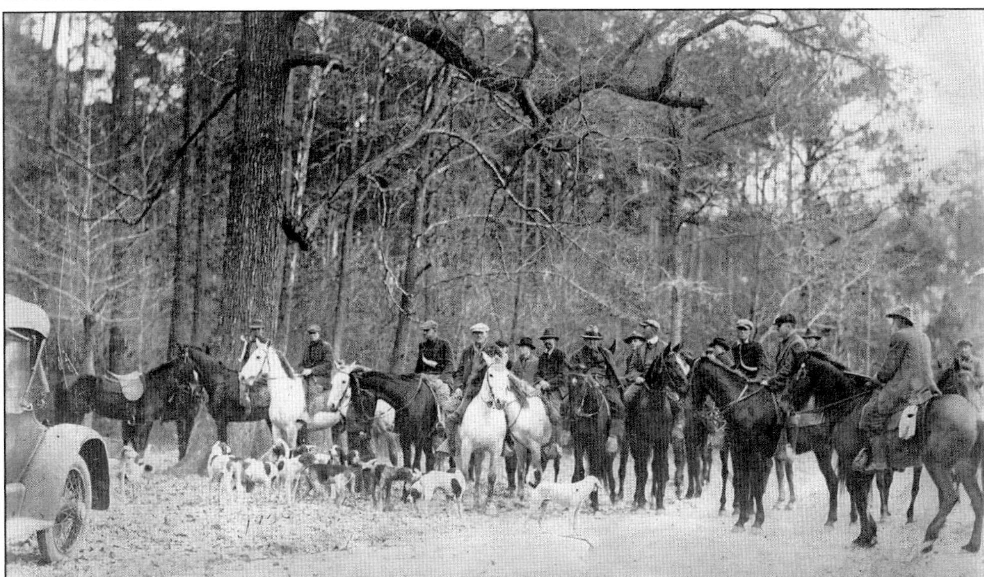

THE HUNT. Keith and Jeff Sinclair and about 15 others on horseback, plus several hounds, mill around before setting off to hunt at Hickman's Chapel in 1908. That the quarry was a fox is indicated by the lack of firearms—the chase, not the kill, was the sport—plus the horns (worn by two huntsmen) for calling the hounds. Foxhunting was important to improve horsemanship, exercise strenuously, and share male companionship.

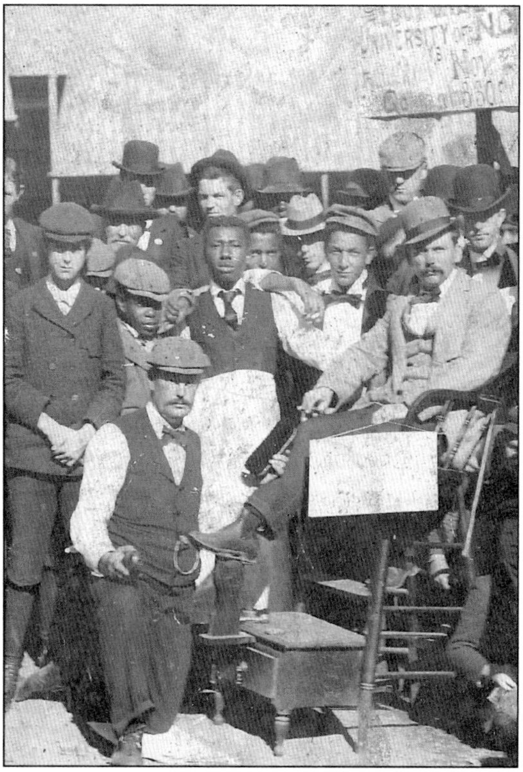

THE WAGER. Two anonymous bettors have taken over the shoe-shine stand of the young man with the apron. The winner (holding the cigar) correctly predicted that Benjamin Harrison would unseat incumbent Pres. Grover Cleveland in 1888, and the loser must shine his shoes. The sign above the stand advertises an upcoming football game involving the University of North Carolina.

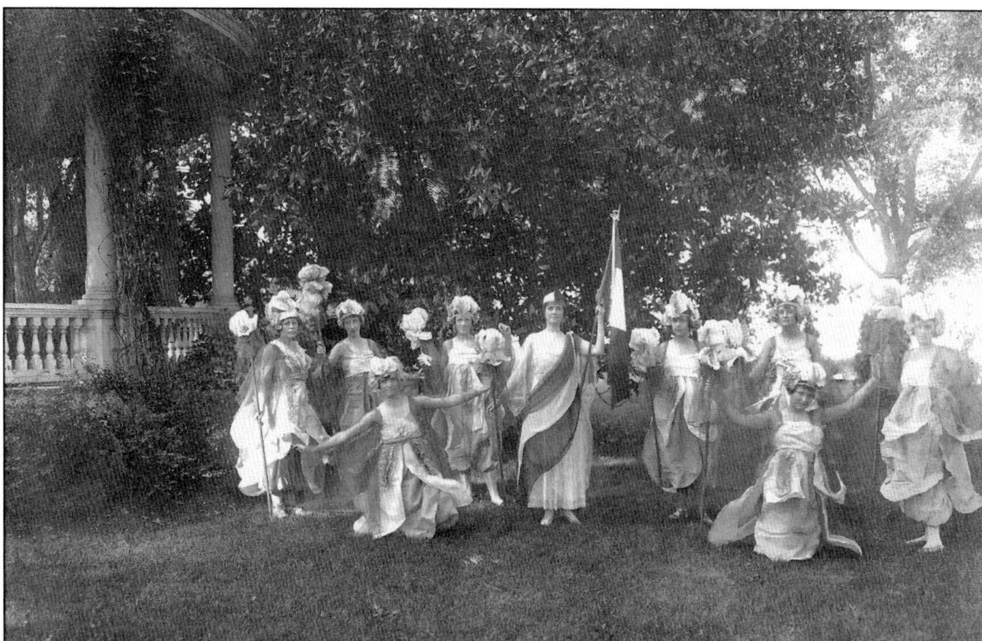

SUPPORT FOR FRANCE. Nine young ladies—including Annie Schmelz, holding the French flag—have donned improvised fancy dress to help sell "liberty bonds" during World War I. The others include Dorothy Booker Andrews, Anne Booker, Virginia Mason, Elizabeth Hudgins, Paige Sclater, and Lavinia Holt; two are unidentified.

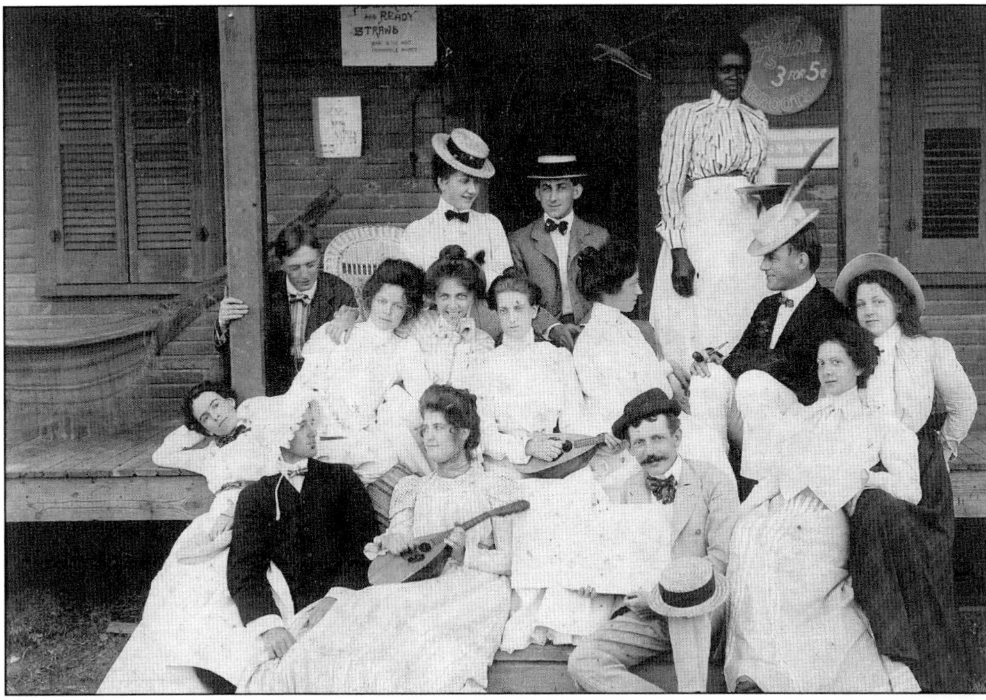

THE MANDOLIN CLUB. Fourteen members of the Mandolin Club pose whimsically at a Buckroe Beach eating establishment in 1899. Those who can be identified include future Hampton assistant postmistress Nancy Jones (far left), Polly Chisman (center left), Lila Chisman (holding mandolin, center), Mae Tabb (second from right), and future Hampton mayors James Bickford (top center) and Thornton Jones (hat with feather).

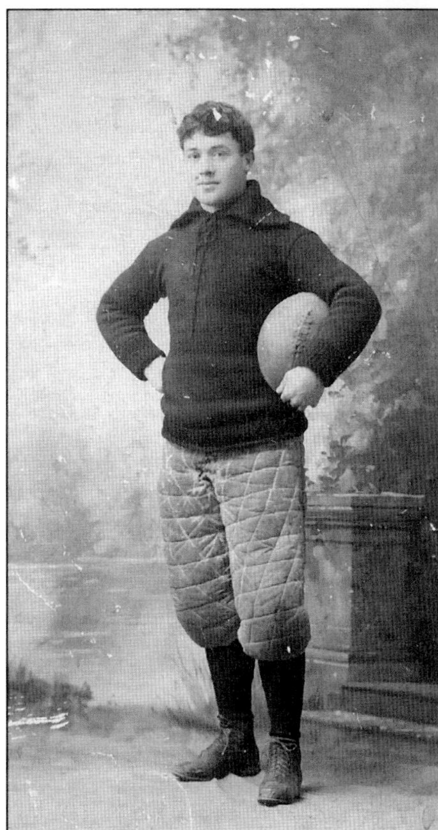

1890S FOOTBALL. Harry Holt was the quarterback on the local semipro team, the Hampton Athletic Club, which under looser rules had contests with college teams, such as Princeton and the University of Virginia. Forward passes were not allowed, little padding was worn, and the biggest-gaining play was the kickoff return with 10 players linking arms in a "flying wedge," shielding the runner. Holt previously quarterbacked the VMI football team.

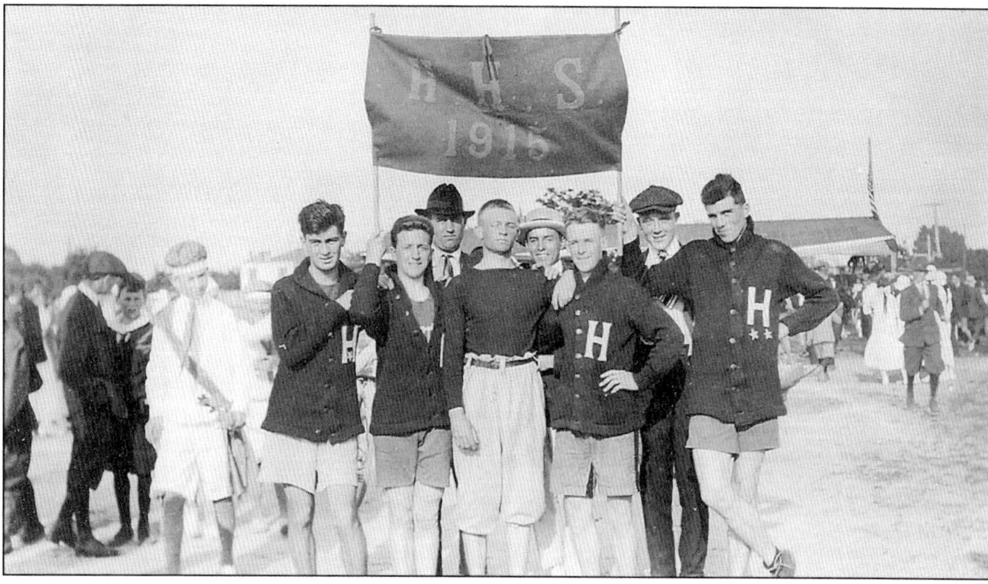

TRACK AND FIELD. Hampton High School is celebrating its annual field day in 1916. Coach Linwood Topping wears the dark hat. In front of him, from left to right, are future Hampton mayor George Bentley, Fenton Batten, Jesse Wilson, Frank Cumming (face only), Emory Ammons, John Driscoll (with cap), and Noah Tucker.

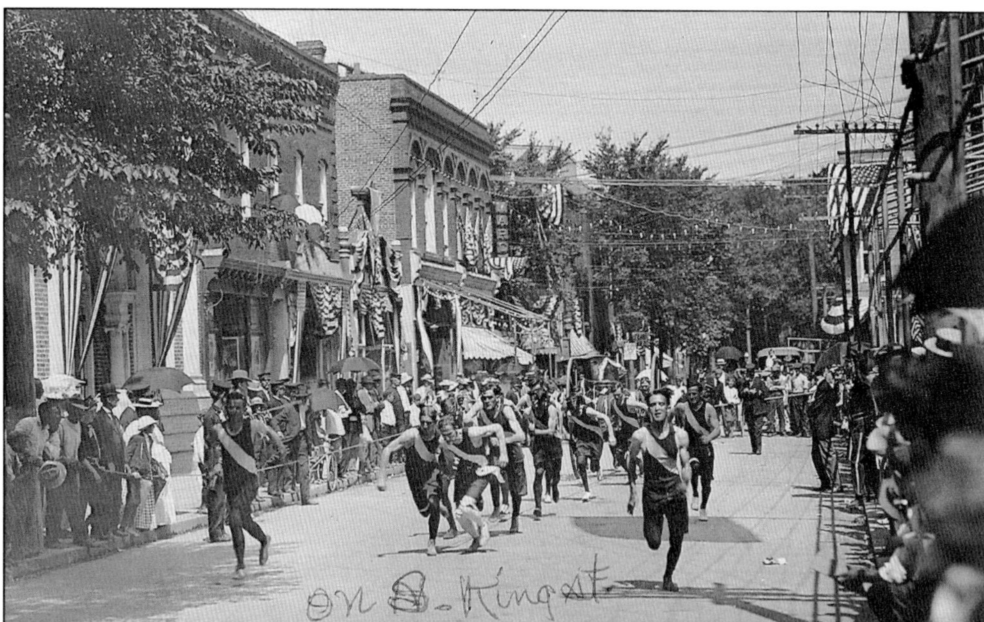

THE HOSE RACE. Competition kept young men interested in joining fire companies. Each company tried to be first at a fire. This 1909 photograph shows men from a company racing down King Street carrying a fire hose. The company that most quickly connected its hose to a water source and got water at the other end was the winner. The top-hatted timekeeper is at the right, while straw-hatted citizens cheer.

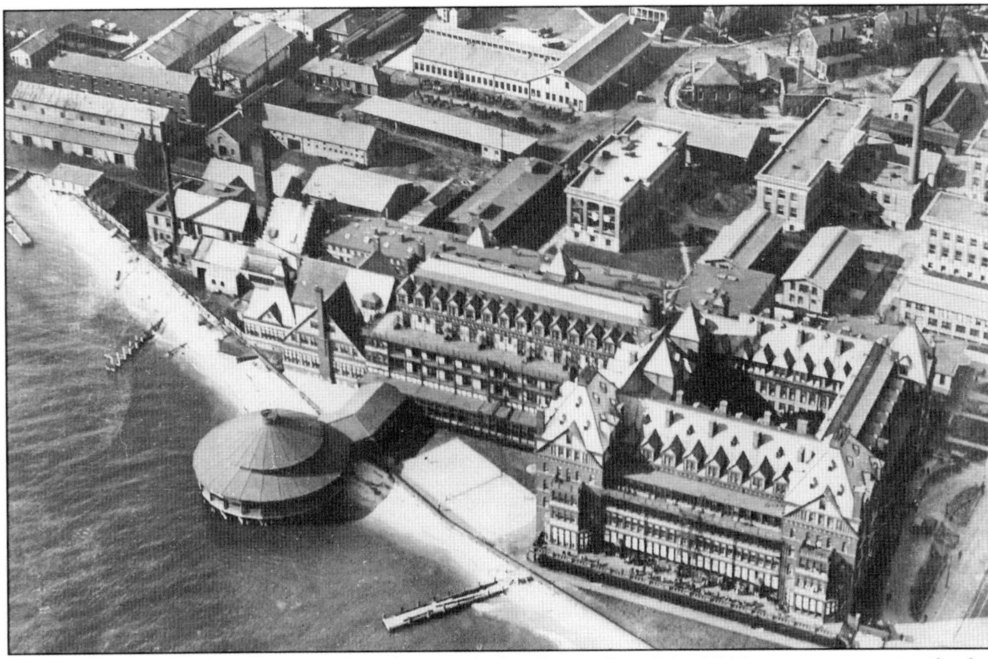

THE FIRST CHAMBERLIN. Completed in 1896, this luxury hotel had 554 rooms, extensive baths, and other facilities for health, including a heated indoor pool filled with saltwater, a business center with telephone and telegraph connections, an immense dining room featuring seafood and an orchestra in the balcony, broad piazzas overlooking the water, and a round pavilion built over the water for cool, breezy summer dancing. It burned down in 1920.

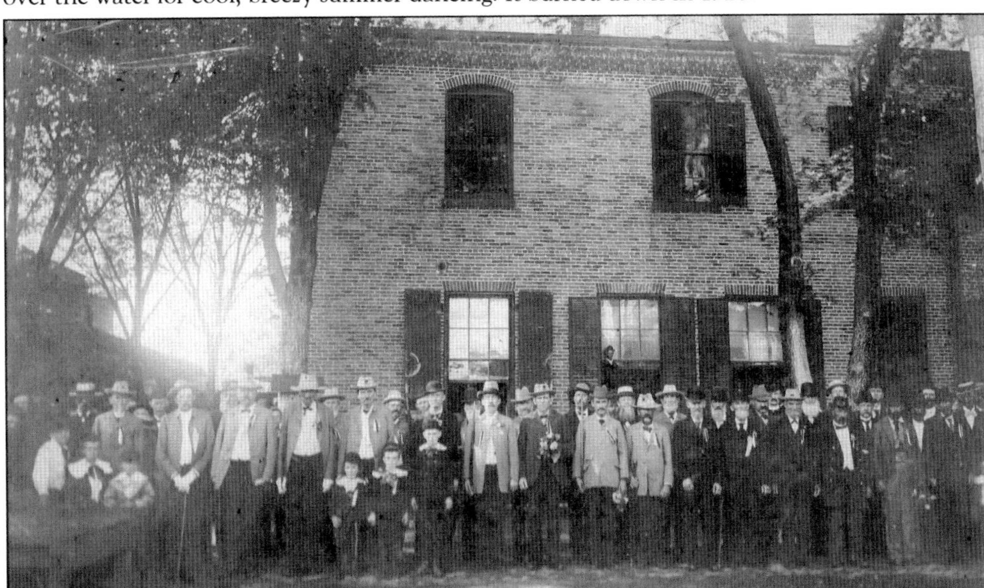

GUARDING MEMORIES. By the 1890s, the horrors of the Civil War had faded and the wartime experience had become romanticized. At least 40 Confederate veterans, wearing uniforms and ribbons, each with a covered head, stand at attention in front of the Hampton courthouse. Ironically, the courthouse had been razed in the Civil War and rebuilt. Several youths also stand at attention, drinking in the emerging tradition.

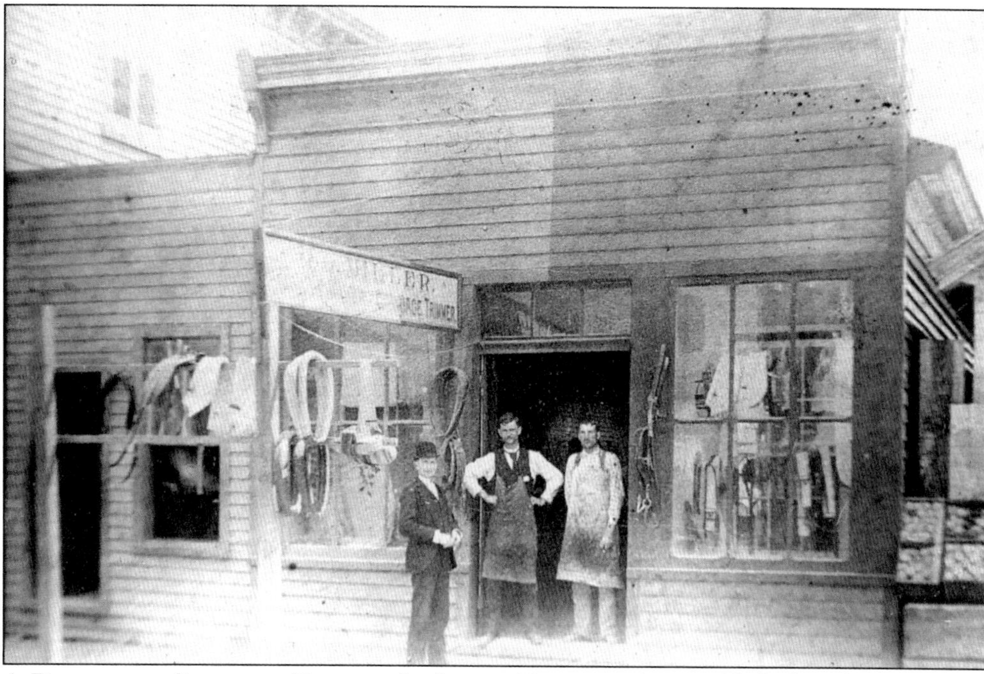

A DOWNTOWN SADDLERY. Horses and riding tackle were indispensable before about 1910 and were useful long after that. Jesse D. Miller stands in the doorway of his harness shop on Queen Street in what is likely one of the earliest street scenes in the Hampton History Museum collection. The person formally dressed for riding, as well as Miller's assistant, are unidentified.

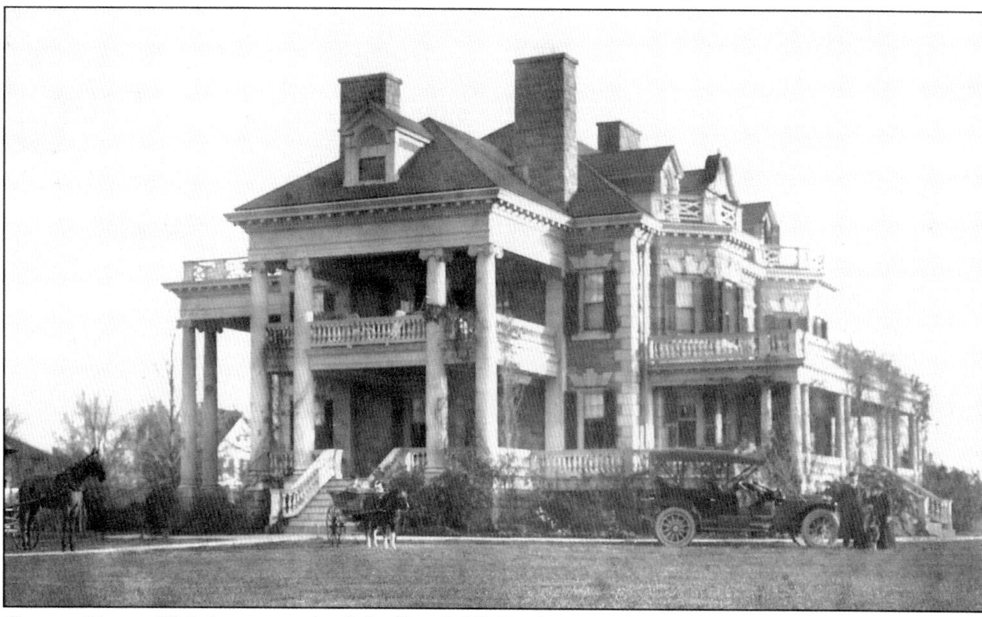

CEDAR HALL. This home was built by Frank W. Darling on Hampton River at the confluence of Sunset Creek. The land was a part of the Little England plantation, which became a fashionable residential neighborhood. Darling persuaded the town to build Bridge Street and a bridge to connect this section with downtown. In this 1910 photograph, Frank, Mary Gorton, and Grace Darling (child) stand in front of the automobile.

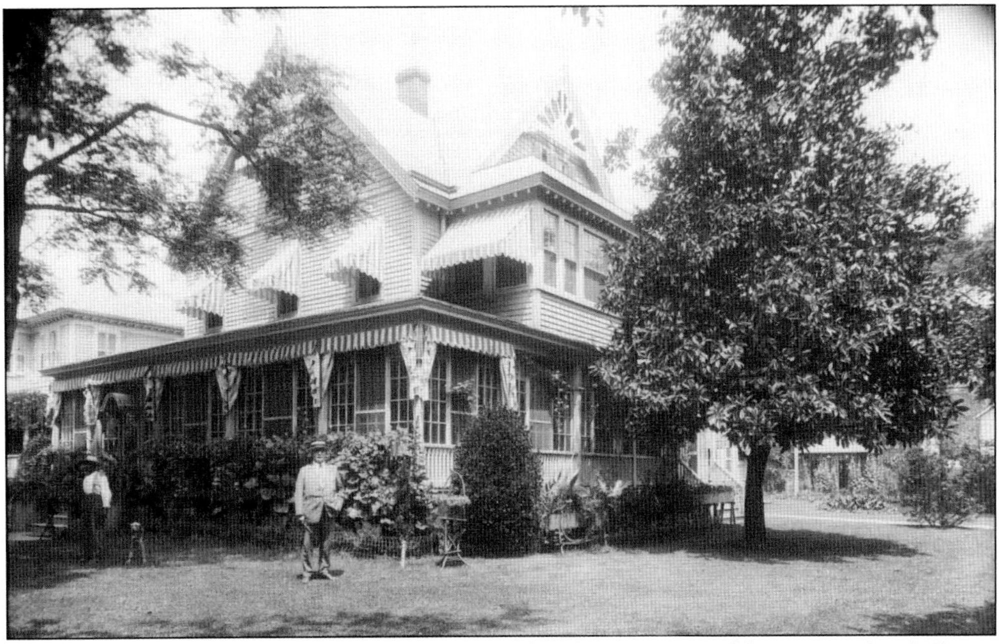

PASTURE POINT. Another fashionable new neighborhood grew up west of downtown when Jefferson Sinclair's Pasture Point Farm was subdivided into lots in the late 1880s. Spacious homes such as this, owned by entrepreneur and Fort Monroe postmaster John B. Kimberley, grew up along Mallory Avenue (now Pembroke Avenue). Kimberley also owned a dairy farm.

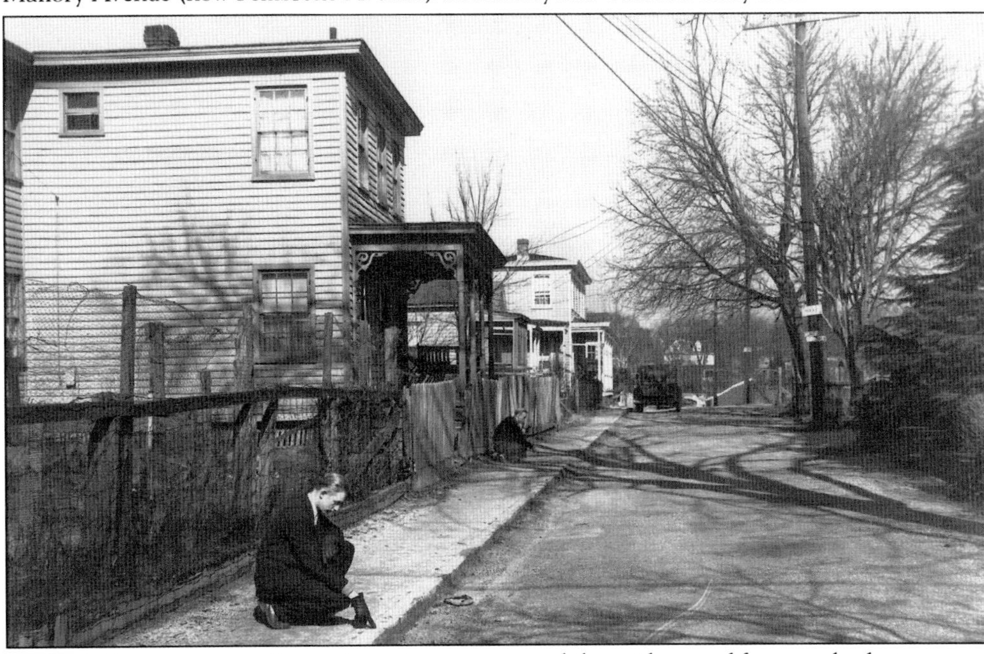

PEE DEE. Two insurance adjusters investigate an automobile accident, and fortunately, the insurance company hired Ethelbert Cheyne as the photographer; he took this fine 1939 study of a Hampton working-class neighborhood, which former resident Carolyn Hawkins remembers as integrated. Frame houses have small yards for gardens or children at play. The white house seemingly at the end of Bayley Street is actually across Wilson's Creek in Pasture Point.

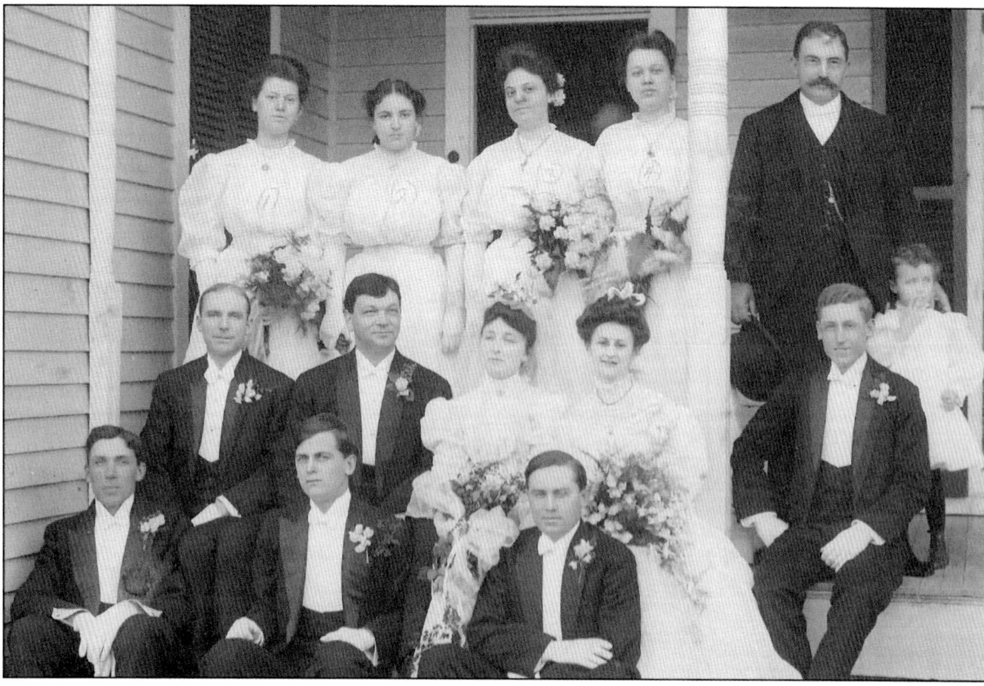

A WEDDING. This is the wedding party of the couple in the center, Mr. Beasley (perhaps Robert) and Mamie, formerly Rowe. The upper rank is formed from four Rowe women—(left to right) Mamye, Edna, Alice, and Elizabeth—plus an uncle, John Rowe, and Ruth, perhaps his small daughter. From left to right, Horace Face, Annie Whitley, and Hamilton Richardson flank the marital couple, while Jack Horseman, Paul Tabb, and Jack Wyatt sit on the bottom step.

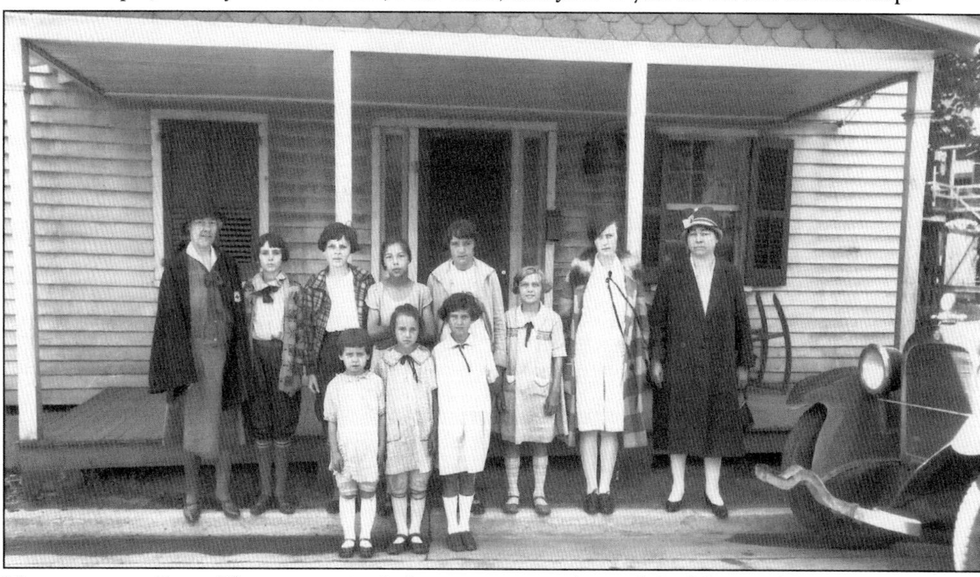

VISITING THE SICK. The women in dark coats are members of the Visiting Nurses' Association. Under the supervision of a nearby hospital, this group sent nurses to poor people unable to visit the hospital. Basic services included bedside care, the execution of physicians' orders, and education and counseling on health care matters. The reason why so many girls are in what appears to be a single-parent home is unknown.

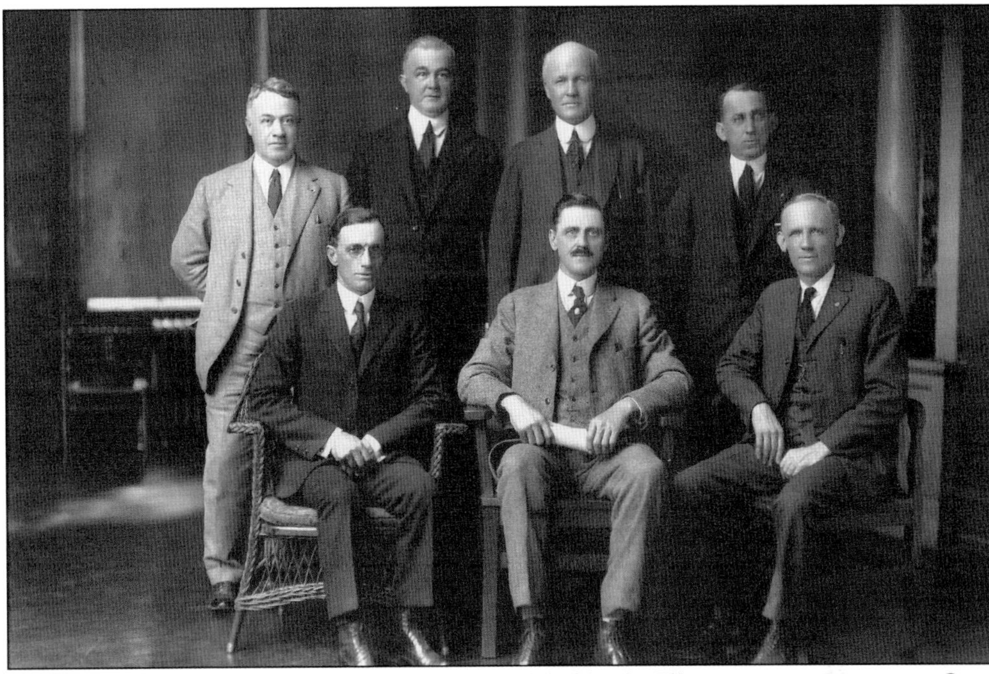

CIVIC ASSOCIATIONS. Closely akin to secret civic clubs like the Elks were civic associations. Open about membership, these associations usually met at lunchtime each month, undertook various civic projects, and gave the town's business, church, and government leaders opportunities to converse informally. This 1922 photograph of Rotary Club officers includes, from left to right, (first row) Richard M. Booker, M. Otto Lackey, and John Weymouth; (second row) Harry Holt, Harry Houston, Matthew Armstrong, and James Bickford.

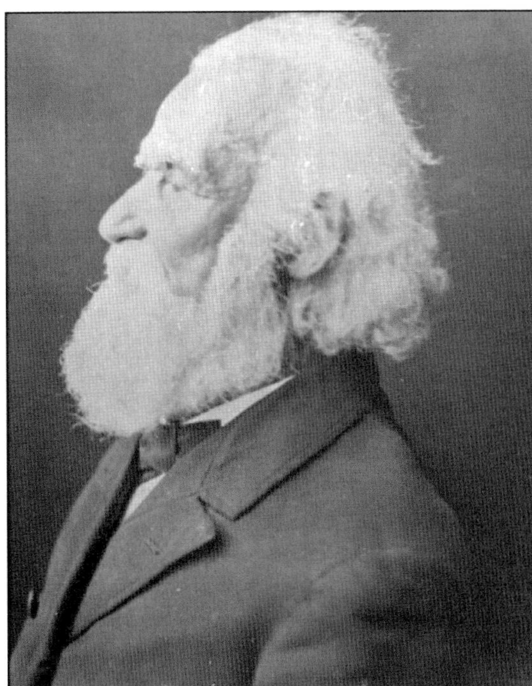

BLACK POLITICAL LEADERSHIP. William Roscoe Davis served his community in many social and political ways during Reconstruction. The child of a sailor and a slave, he was literate, eloquent, and courageous. An antebellum entrepreneur in a pleasure-boat enterprise, Davis was sent north to speak about contrabands' terrible conditions during the Civil War. At its end, he became a respected pastor. He served as a member of the Hampton City Council in the 1890s.

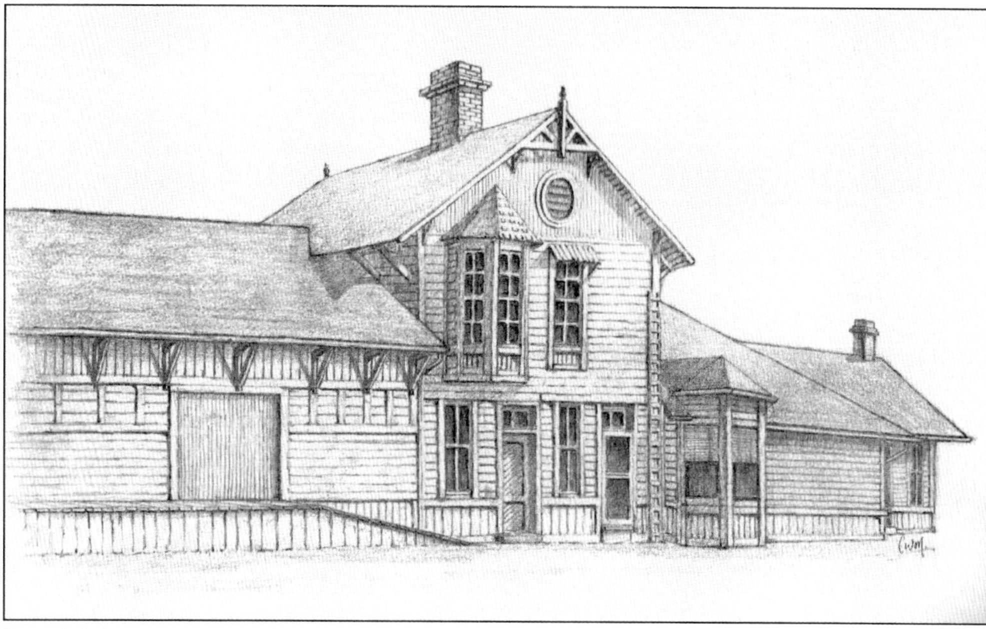

THE C&O. Hampton's railroad station on the Chesapeake and Ohio Railroad (C&O) spur from Newport News to Fort Monroe was located at the north edge of town behind Pasture Point. The sketch shows the station as of about 1891. Until the 1950s, rail was a popular and important way to travel, as well as to take shopping trips to Richmond, the regional entrepot.

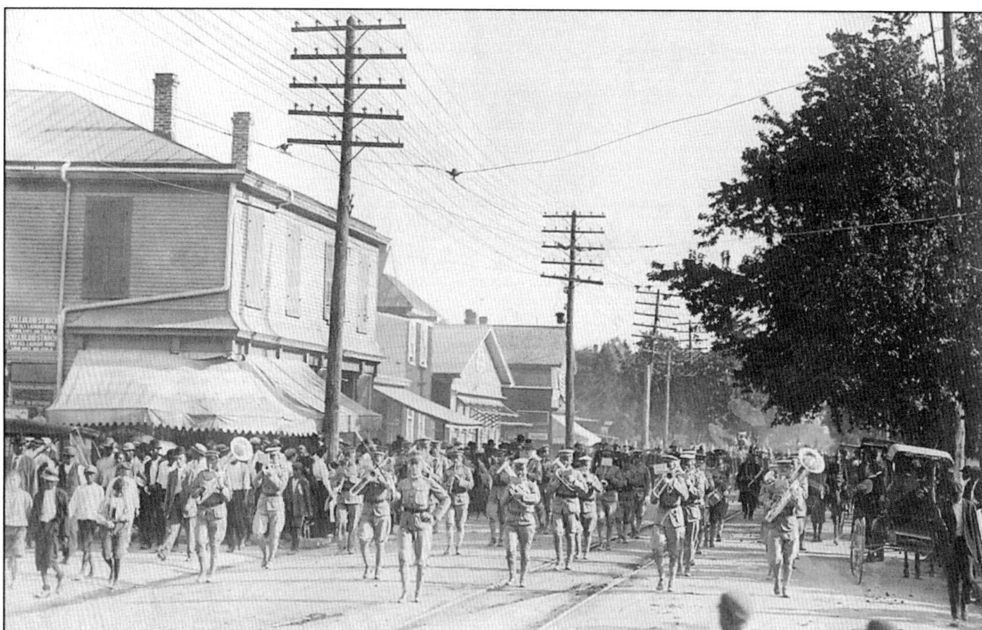

EVERYBODY LOVES A PARADE. The Fort Monroe Band leads the Hampton firemen and their fire pump on a parade past Thomas S. Tennis's grocery store on Armistead Avenue amid the enthusiastic support and accompaniment of children and other residents. Parades and other outdoor civic entertainment were more frequent in the days without radio or television.

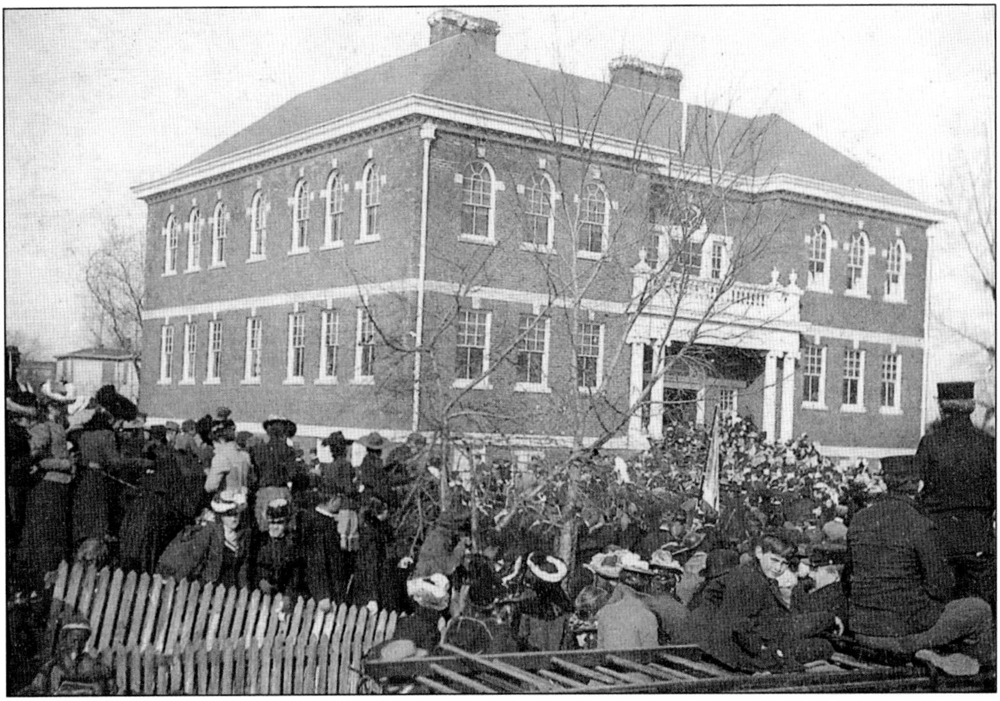

SYMS-EATON ACADEMY. Hampton's citizens flock to the opening of the new elementary school on February 13, 1902. There was a parade, and local shopkeepers gave a half-holiday because the occasion was so important. Named for two local 17th-century donors of property for the free education of local poor children, the school served the town's white children for 38 years.

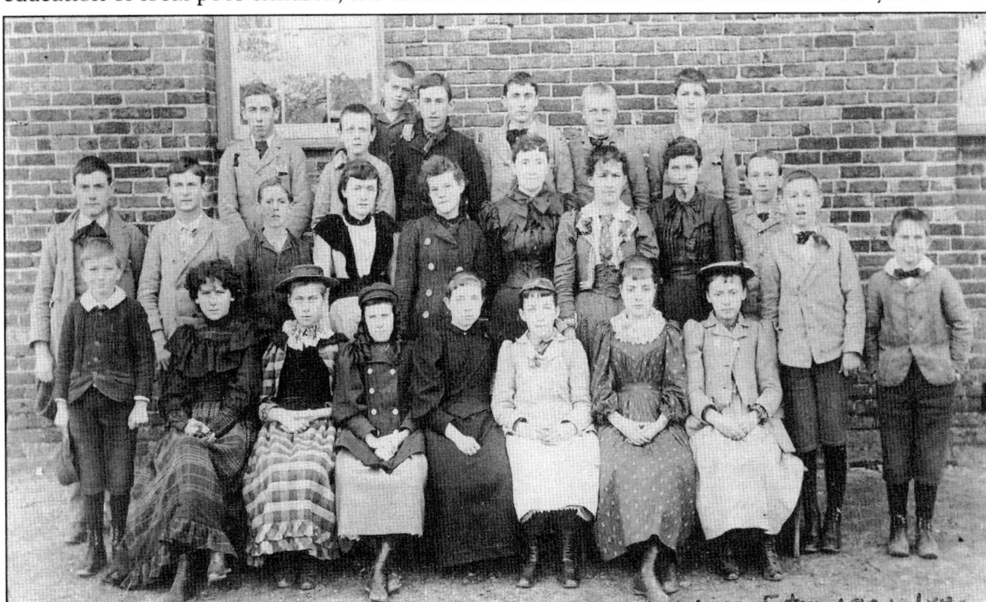

A SYMS-EATON CLASS. Having apparently been sternly instructed by their teacher, these young men and women from an older grade have riveted their somewhat apprehensive attention on the camera. Syms-Eaton taught the first seven grades. After 1952, the building housed the city's board of education until it was demolished for urban renewal in 1977.

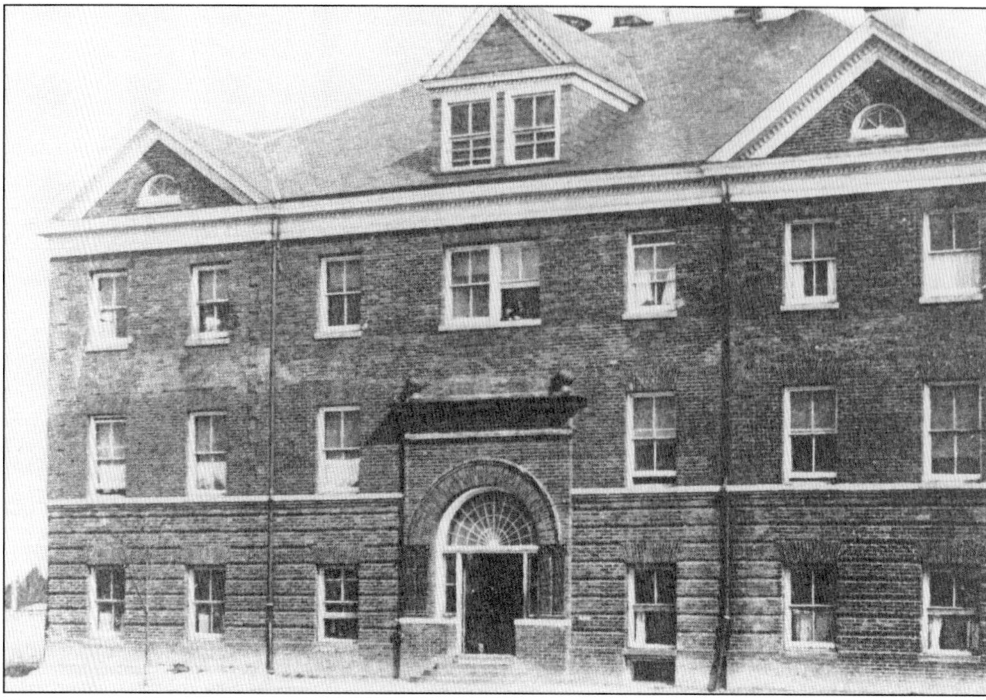

The First Hampton High School. West End Academy offered instruction for all grades, including high school classes, when it opened in 1899 on Victoria Boulevard. An addition, built in 1914, was used exclusively for high school classes and was officially called Hampton High School. A completely new Hampton High School was built in 1922 nearby on Jackson Street, and this building became John M. Willis Elementary (renamed Willis-Syms-Eaton in 1940).

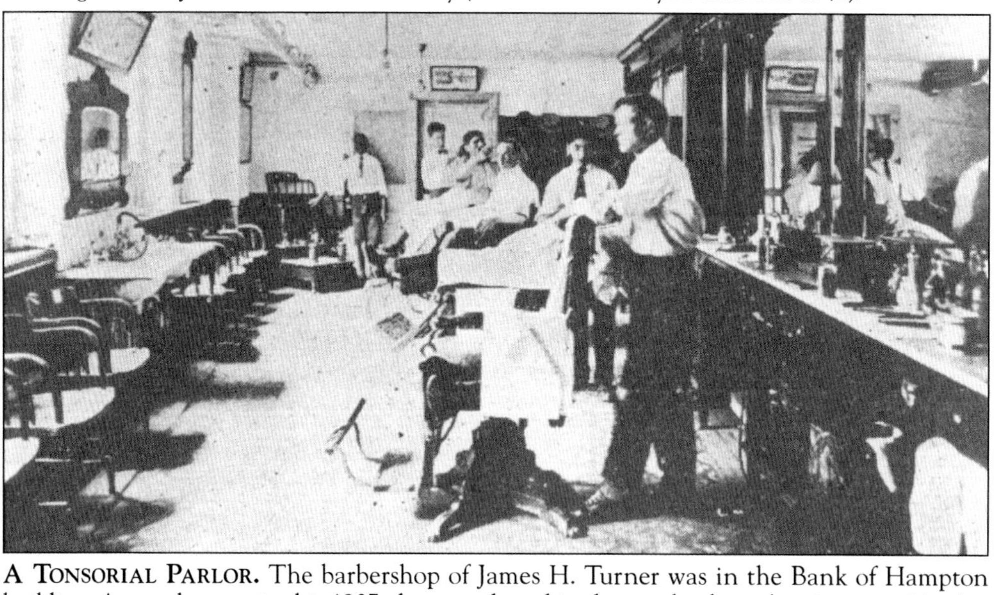

A Tonsorial Parlor. The barbershop of James H. Turner was in the Bank of Hampton building. As can be seen in this 1907 photograph and in the words of an advertisement, "At this most modern and progressive establishment are four handsome scientific artists, each a professor in his line and man of rare judgment." Turner, formerly an employee, rose to manager and later bought out A. C. Dykes.

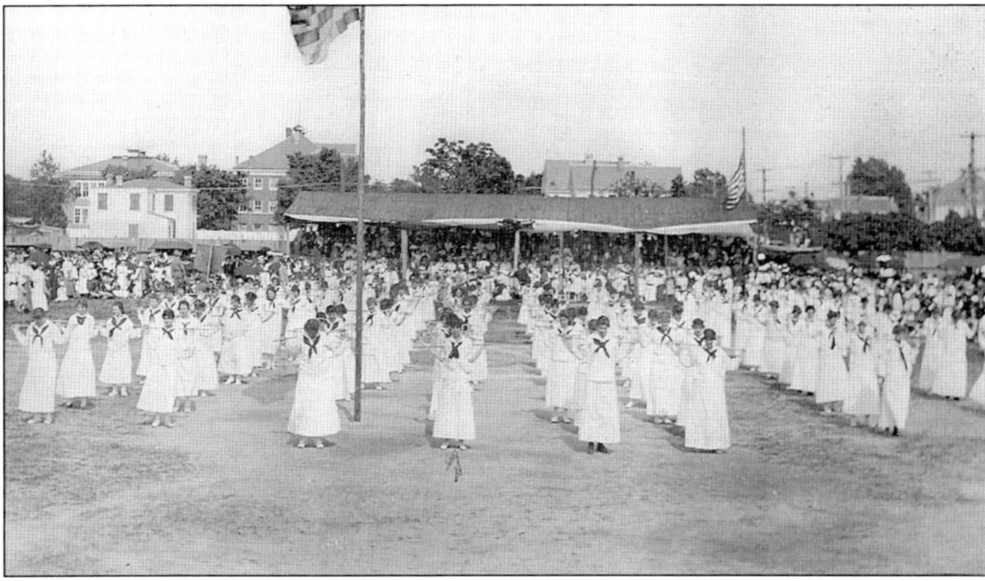

HAMPTON STUDENT CELEBRATION. These two photographs of Hampton High School students engaged in a series of ceremonies were probably taken in the late 1910s at the football field now known as Darling Memorial Stadium. The brick buildings at top left of the above picture are West End Academy (later John M. Willis Elementary) and its annex, the first Hampton High School. With large numbers of onlookers seated on bleacher seats, plus students dressed entirely in white, these were probably elaborate graduation festivities at a time when some students rode to school on horses and few went on to college. Perhaps, however, these were May Day ceremonies, popular at the time.

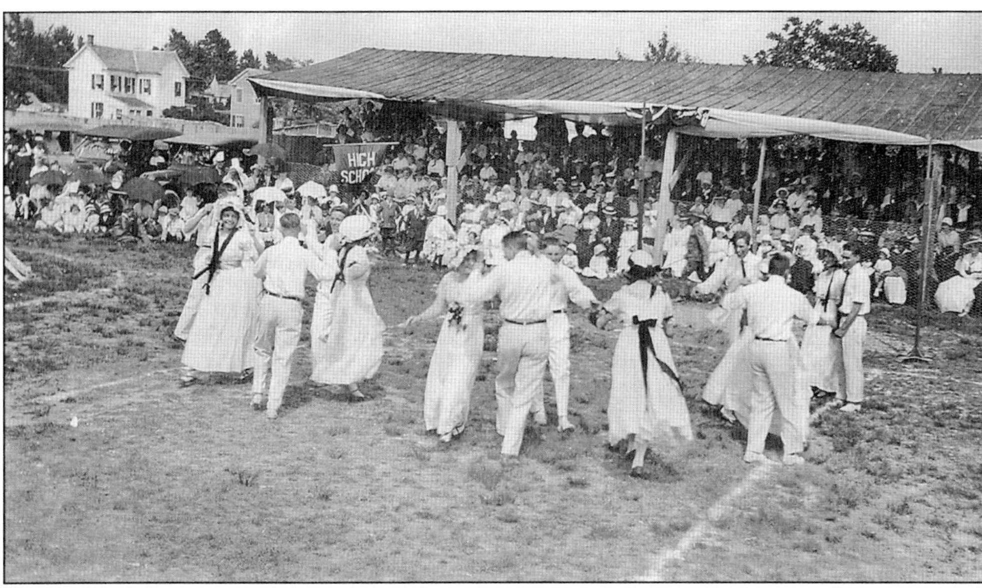

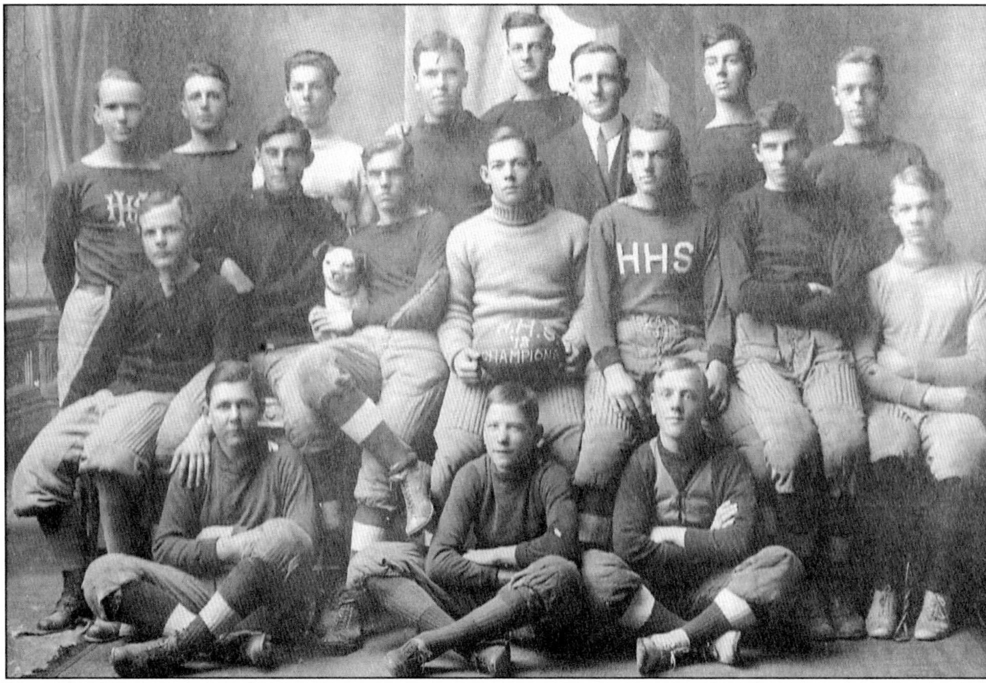

1912 STATE CHAMPIONS. Hampton High School has a long and proud tradition of football prowess, extending to the present. Equipment has greatly improved, and the number of players and coaches has risen drastically since this championship team of 1912, the first of many. Harry Morrow is the coach, probably a volunteer, and next to him (right) is John Bentley, a future Episcopal bishop.

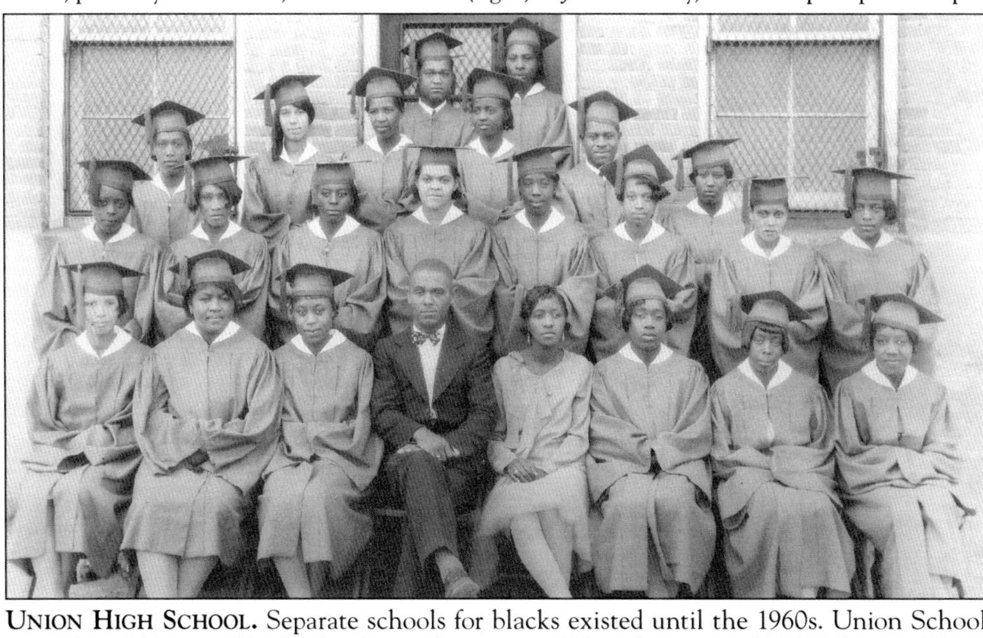

UNION HIGH SCHOOL. Separate schools for blacks existed until the 1960s. Union School, opened in 1922, gained high school accreditation in 1925 under principal Y. H. Thomas. This is the graduating class of 1927. The George P. Phenix Training School, a project of the Hampton Institute's education department that was located on its grounds, replaced the Union School in 1932. It was later closed by the Hampton Institute, helping force integrated schools to exist.

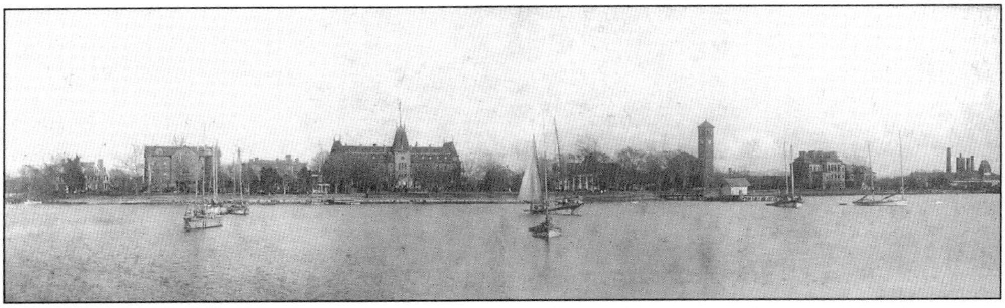

HAMPTON INSTITUTE GROWING. Situated on many beautiful acres on the east side of Hampton River with a fine view down river of Hampton Roads, Hampton Institute (now Hampton University) hit its stride by the 1890s. Buildings still visible today include (from left to right): Moorings Hall, Kelsey Hall, the Virginia Cleveland Hall, the Mansion House (formerly Little Scotland), Memorial Church (with clock tower), and the Academy Building.

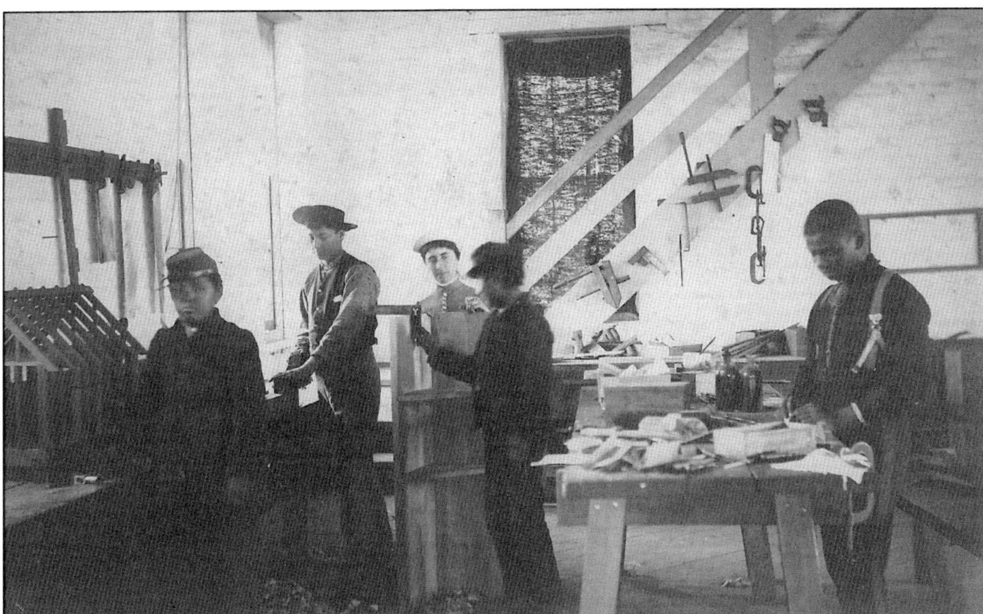

WOODWORKING. Although some thought it arrogant to teach former slaves how to work, Hampton Institute was founded upon the notion that, as historian Robert Engs said, "the black man needed, above all, to acquire 'habits of labor,' " that is, to bend their will to the boss, though they had escaped masters. Here instruction is being given by a "Miss Park" to (left to right) Willie Harrison, John Hans, Solomon Yellow Hawk, and ? Barnett.

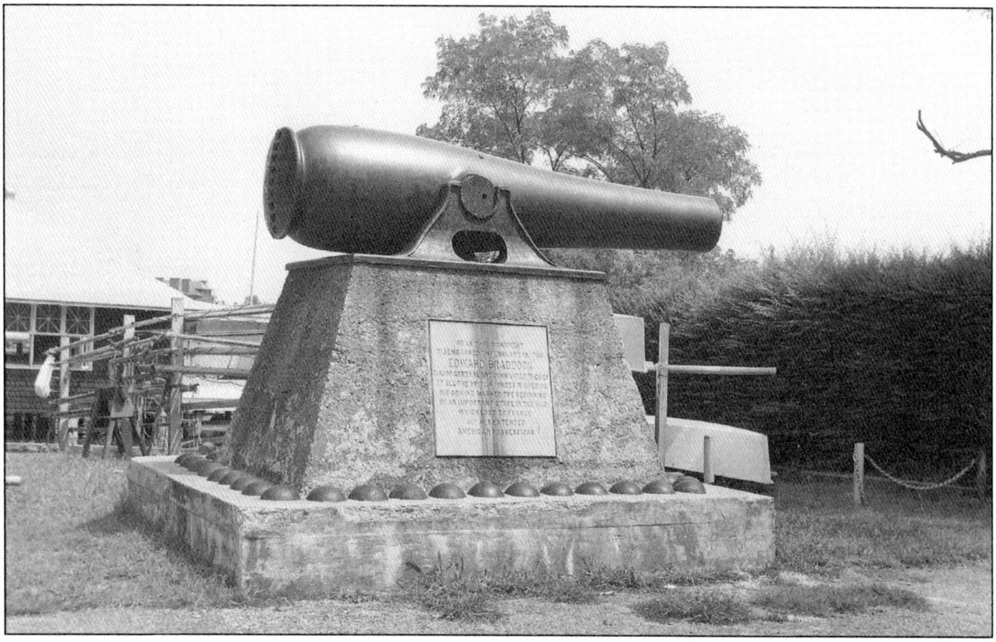

HAMPTON AS MILITARY EMBARKATION POINT. Gen. Edward Braddock and hundreds of British troops disembarked in Hampton on February 12, 1755, to fight in the French and Indian War. The cannon, dating from the post–Civil War period, was set up in May 1916 by the Colonial Dames to commemorate the occasion. The monument was later moved from this site near the water to the intersection of Victoria Boulevard and Bridge Street.

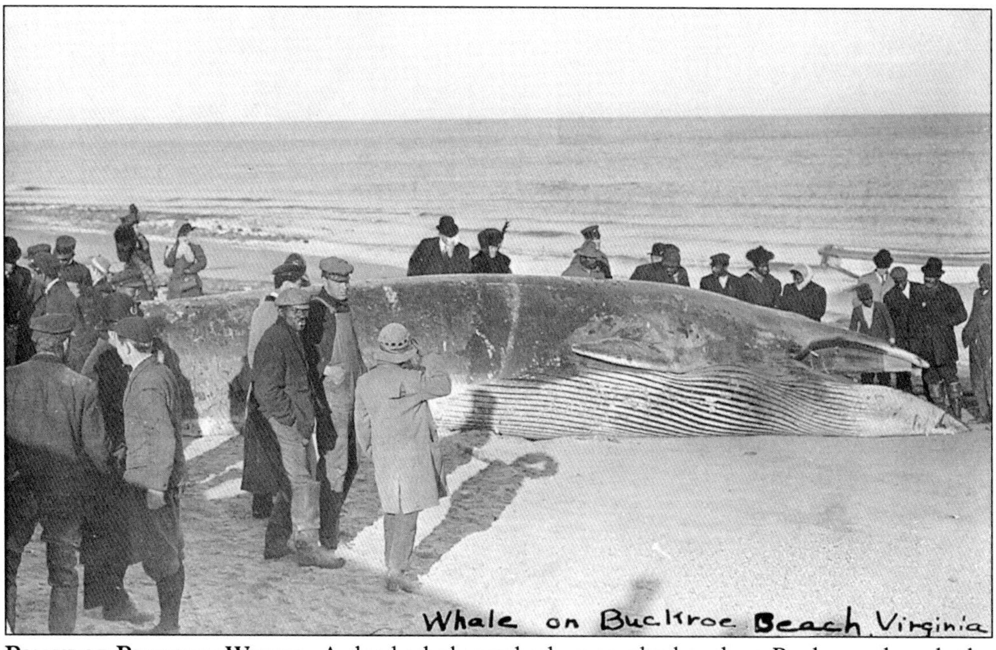

BUCKROE BEACHED WHALE. A dead whale washed up on the beach at Buckroe, though the date is unknown. A note on the back of the postcard from which this picture was taken reads: "The people are not weeping over the whale but during the last days they had to protect their noses from the odor."

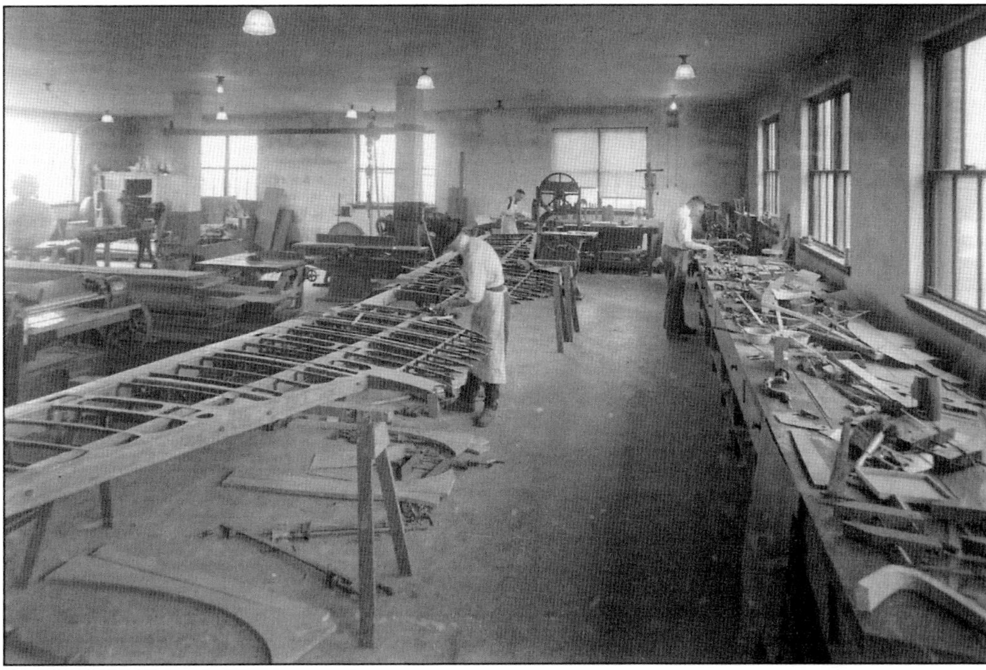

NASA'S FORERUNNER. The National Advisory Committee on Aeronautics (NACA) was sited north of Hampton, along with the army's new air base, at Langley Field in 1917. NACA was the nation's first center for aeronautical research, some of which is being pursued in this June 1922 photograph. With the space competition crisis in the late 1950s, NACA became the National Aeronautics and Space Administration (NASA), and the first astronauts were trained here. (Courtesy of Langley Research Center, NASA.)

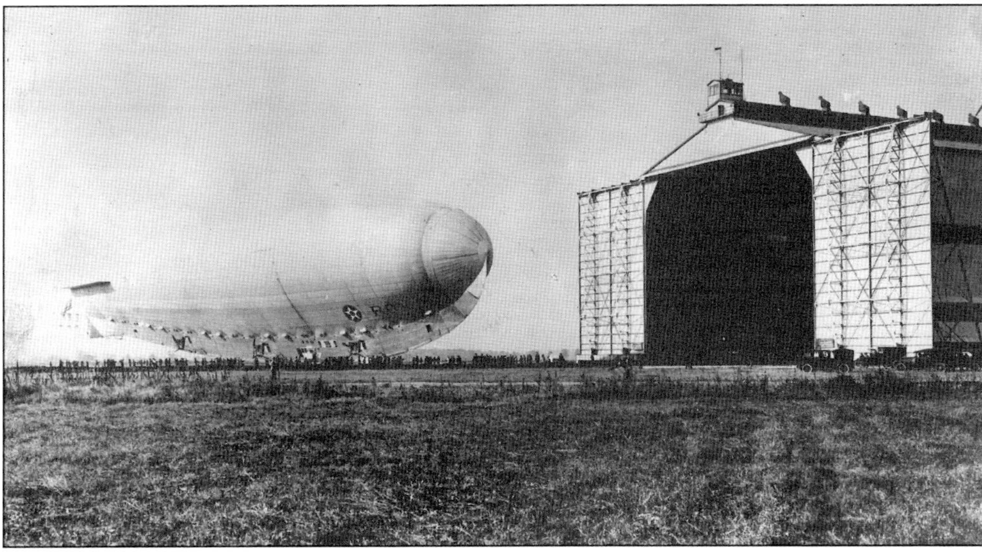

THE *ROMA*. Dirigibles were thought to be aerial observation platforms extraordinaire. This photograph shows the enormous Italian-made *Roma* and her hangar at Langley Field in November 1921. Filled with flammable hydrogen gas, however, the airships were vulnerable to the slightest spark. When its rudder failed on its fourth trouble-plagued test flight on February 21, 1922, the *Roma* hit power lines and exploded, killing 34 of its 45 crewmen.

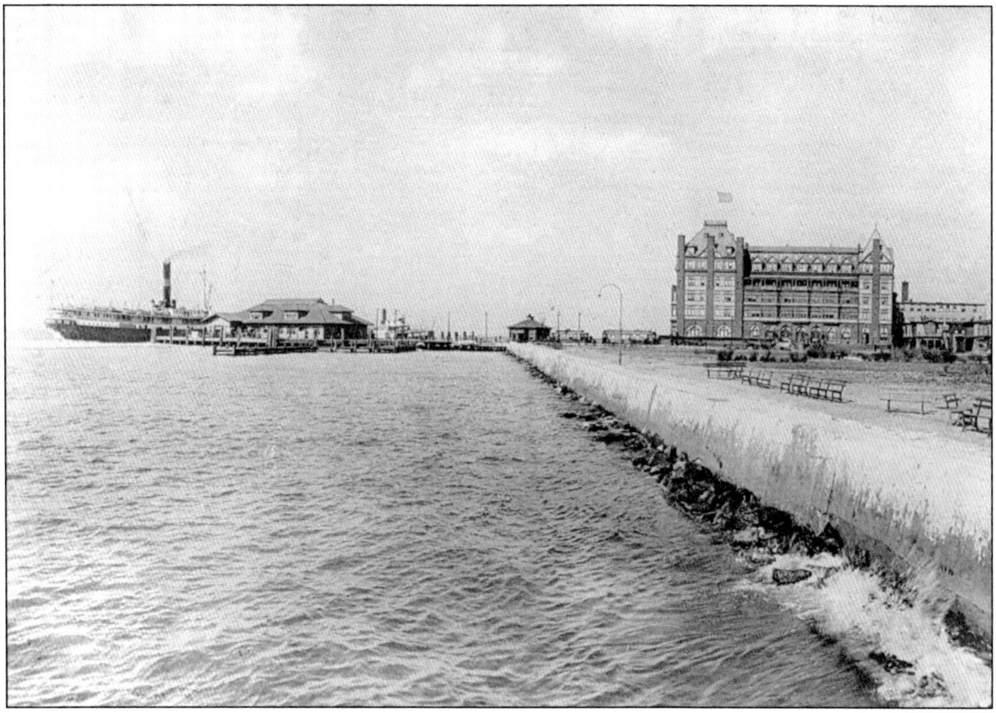

THE SEA WALL. Waters of the Chesapeake Bay lap up against a necessarily stout sea wall beyond the first Chamberlin Hotel and its wharf. Large steamships, such as the one shown in this *c.* 1903 photograph, stopped here en route to Washington, D.C., Baltimore, and New York. The trolley tracks extended onto the wharf.

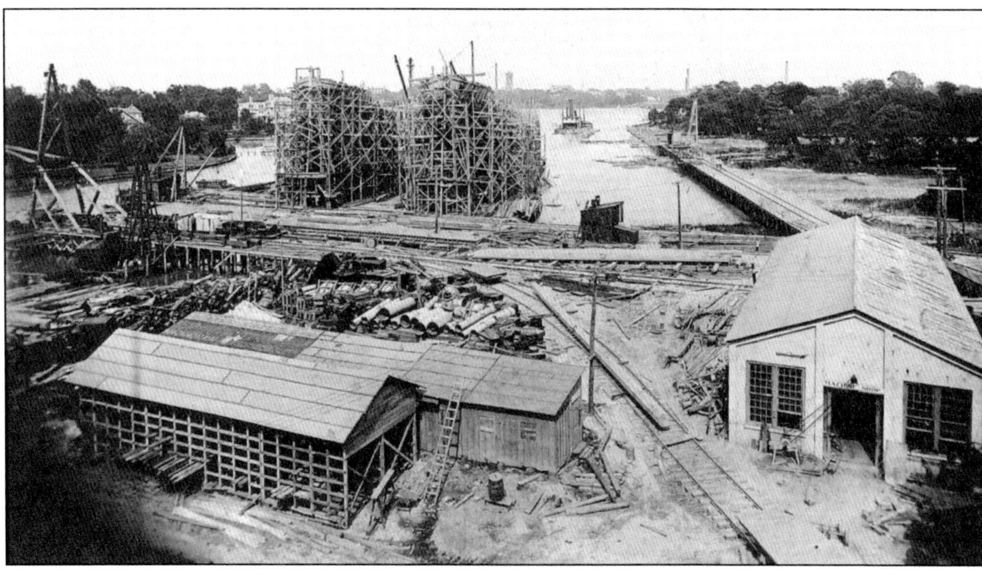

SHIPBUILDING. Hampton's biggest employer in the late 1910s was the Newcomb Lifeboat Company on Sunset Creek, where 500 people worked. During World War I, it built submarine chasers and cargo ships for the navy. This 1918 photograph shows two of the latter under construction, the *Kahoka* and the *Luray*. The company boasted of its stock plan that allowed "employees to share in the business's profits."

Eight

Hampton's Renewal

The 1930s did not start well for Hampton. In the depths of the Great Depression, which caused the closing and reorganization of the Bank of Hampton, Hampton suffered grave destruction from the great storm of August 1933. Banks closed everywhere, and economic disaster brought widespread suffering.

World War II brought a return of prosperity, ending the Depression, although total mobilization for the war also meant a relative scarcity of consumer goods, such as automobiles and metal products. Meat and gasoline were among items that had to be purchased with ration cards. Many women left home to work for the first time. The Newport News shipyard employed many Hamptonians, and many others went off to war. People feared attacks from German submarines surfacing in the harbor. Warplanes roared overhead ceaselessly, while amphibious landings on South Pacific islands were practiced at Grandview Beach.

Postwar mushrooming growth characterized Hampton and the entire Hampton Roads region. The 1950s brought space exploration activity to Langley Field. The most prosperous period in U.S. history saw waves of consumer products, from washing machines to televisions and computers. Paradoxically, as Hampton geographically and economically became a segment of an unbroken giant megalopolis, including the new city of Poquoson and five cities on the other shore of Hampton Roads, its own individuality and economy declined.

In 1952, Hampton was consolidated with the town of Phoebus and Elizabeth City County. However, consolidation with Newport News was voted down. The town, so proud of its venerable and distinctive heritage, has once again struggled to discover a new identity. The question has proved trying and difficult, as it has in many urban places in the United States. Determined to leave the past behind, Hampton has been redeveloped in order to secure its path into the future.

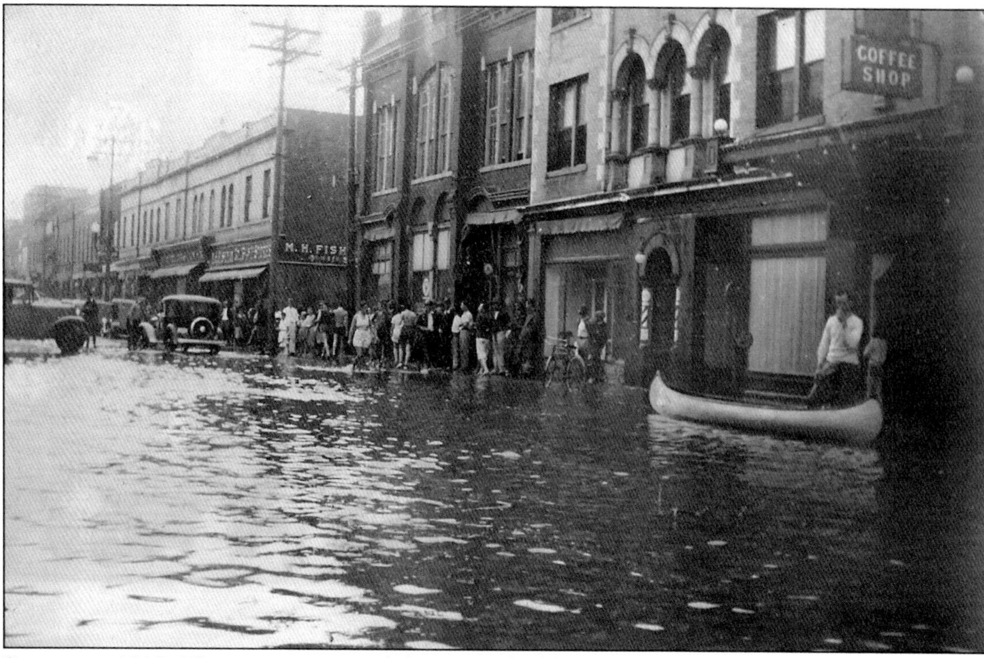

STORM OF 1933. The greatest natural disaster to befall Hampton in modern times was the great hurricane, which made a direct hit on the area on August 23, 1933. Hurricanes were not given names then. Some streets were deep in water, such as Queen Street in front of the Langley Hotel (above). Agnes Chambers, secretary for P. K. Hunt at Elliott Seafood, got to work in a rowboat.

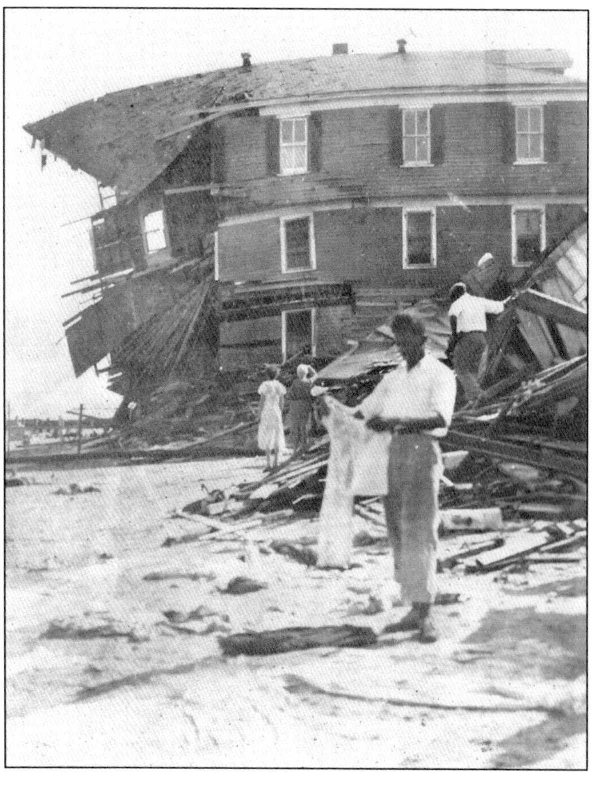

DESTRUCTION AT BUCKROE. Damage from the great storm was much worse in Phoebus and Buckroe. Here people rummage through the ruins of their houses near the smashed edifice of the Bay Shore Hotel in Buckroe. Hampton has suffered from many hurricanes. Hurricane Hazel ruined Grandview Beach in 1954, while Hurricane Flossie destroyed the Back River Lighthouse at Grandview in 1956. Hurricane Isabel in 2003 was only the latest.

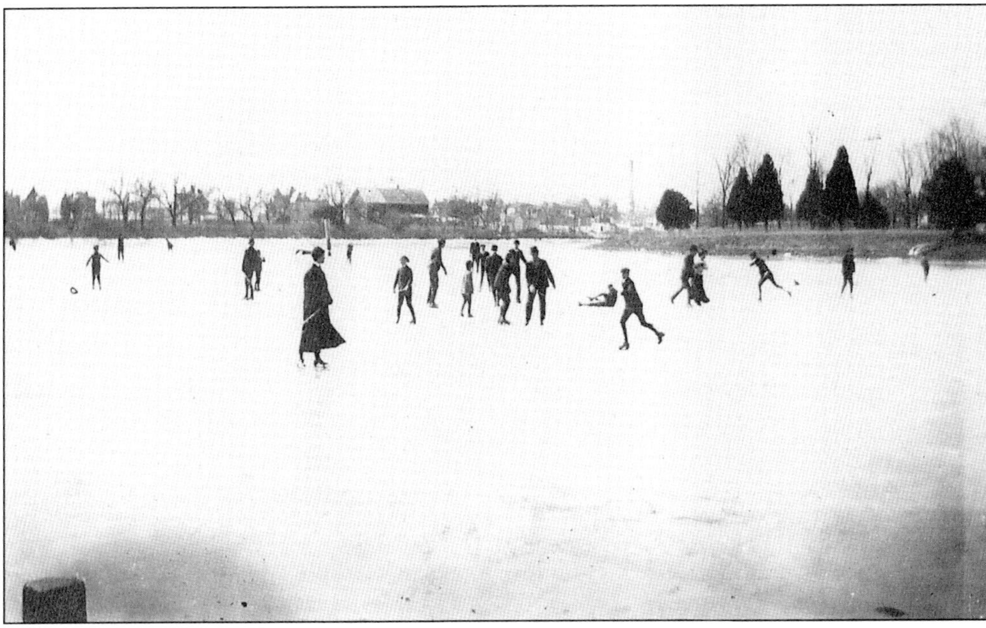

Skaters on Hampton River. The weather was noticeably colder on average during early-20th-century winters in Hampton. The upper reaches of Hampton River stayed sufficiently frozen to support ice skaters for 10 days in 1905, for example (shown in the photograph), while about the time of World War I, an automobile reportedly sank through the ice in an attempt to drive across a frozen Hampton Roads.

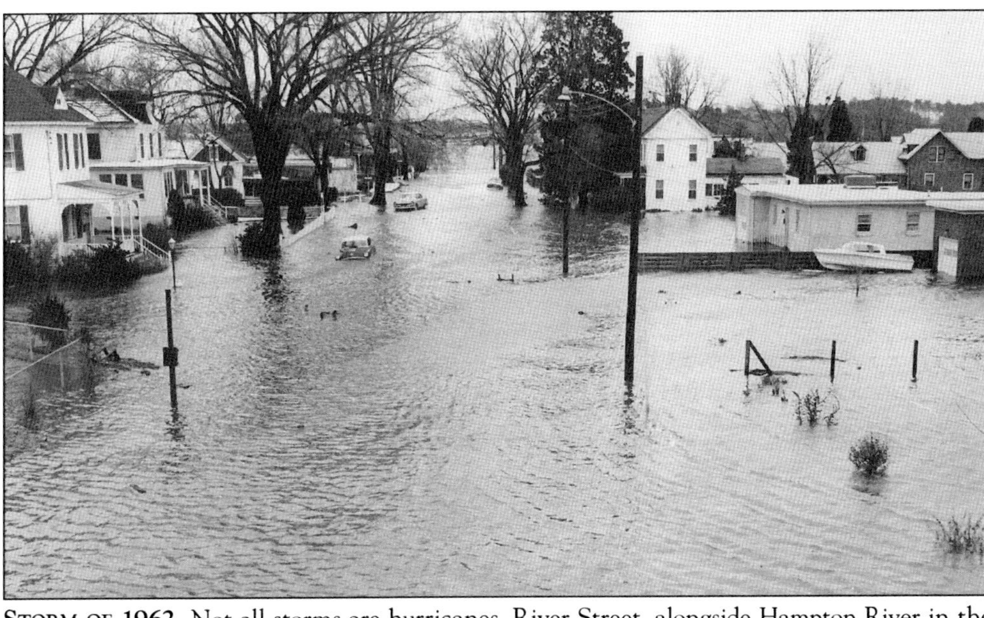

Storm of 1962. Not all storms are hurricanes. River Street, alongside Hampton River in the Pasture Point neighborhood, flooded during the high tides brought on by the Atlantic coast's Ash Wednesday storm of March 6–8, 1962. Water ran 8.5 feet above normal at this place, according to the Associated Press. As a result, some cars have been partially submerged. (Courtesy of William E. Rouse Research Library.)

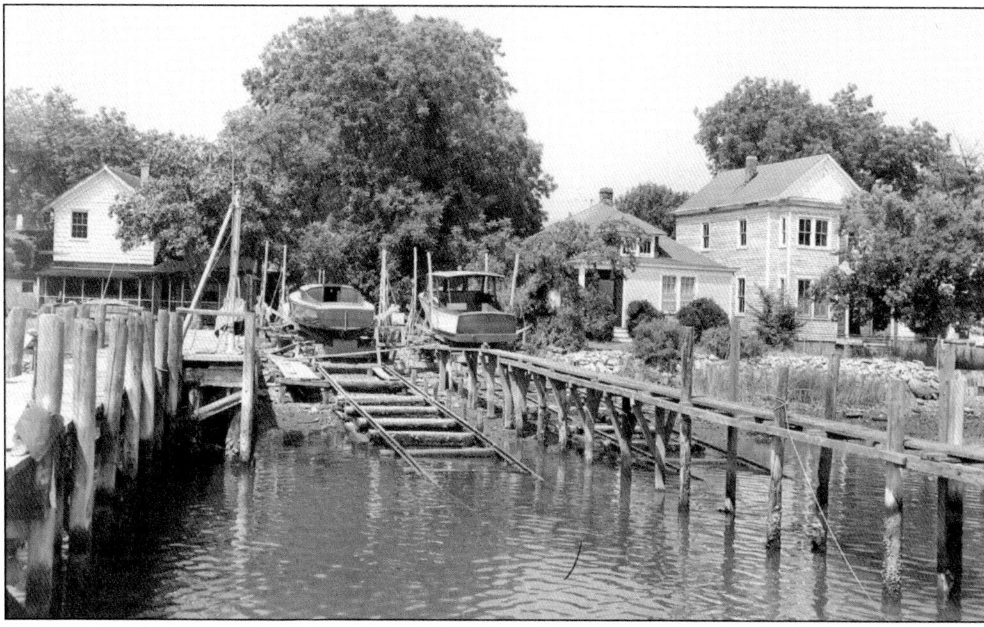

A Marine Railway. After serving in the navy in World War II, Capt. Edward Haldeman purchased this marine railway in the middle of Pee Dee's Hampton River waterfront. Haldeman and his family lived in the house on the left. He soon sold his railway to Vincent Serio, who moved his boatbuilding operation there. Serio was famous as the designer of the Hampton One Design competitive sailboat. (Photograph by Donald Ransone Taylor.)

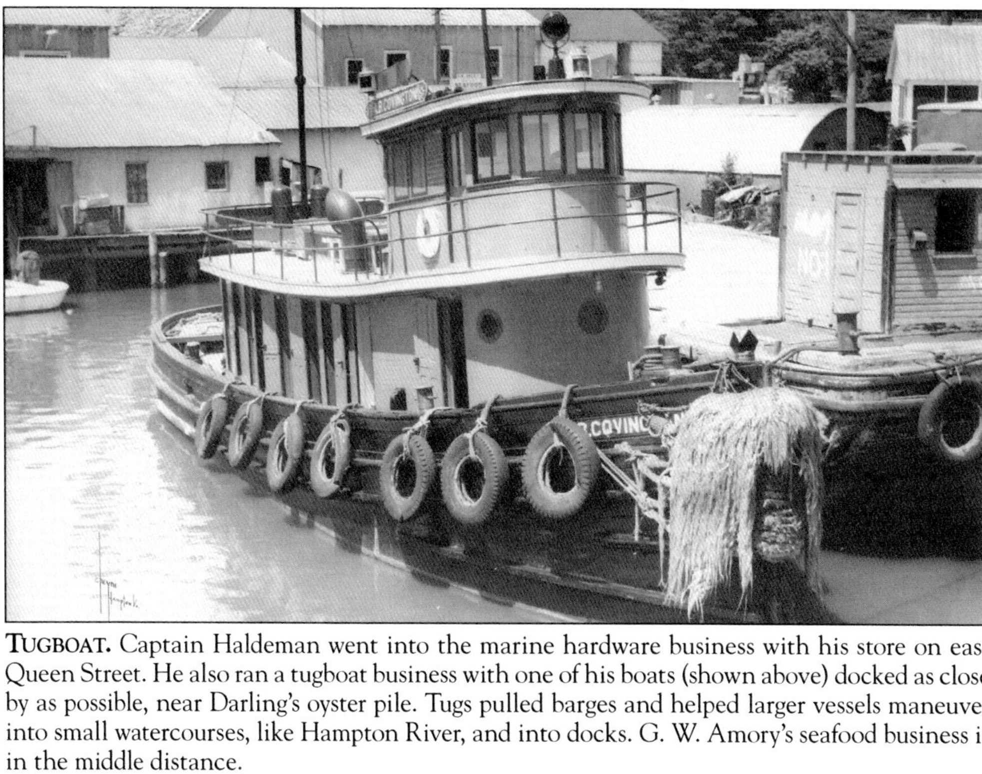

Tugboat. Captain Haldeman went into the marine hardware business with his store on east Queen Street. He also ran a tugboat business with one of his boats (shown above) docked as close by as possible, near Darling's oyster pile. Tugs pulled barges and helped larger vessels maneuver into small watercourses, like Hampton River, and into docks. G. W. Amory's seafood business is in the middle distance.

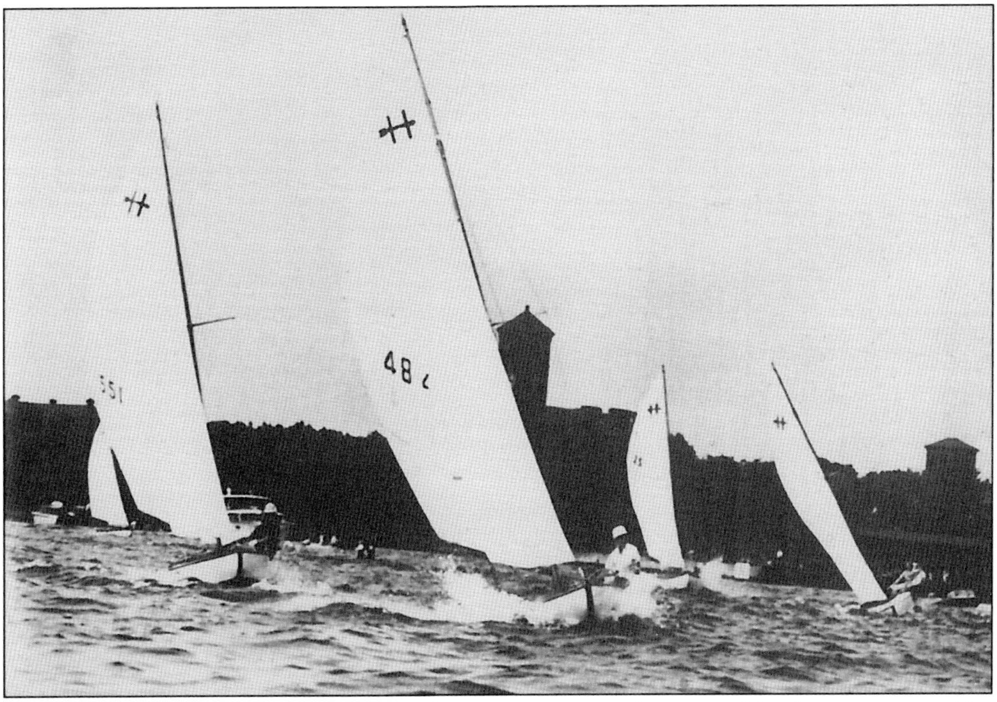

HAMPTON ONES. Vincent Serio's boat design was immensely successful—fast, maneuverable, and easy for one experienced yachtsman to handle. Here several Hampton Ones are sailing out of Hampton River to race in Hampton Roads. Eddie Williams is at the helm of No. 551, while E. Ralph James Jr. is in No. 484. The Hampton One has been a favorite in sailboat racing throughout the Chesapeake Bay region. (Courtesy of Eddie Williams.)

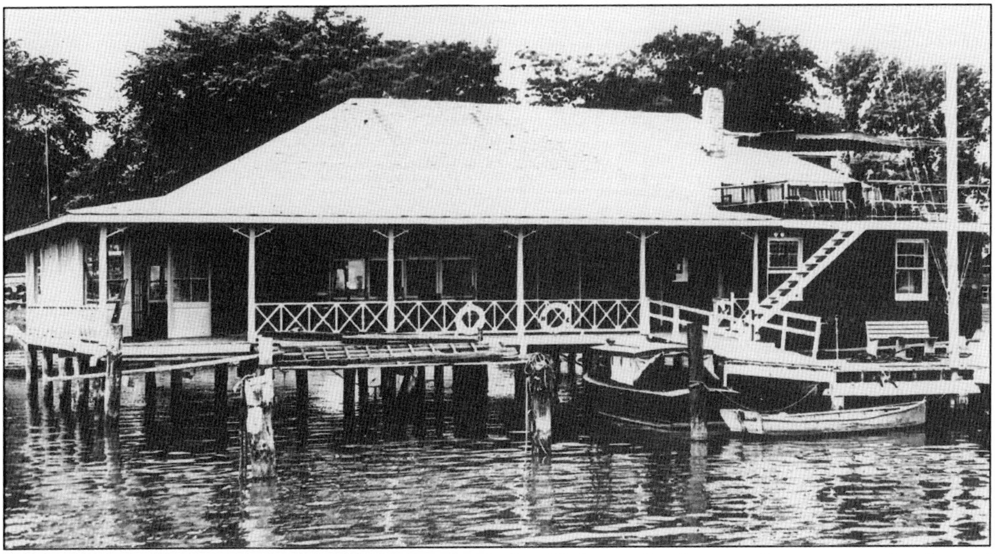

HAMPTON YACHT CLUB. The old Hampton Yacht Club was built over the water at the foot of Victoria Boulevard. Regattas of various classes of sailboats were held here on several weekends each summer, and many families enjoyed relaxing times in its dilapidated facilities. It has been replaced by a safer, more fuel-efficient, land-bound structure.

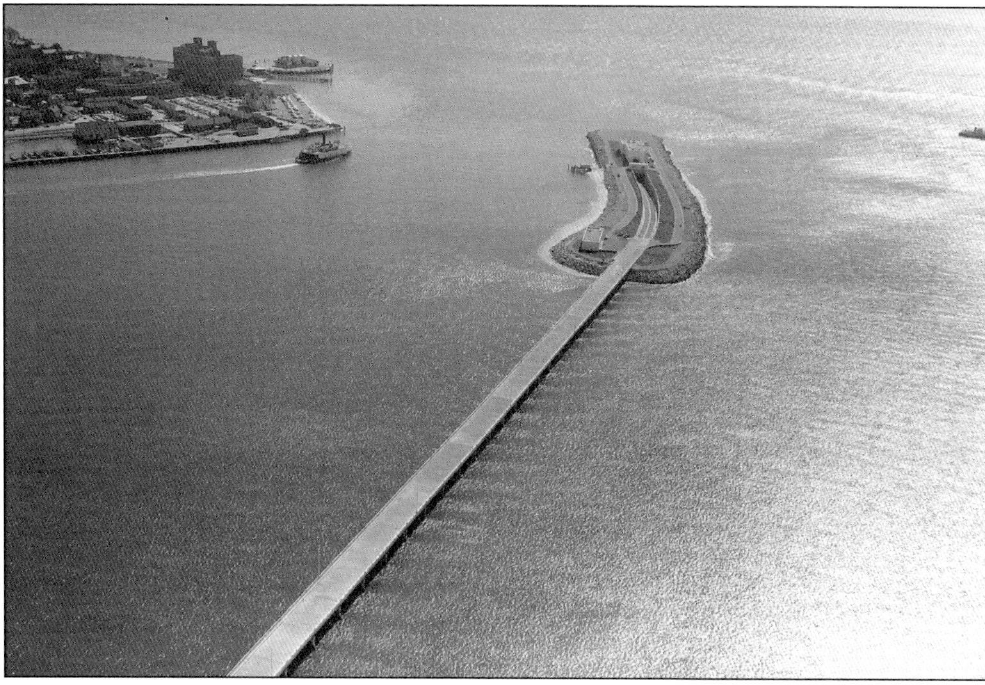

The Bridge-Tunnel. After the 3.5-mile roadway was completed in 1957, one could finally drive from Hampton to Norfolk expeditiously. A second span opened in 1976 when tolls were removed. It replaced vehicular ferries, one of which is passing Old Point Comfort in the photograph. (Courtesy of William E. Rouse Research Library.)

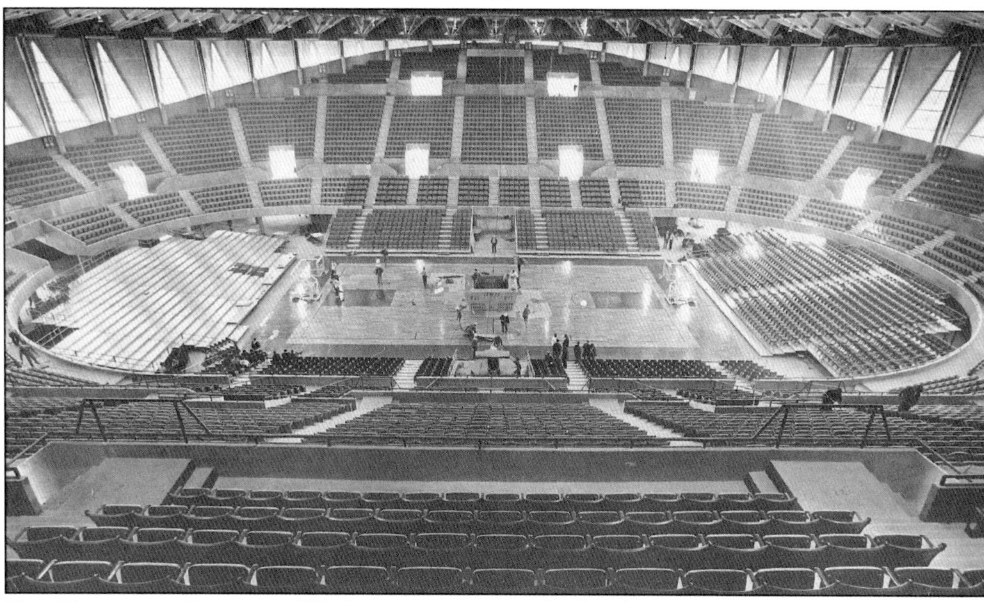

The Hampton Coliseum. Workmen are putting the finishing touches on the new Hampton Coliseum. It opened on December 1, 1969, seating more than 8,000 for a college basketball game. Jack Benny performed at the official opening on January 30, 1970, Elvis Presley appeared in concert on August 1, 1976, and the Rolling Stones appeared on December 18, 1981. (Photograph by Bea Kopp; courtesy of William E. Rouse Research Library.)

USO Dance. Founded in 1941, the United Service Organization (USO) tries to brighten the lives of military personnel. This picture taken during World War II shows USO volunteer Nell Whittenberry at a dance the organization sponsored at Langley Field. The white USO Club was near Locust Street, while the black USO was at the corner of King and Mallory. (Courtesy of USO of Hampton Roads.)

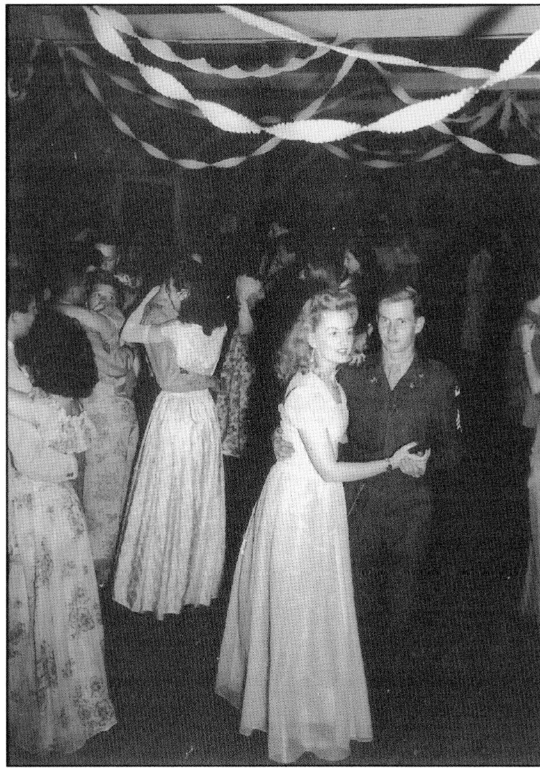

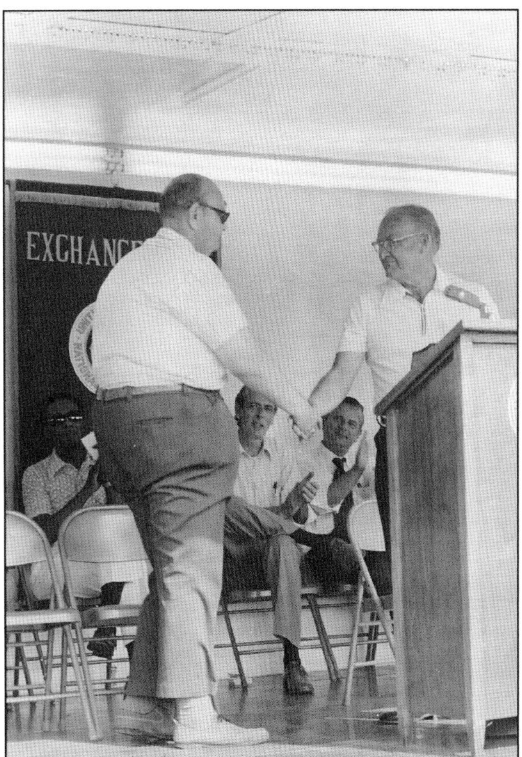

A Well-Deserved Civic Award. E. M. "Tiny" Hutton receives an award at an Exchange Club meeting in the 1950s. Hampton politician Dick Bagley is an onlooker. An employee of station WVEC and an aide to congressman Thomas Downing, Hutton was a local historian, a Civil War buff, a great storyteller, a genealogical researcher, and a collector.

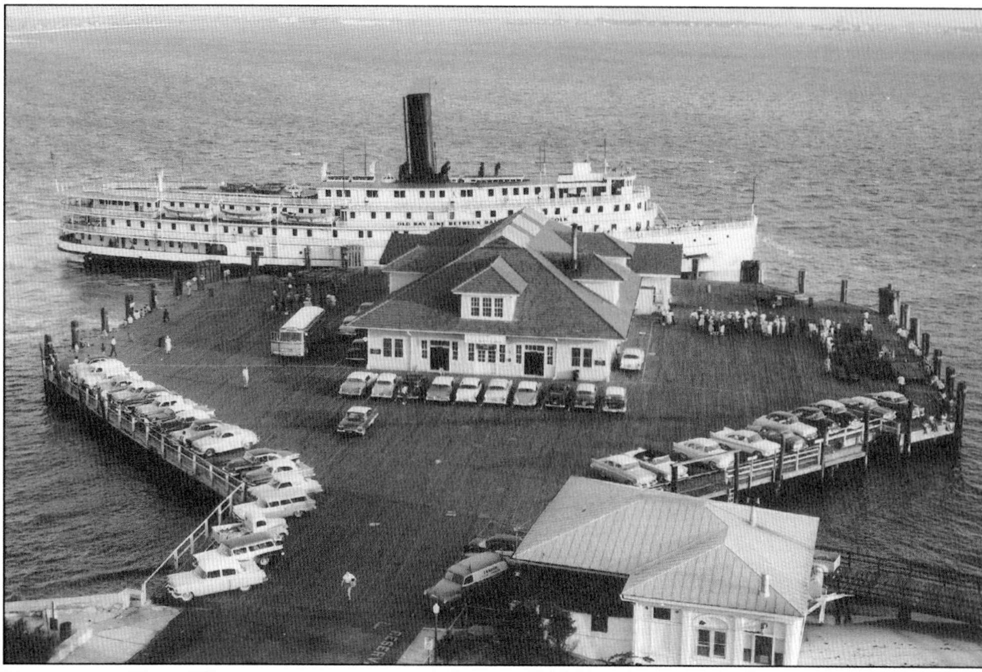

END OF AN ERA. The water astern is roiled as an Old Bay Line steamship begins to pull away from the wharf at Old Point Comfort on June 25, 1958. Discharged passengers head for their cars or the bus, while onlookers wave to their departing friends and loved ones. Meanwhile, people are fishing from both sides of the wharf. Hampton's steamship service terminated in 1959.

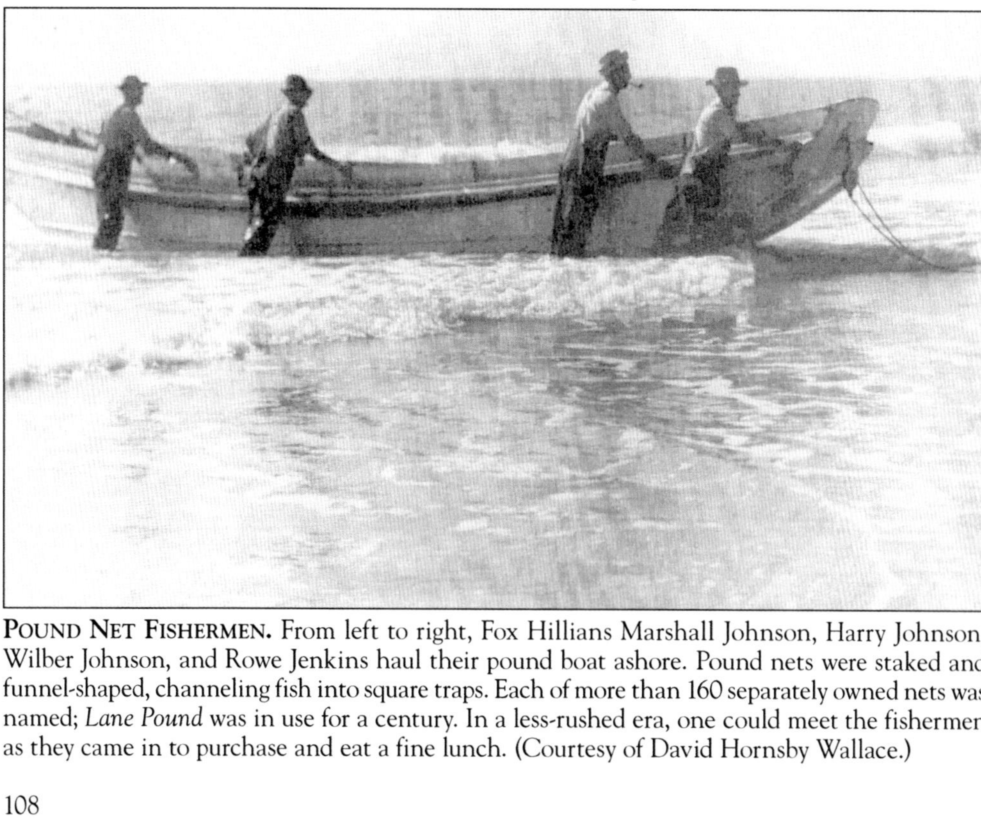

POUND NET FISHERMEN. From left to right, Fox Hillians Marshall Johnson, Harry Johnson, Wilber Johnson, and Rowe Jenkins haul their pound boat ashore. Pound nets were staked and funnel-shaped, channeling fish into square traps. Each of more than 160 separately owned nets was named; *Lane Pound* was in use for a century. In a less-rushed era, one could meet the fishermen as they came in to purchase and eat a fine lunch. (Courtesy of David Hornsby Wallace.)

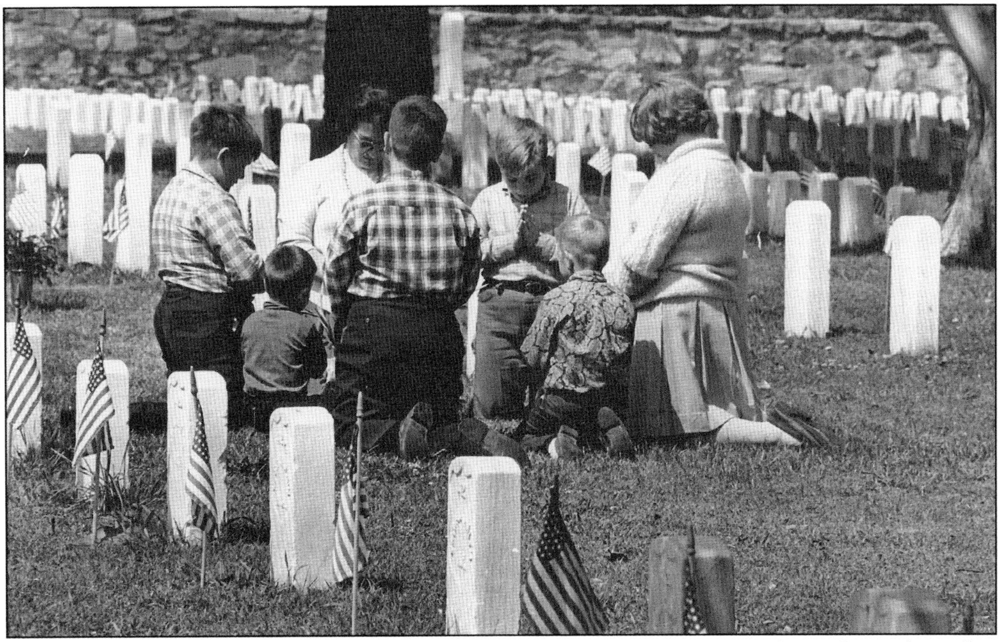

A Lost Loved One. A family of seven kneels in the grass, deep in prayer for a relative buried in Hampton National Cemetery. Established originally for Union soldiers who died in Hampton's Civil War military hospitals, the cemetery near Hampton University has received the remains of veterans of all wars since then. (Courtesy of William E. Rouse Research Library.)

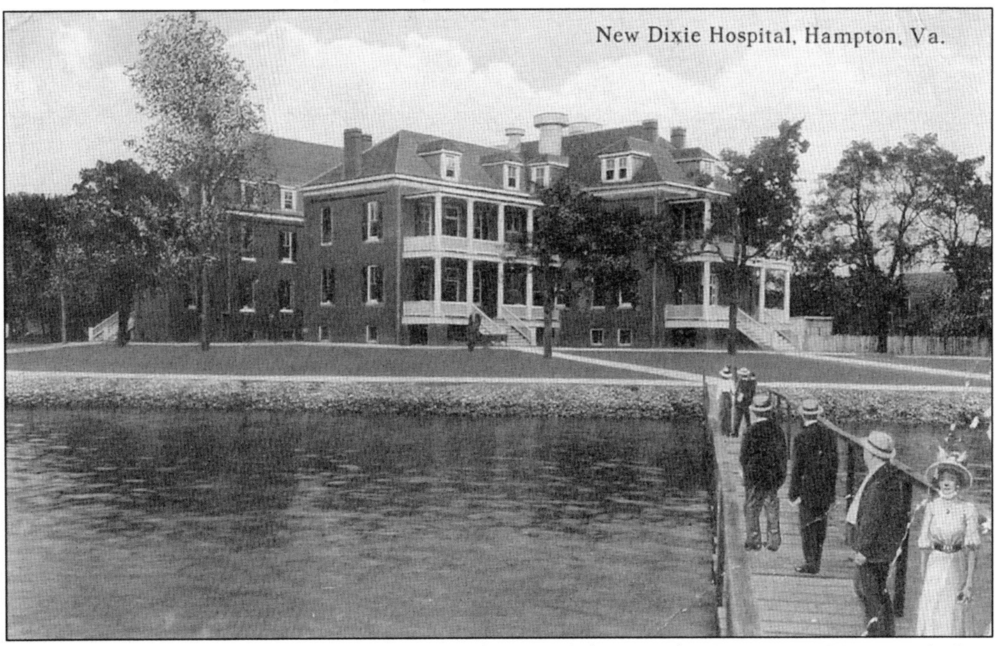

Dixie Hospital. Named for a horse, not the Confederacy, the Dixie was Hampton's first hospital, founded in 1892 on the Hampton Institute grounds as a training school for nurses. The magnificent new structure shown above was opened on June 24, 1913, on the nearby site of Pres. John Tyler's Villa Margaret. After additions in 1932 and 1943, the hospital was moved to Victoria Boulevard in 1959.

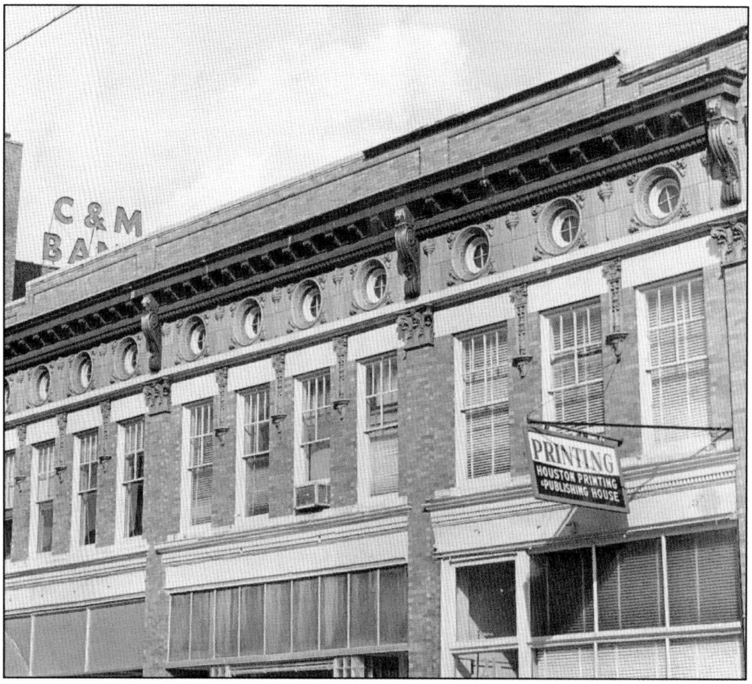

THE KECOUGHTAN BUILDING. This was one of the first office buildings to be built in Hampton, on south King Street, replacing most of the Barnes Hotel. In 1905, Harry R. Houston moved his printing and publishing business there, where it filled the third of the building to the right, as it still did in this 1967 photograph. Houston published the weekly *Hampton Monitor* newspaper for many years.

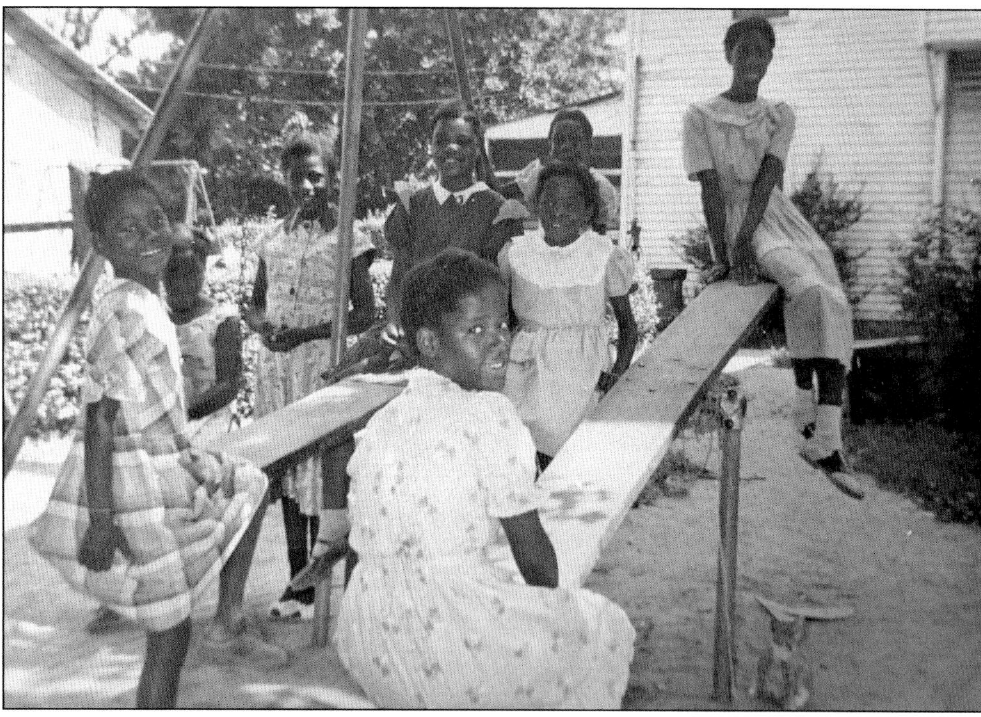

WEAVER HOME GIRLS. These young women enjoy playtime at the Weaver orphanage, for, as an anonymous biographer of founder Anna Weaver said, "They would not have had a chance otherwise." Encountering difficult financial spells, the institution received generous aid, including two cows from one friend, a barn built by volunteer young men, and a workhorse donated by the Hampton Institute faculty. Many residents went on to responsible and important lives.

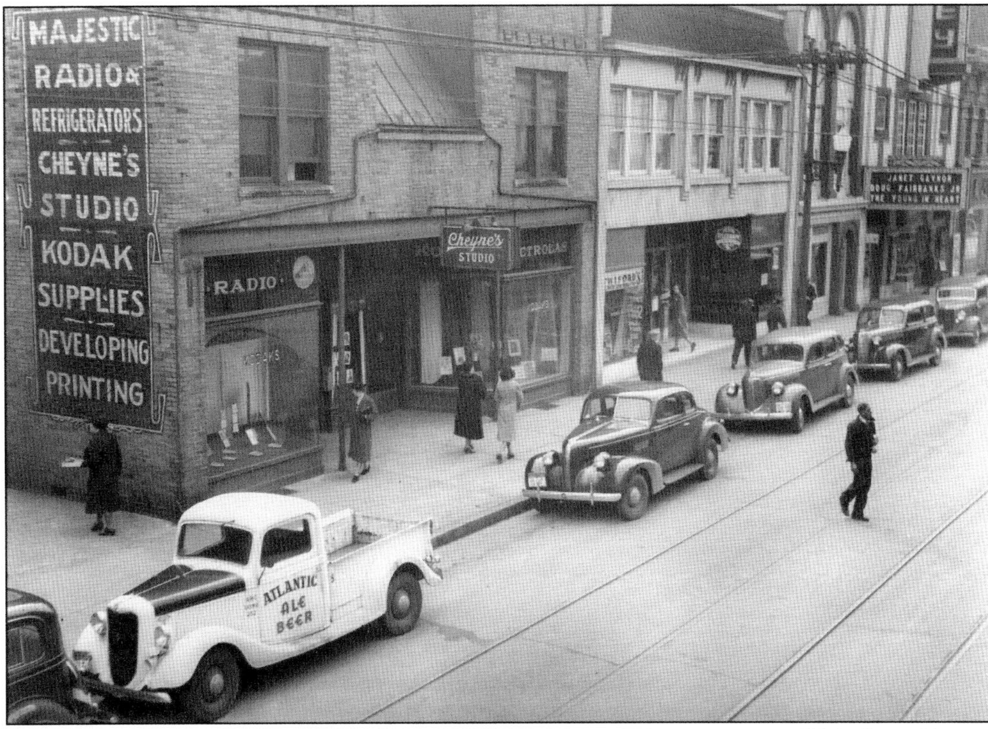

CHEYNE'S STUDIO. Many Hamptonians prized the delicate, clear portraits of Ethelbert Cheyne and his son "Happy," but as this 1938 study shows, they had to sell cameras, record players, radios, and even refrigerators to survive. The portraits were made under this slanted skylight. Janet Gaynor and Douglas Fairbanks Jr. are wowing local moviegoers nearby. The Hampton Stationery Company is today located in Cheyne's building.

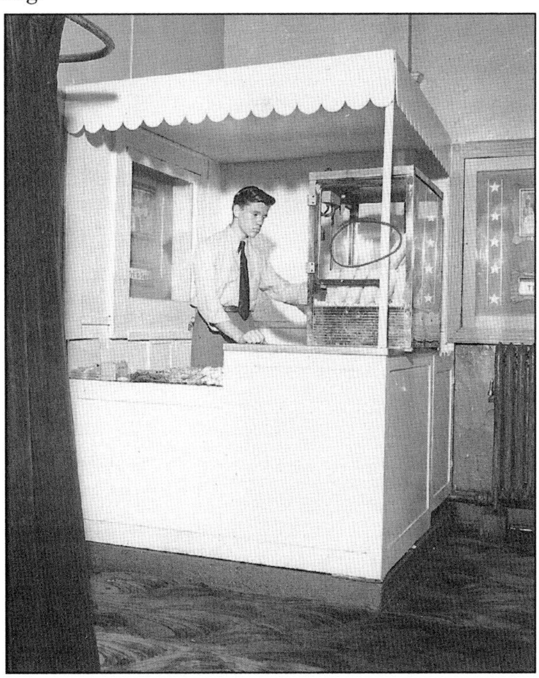

THE LANGLEY THEATER. Hampton's movie palace received the name of the local army air base. The silver screen proved an exciting entertainment draw for Americans from the 1910s onward, and Hampton was no exception. The popcorn vendor gets his supply ready for expected moviegoers in the Langley's lobby. The curtain shielded the theater proper from the light of the lobby. Inside, appointments were elegant.

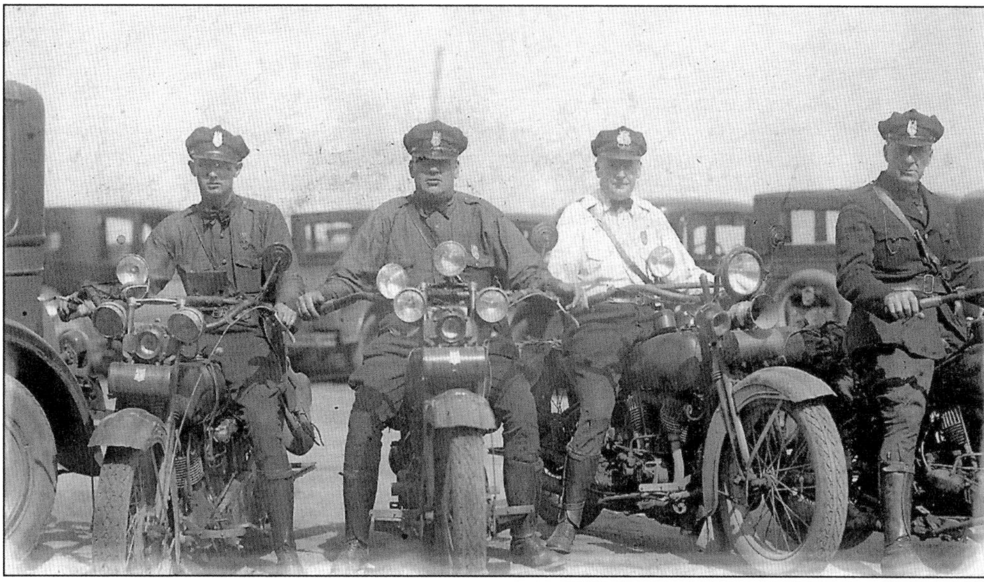

HAMPTON'S FINEST. Hampton's police force began soon after the town's incorporation in 1887. A force of three had increased to six officers by 1920, when E. C. Eaton became the first police chief. Henry Curtis began service on the force in 1906 and was chief from 1928 through 1945. Here four (perhaps all) of Hampton's police force pose on their motorcycles, perhaps at a sporting event.

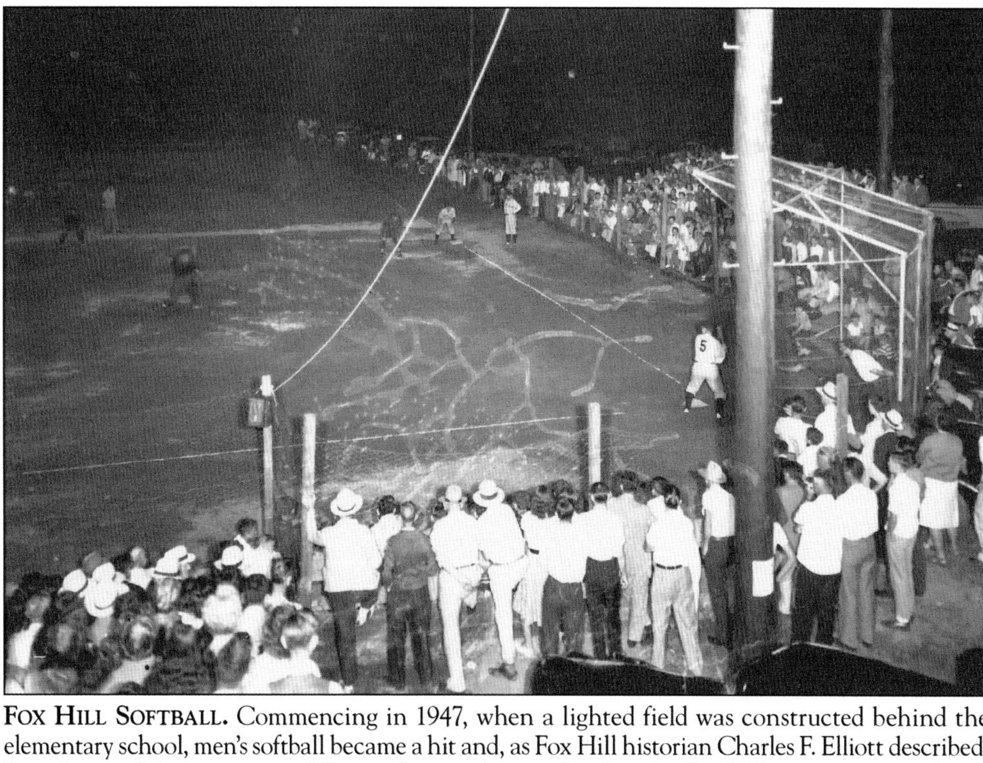

FOX HILL SOFTBALL. Commencing in 1947, when a lighted field was constructed behind the elementary school, men's softball became a hit and, as Fox Hill historian Charles F. Elliott described, "a real part of the community." Soon adopting fast-pitch rules, the Fox Hill teams competed well nationally, becoming one of the strongest fast-pitch teams in the country and advancing to the softball World Series five times between 1965 and 1975.

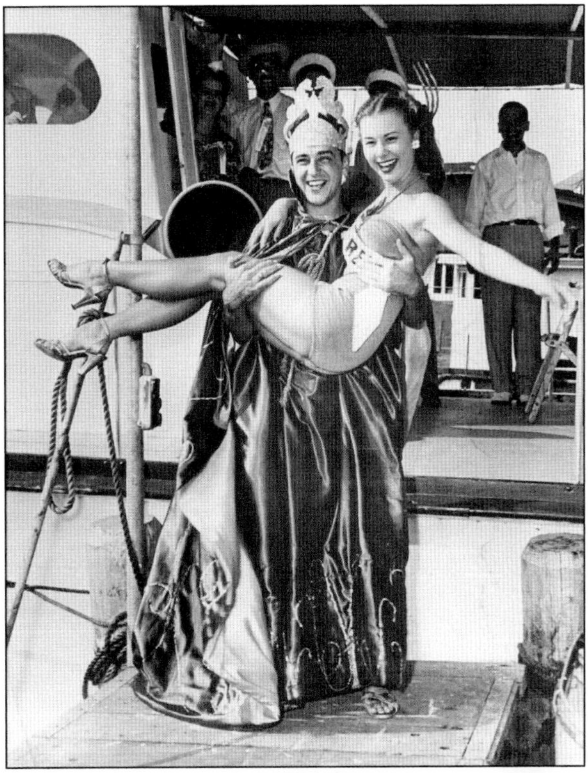

QUEEN LORELEI III. Mitzi Gaynor, having just turned 20 and fresh from the hit musical *My Blue Heaven*, which starred Betty Grable, was the queen of the third National Seafood Festival, a celebration Hampton held each September in the late 1940s and 1950s. Andy Roberts from Phoebus, a singer and local television personality, was King Neptune in 1950. The queen's coronation ceremony was emceed by E. M. "Tiny" Hutton.

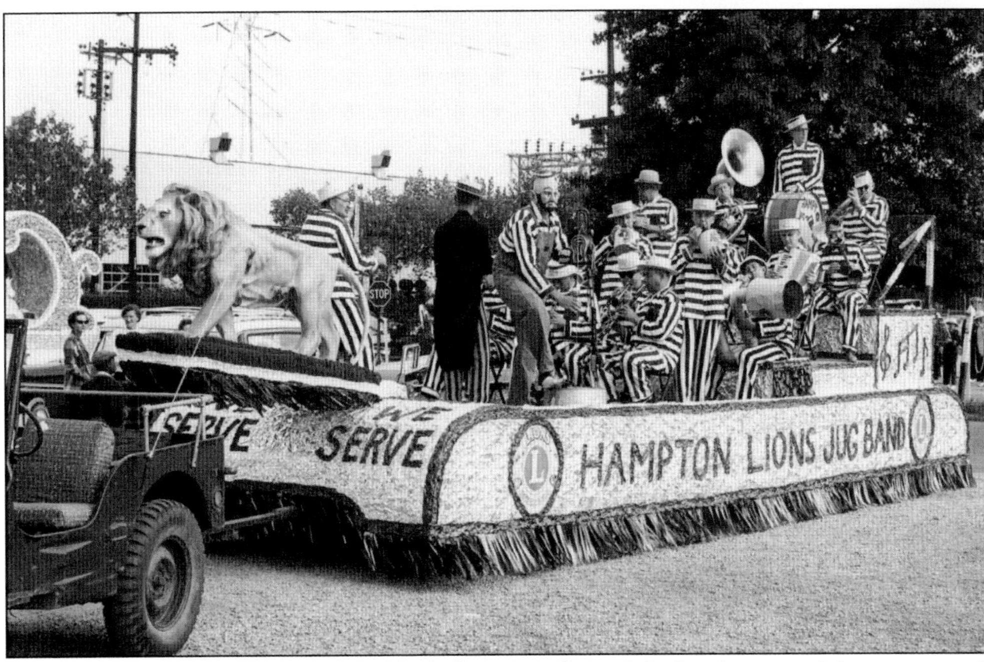

THE JUG BAND. Each seafood festival had a large parade, and the local service clubs participated. Here the Lions Club float and its participants, the Jug Band, are getting tuned up for the 12th festival in 1959. Dressed as clowns in uniforms any self-respecting prison would reject, the Jug Band performed in other venues as well, including trips to international Lions Club conventions.

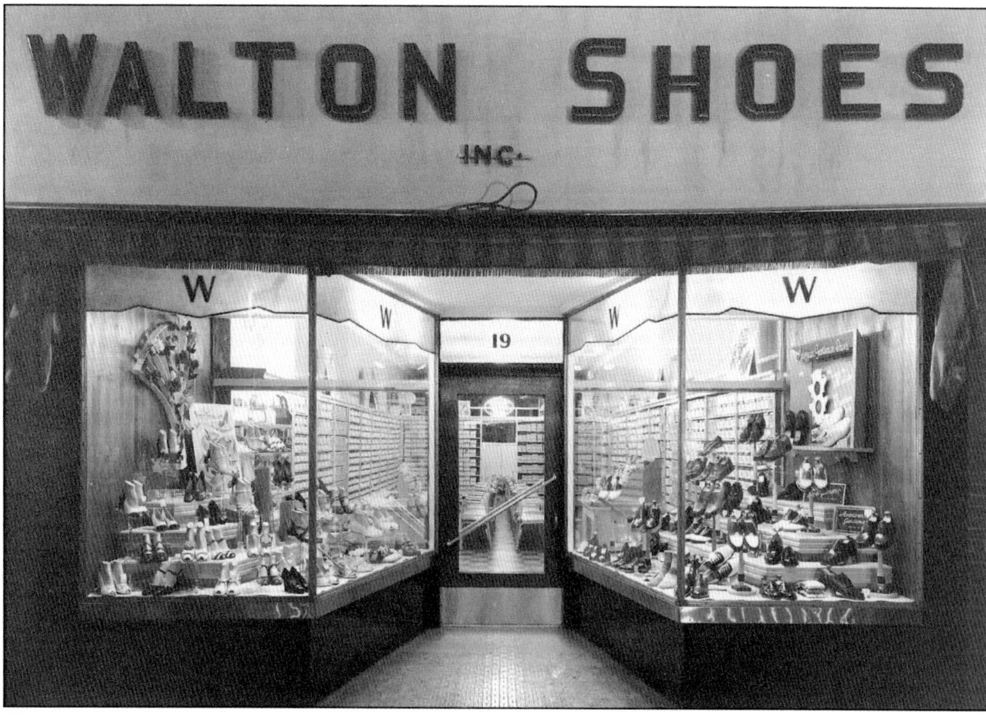

THE ICONIC HAMPTON SHOE STORE. Many Hamptonians purchased their footwear from Doc Walton at this store at 19 East Queen Street near "the crossing." A smile and personal service were its hallmarks, as Doc knew all his customers. Note the two-tone saddle oxfords, which were in vogue for men and women in the 1950s.

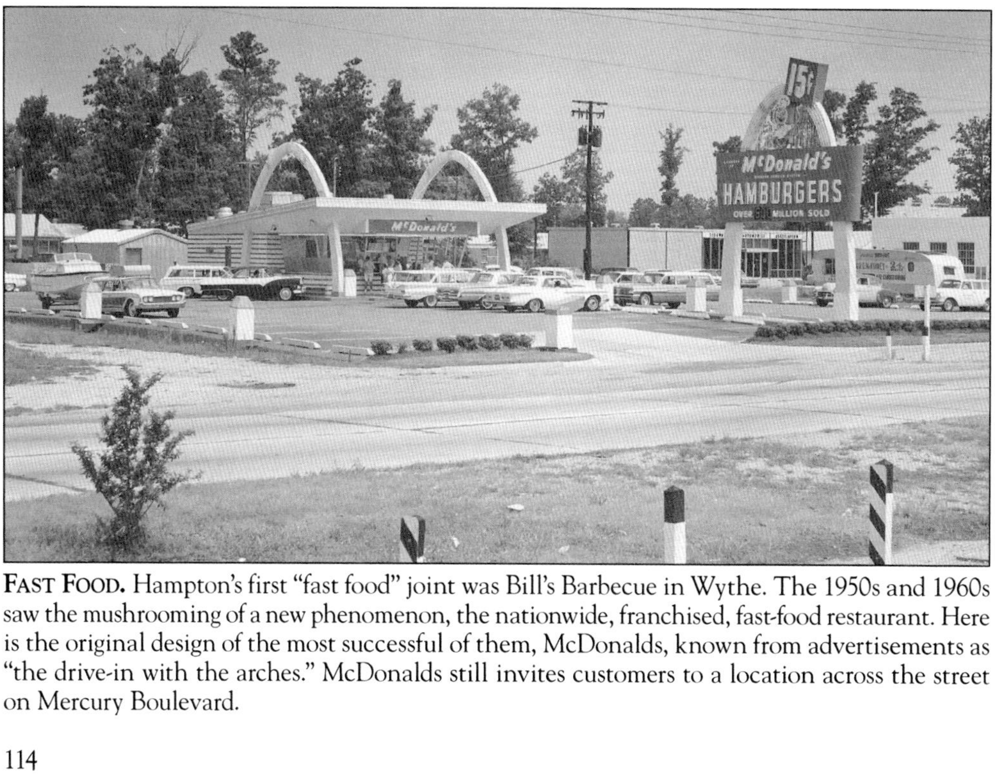

FAST FOOD. Hampton's first "fast food" joint was Bill's Barbecue in Wythe. The 1950s and 1960s saw the mushrooming of a new phenomenon, the nationwide, franchised, fast-food restaurant. Here is the original design of the most successful of them, McDonalds, known from advertisements as "the drive-in with the arches." McDonalds still invites customers to a location across the street on Mercury Boulevard.

History as Community Project. Sis Evans and Rufus B. Easter were among those who led the formation of an active local history group, the Hampton Heritage Foundation. They obtained a grant for the first archaeological excavations and greatly accelerated the collection of papers, photographs, and other materials that formed the basis of the Syms-Eaton Museum's collections, the ancestor of the Hampton History Museum and its collections.

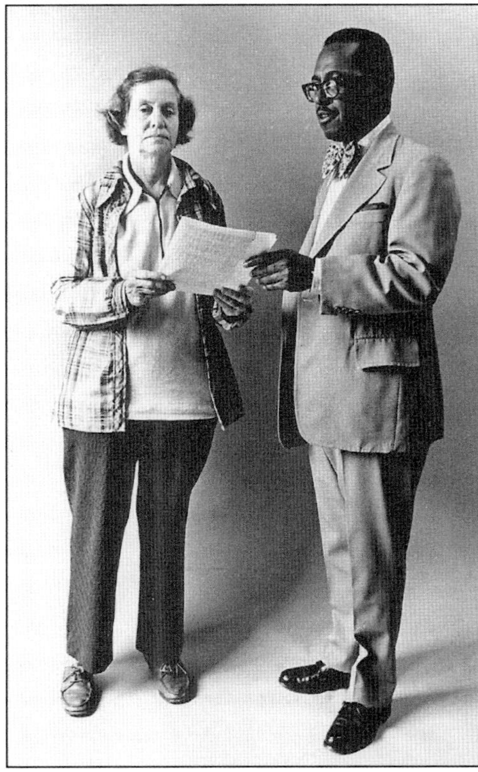

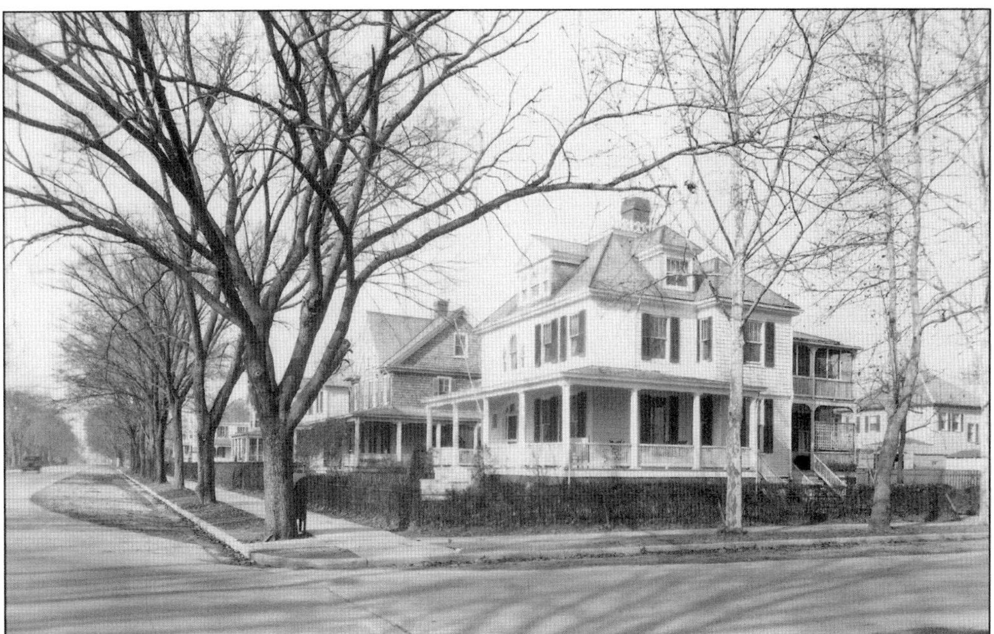

The Fashionable West End. The Pugh home, located at the corner of Victoria Boulevard and Bridge Street, was one of many large frame houses in wide, shady yards in the subdivision that grew up on what had been the Little England plantation on the west side of Hampton River. This 1926 photograph shows the broad streets not yet fully paved.

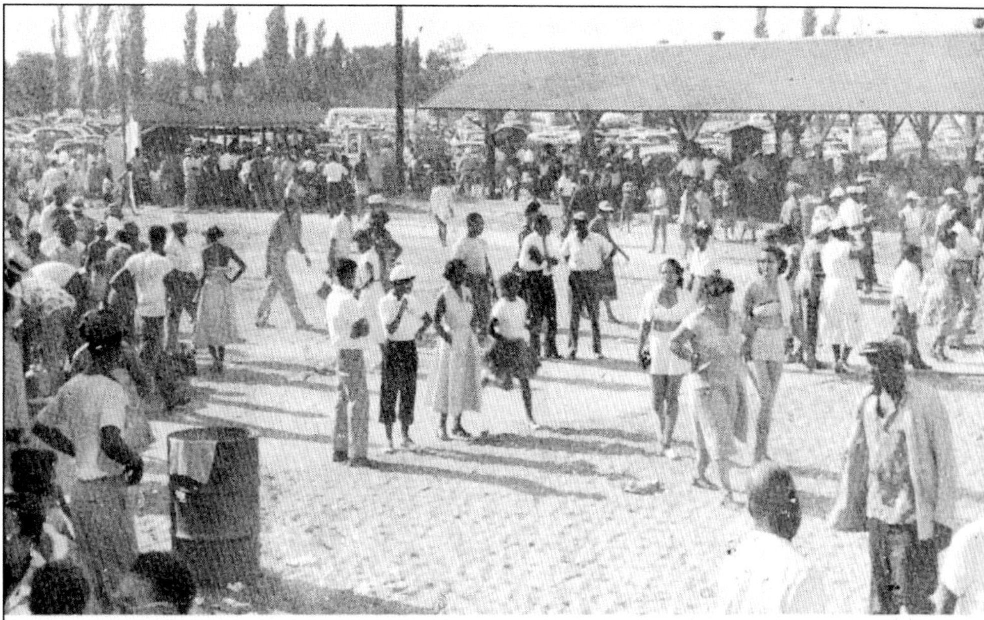

BAY SHORE MIDWAY BUCKROE BEACH, VA.

BAY SHORE MIDWAY. Buckroe had enticing beaches, and black residents desired to share in the fun. Bay Shore was developed in the 1890s and became, as Hampton historian Colita Fairfax said, "the mecca of the black vacationist," as it was the only resort in this area open to blacks. Decimated in the 1933 storm, Bay Shore revived and operated through 1973. Redd Foxx, Ella Fitzgerald, and Louis Armstrong performed there.

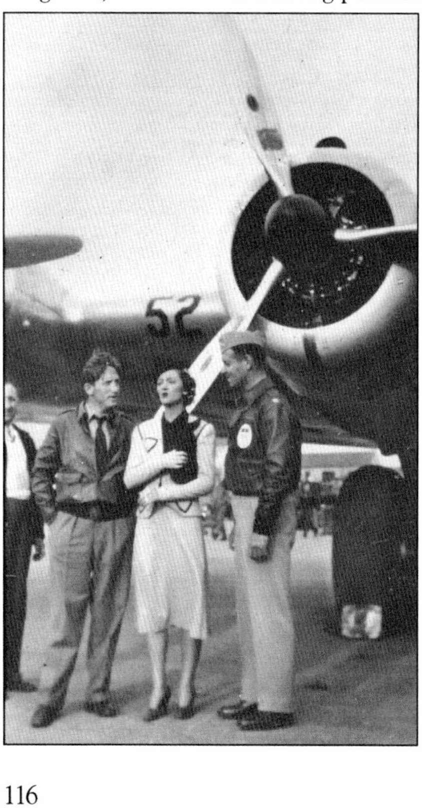

STARS OVER LANGLEY. Spencer Tracy, Myrna Loy, and Clark Gable land at Langley Field in 1937 to complete the filming of *Test Pilot*. Lionel Barrymore also starred. The movie climax, in which Gable and Tracy crash land a still-experimental Boeing B-17, was shot at Langley. While Gable was doubled in these flying scenes, he later served in the army's air corps, flying combat missions in Europe in World War II.

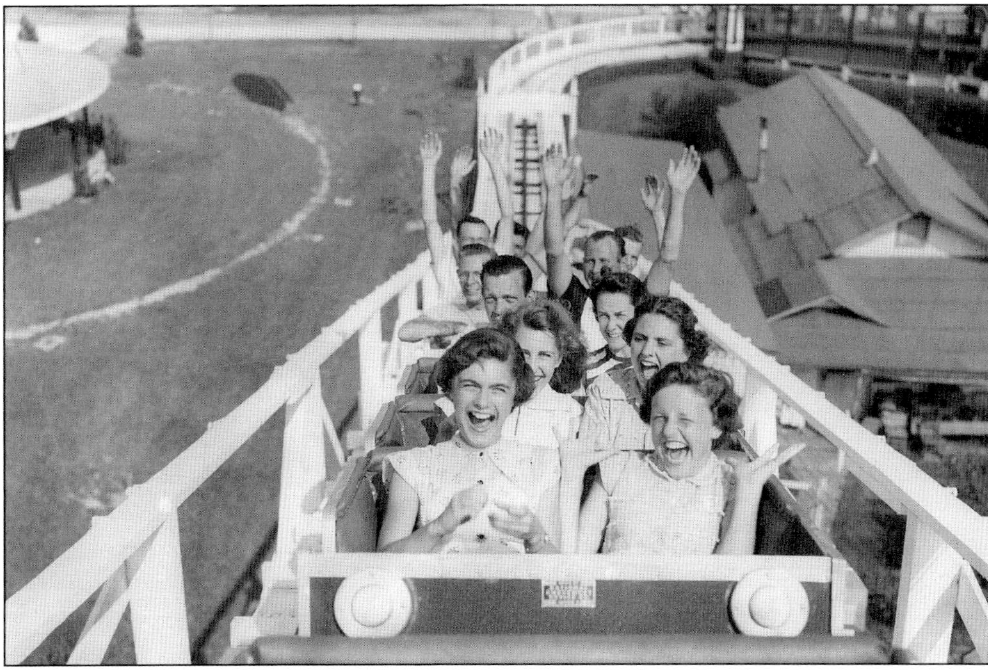

Roller Coaster. A favorite summer pastime was the Buckroe Beach amusement park, and this ancient roller coaster was at its heart. Everyone screamed, everyone lifted their arms, everyone shut their eyes, and everyone had a great time. It is a shame that the amusement park is no longer there.

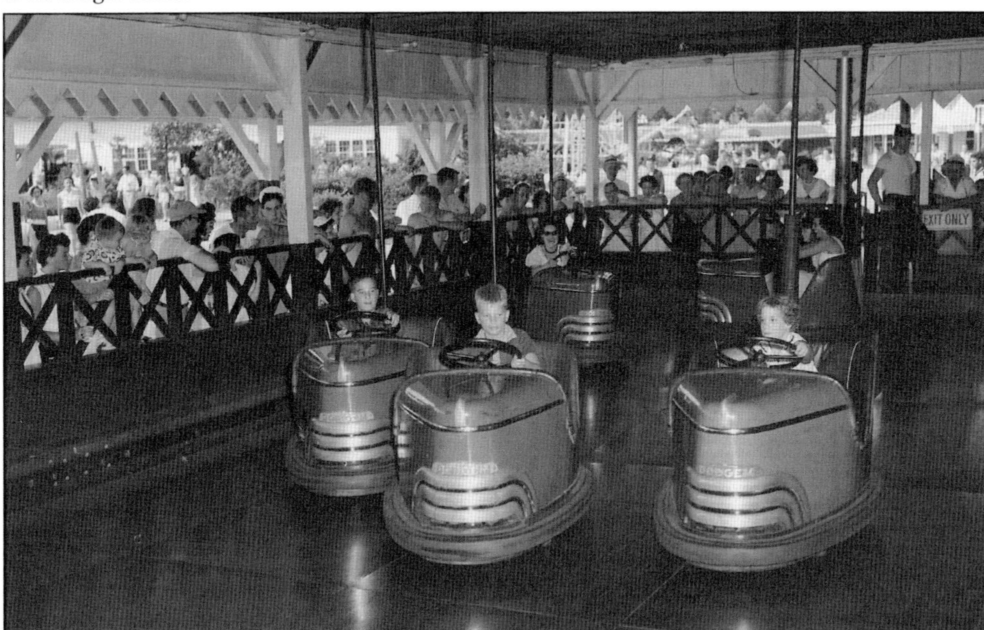

Bumper Cars. People wait in a long line to ride the bumper cars in this midsummer photograph from the Buckroe Beach amusement park. Like the mom in the back and the kids in the foreground, everyone becomes a serious, dedicated demolition derby entrant when they take the wheel of a bumper car, loving the crashes and the narrow escapes.

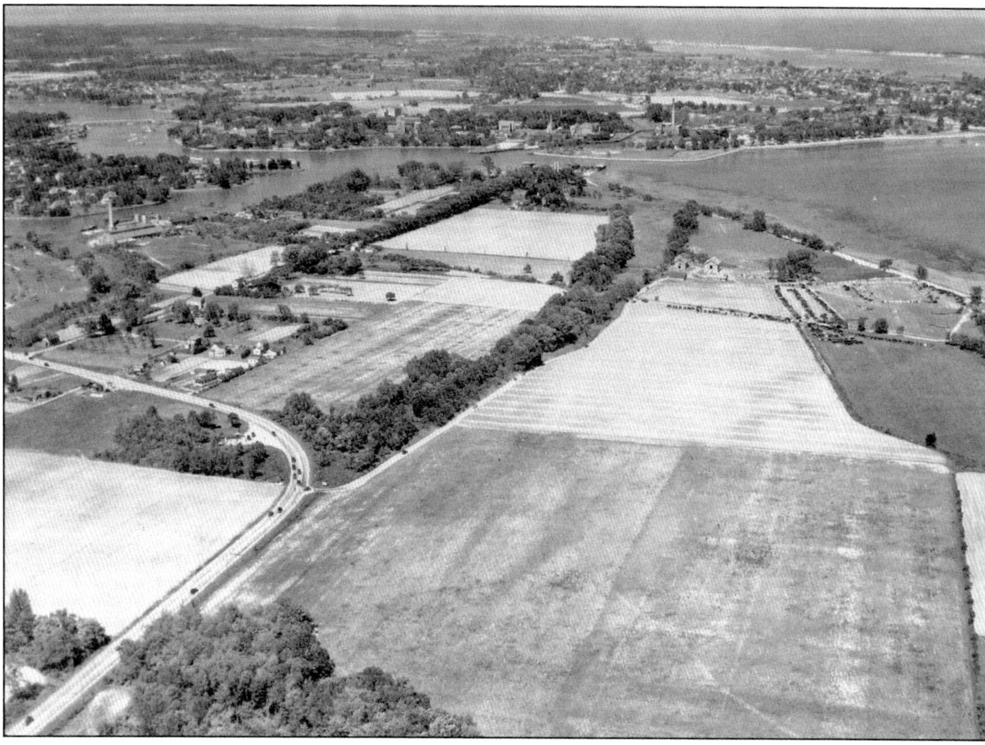

Merrimac Shores. This aerial view, probably from the early 1940s, shows Kecoughtan Road turning past vast farm acreage that would soon be developed as Southampton, Sussex, and the Merrimac Shores community. A horse race is in progress at the waterside track on the Cooper Farm in the upper right center, while one of Hampton's power plants can be seen on the south side of Sunset Creek at the upper left center.

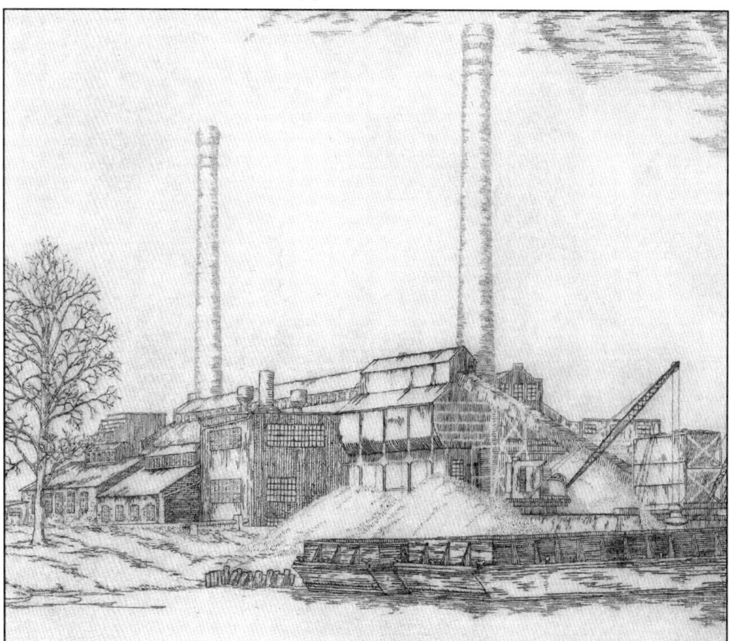

Powerhouse. Early power plants primarily provided electric light service. After 1900, tremendous advances were made in the development and supplying of power to factories. Hampton's largest power plant, located on the north side of Sunset Creek, was built by the Darling firm—which became the Newport News and Hampton Railway, Gas, and Electric Company—to provide power for its trolley cars. It also supplied electricity for consumers.

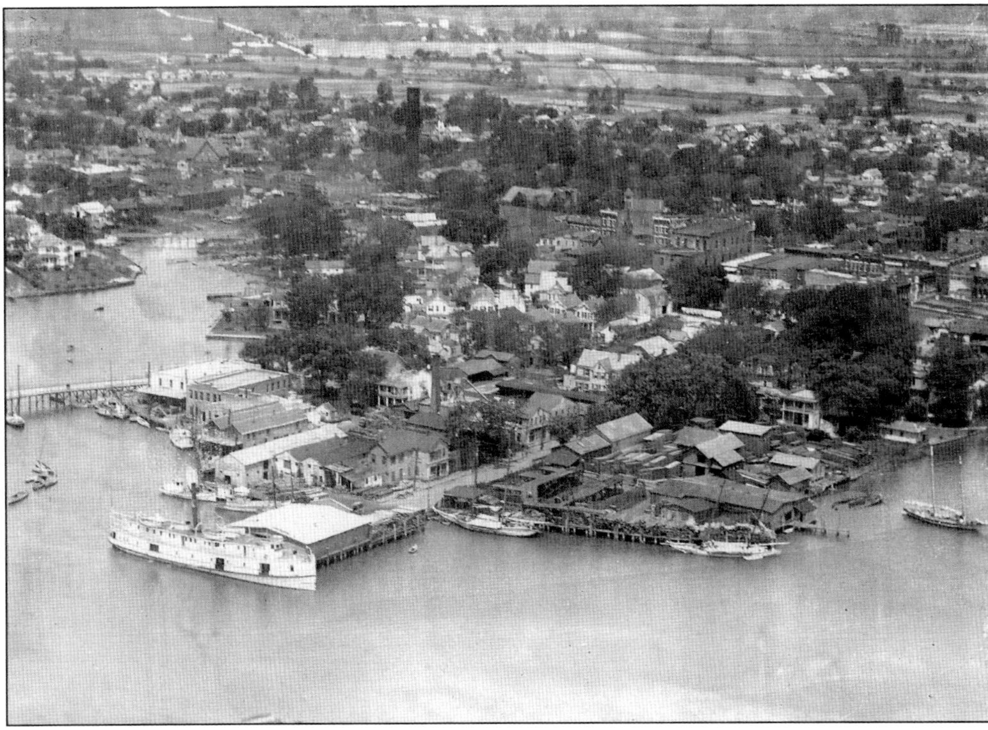

LOST TO MODERNITY. These two pictures present the town of Hampton nostalgically as Crabtown. Seafood and a compact, small town are the focus of the upper picture. Several kinds of boats are anchored or docked. Seafood businesses intermingle with dwellings, plus Heffelfinger's lumberyard at the foot of south King Street. Spacious houses and the bricked outlines of the Queen Street business district cozy up from the landward side. Bridge Street (center left), the old footbridge (above it), and other streets lead easily into suburbs and the farm country beyond. The tranquil photograph at right, centered on oyster boats floating at rest backed by the quiet panorama of the Darling complex on the left and the Schmelz mansion on the right, similarly evokes a sleepier, more intimate Hampton that is irretrievably lost.

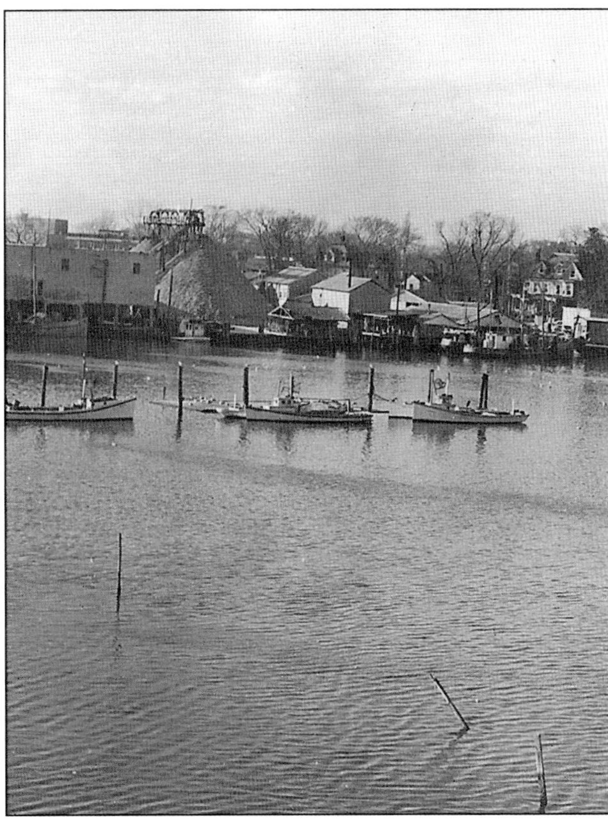

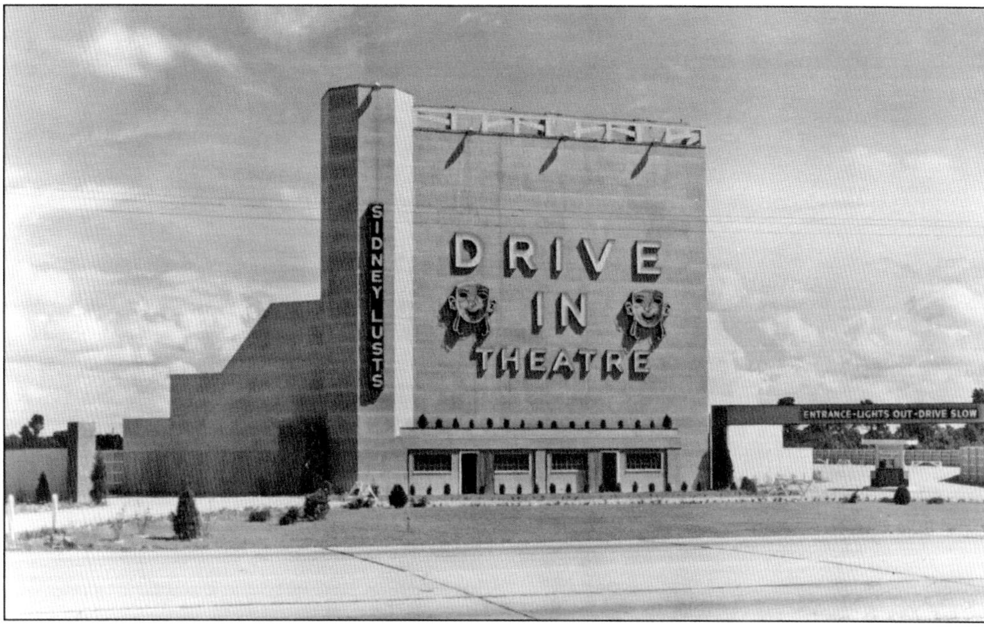

DRIVE-INS. Downtown Hampton's outdoor movie theater, the Sidney Lust Drive-In, opened on then-new Pembroke Avenue in 1948. The invention of in-car heaters in 1950 made outdoor movie attendance a year-round possibility, and drive-ins reached their national peak of popularity in 1958, when more than 4,000 were open. Like most other drive-ins, the Sidney Lust has long been closed.

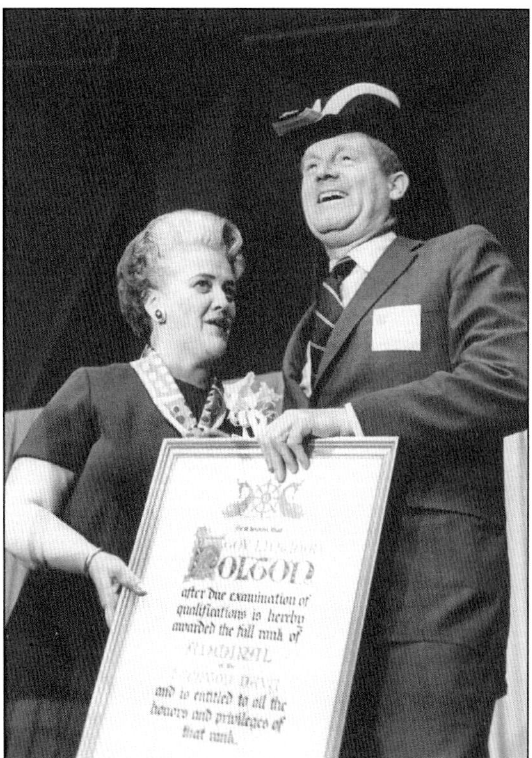

HER HONOR. Ann Kilgore became Hampton's mayor in 1963, the first woman in Virginia to achieve that rank. Here she elevates Gov. Linwood Holton to the rank of admiral in the Hampton Navy. Mayor Kilgore launched a vigorous campaign to increase tourism, and media entrepreneur and visionary Thomas Chisman, with others, convinced the city to commence a redevelopment program, bringing Hampton into the future. (Courtesy of William E. Rouse Research Library.)

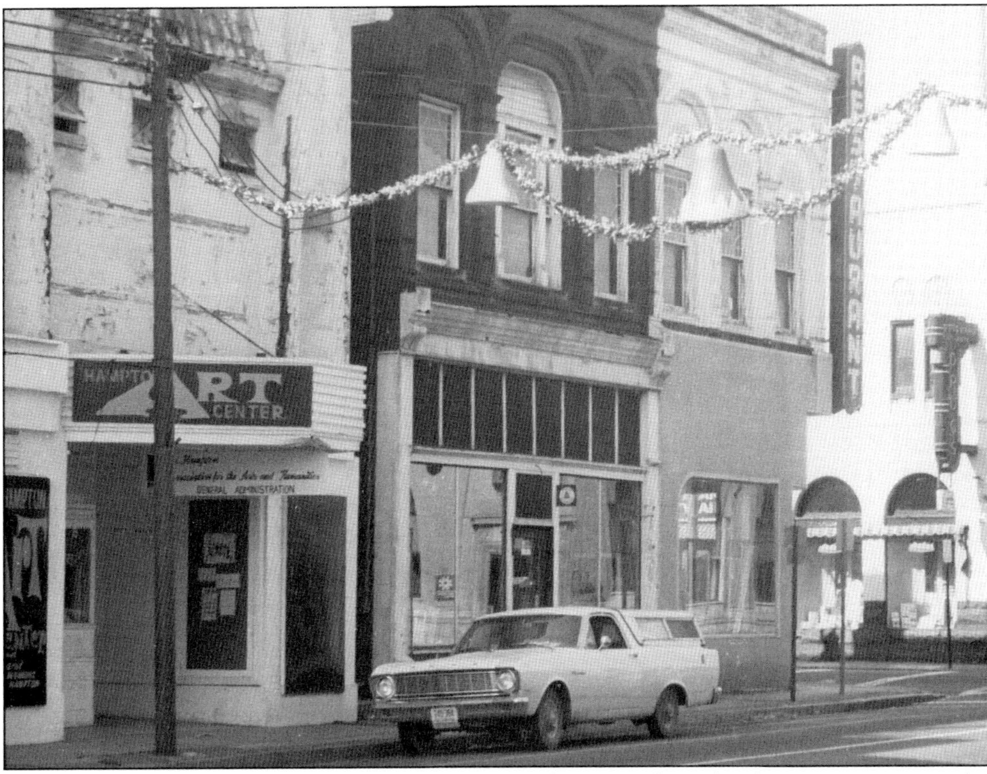

DOWNTOWN NEEDS CHANGE. One of the principal reasons for redevelopment is seen in this photograph: Hampton was becoming run-down. The Art Center on King Street had in brighter days been the Rex Theater (formerly the Apollo, Hampton's first movie house), where the mother of one of the authors parked him every Saturday for two Westerns and a cartoon while she shopped.

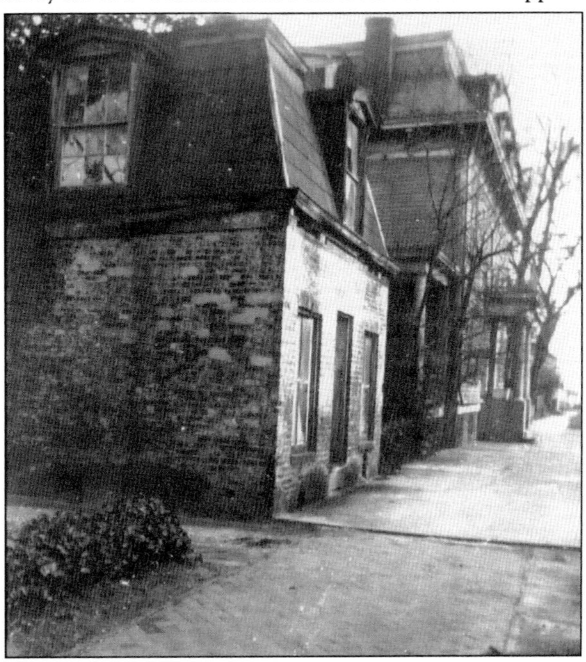

HISTORIC STRUCTURES. While conducting an archaeological investigation, it was determined that the brick structure in the foreground, long thought to be the Colonial customs house, was built early in the 19th century. The larger building had been the pre-Revolutionary Kings Arms Tavern. Kennon Whiting purchased it before the Civil War and remodeled it into his home, which survived Hampton's burning in 1861. Both structures were demolished in the late 1960s.

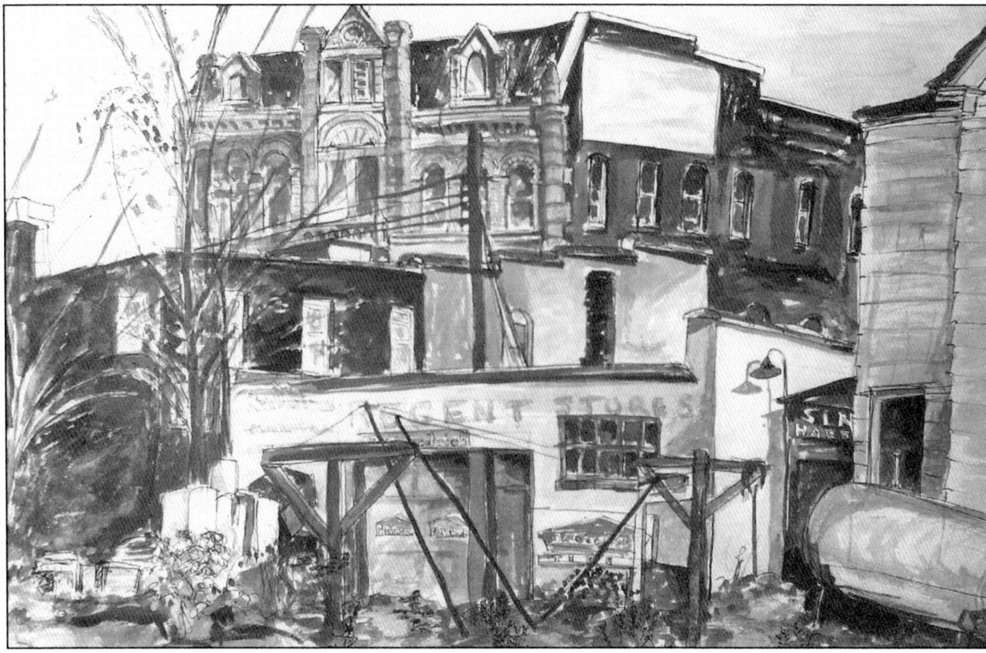

QUEEN STREET SCENES. Sis Evans, one of Hampton's best historians, used her watercolors to render a record of what would be lost through redevelopment. Four of her downtown scenes grace these two pages, courtesy of the Evans family. Above, the four-story "Pythian Castle" towers over other Queen Street buildings (here seen from the rear from Court Street). Built in 1889, as the meeting hall of the Knights of Pythias, its third-floor auditorium long served Hamptonians for large meetings and was the locale for Hampton's first movies. In the picture below, the Langley Theater and the old Bank of Hampton building (built in 1885) were razed during redevelopment, but the grand Masonic Temple was spared and is extant today, housing Wheat First Securities. It was built in 1888.

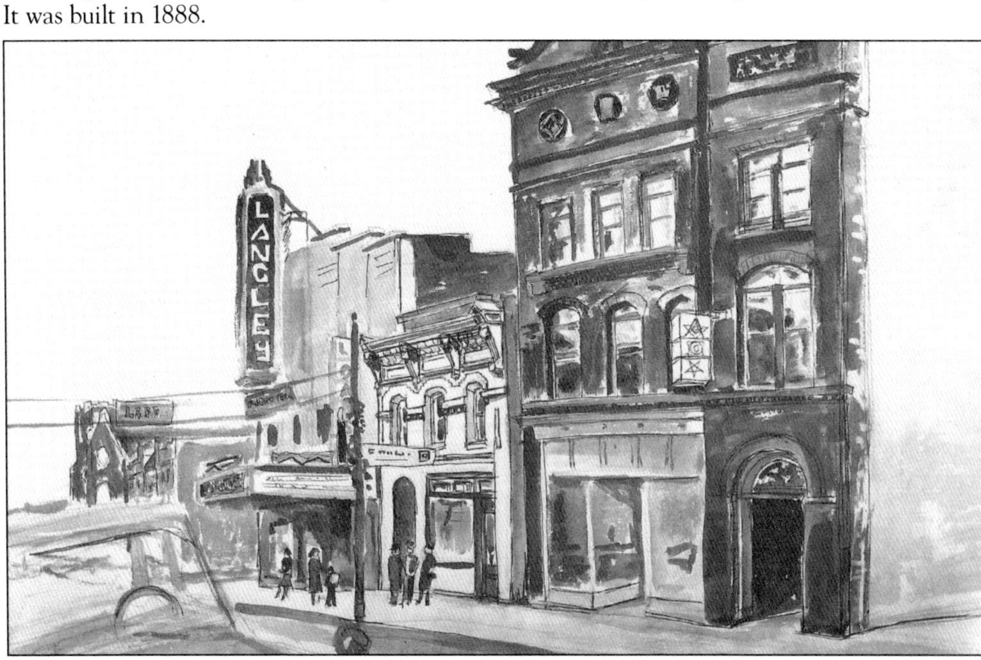

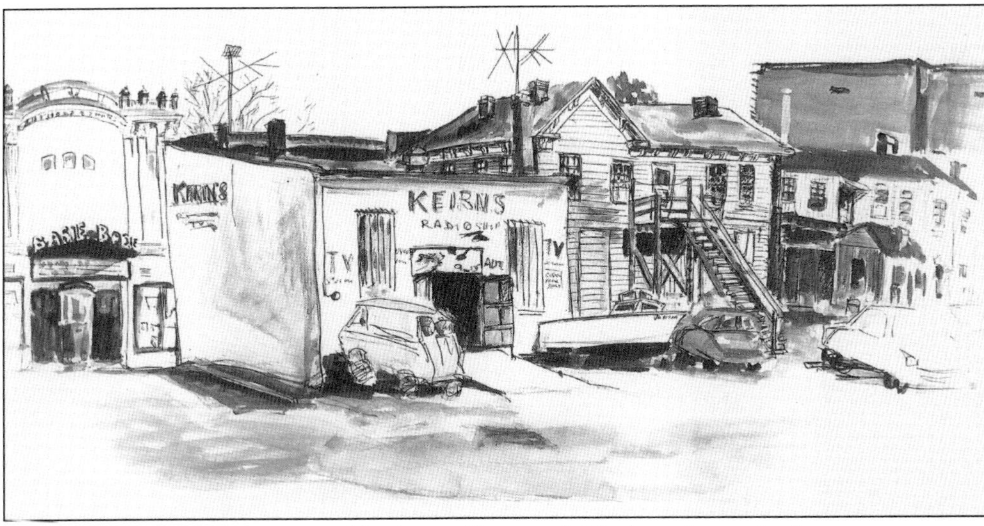

DOWNTOWN NEIGHBORHOODS. The Basie, Hampton's blacks-only movie theater, was on west Queen Street, as shown in the above picture. The tall building to the extreme right was Brittingham's Furniture. Many of the buildings in between (the backs of which are visible) were owned by blacks, particularly by the family of R. M. Smith, a contraband and member of Virginia's House of Delegates in the 1870s. People lived in the apartments over the stores. The picture below shows the houses along Hope Street progressing from Queen Street near Brittingham's Furniture (tall building) to Bridge Street (where the stop sign is). All have been razed. James S. Darling's saw and gristmill was near here in the 1870s.

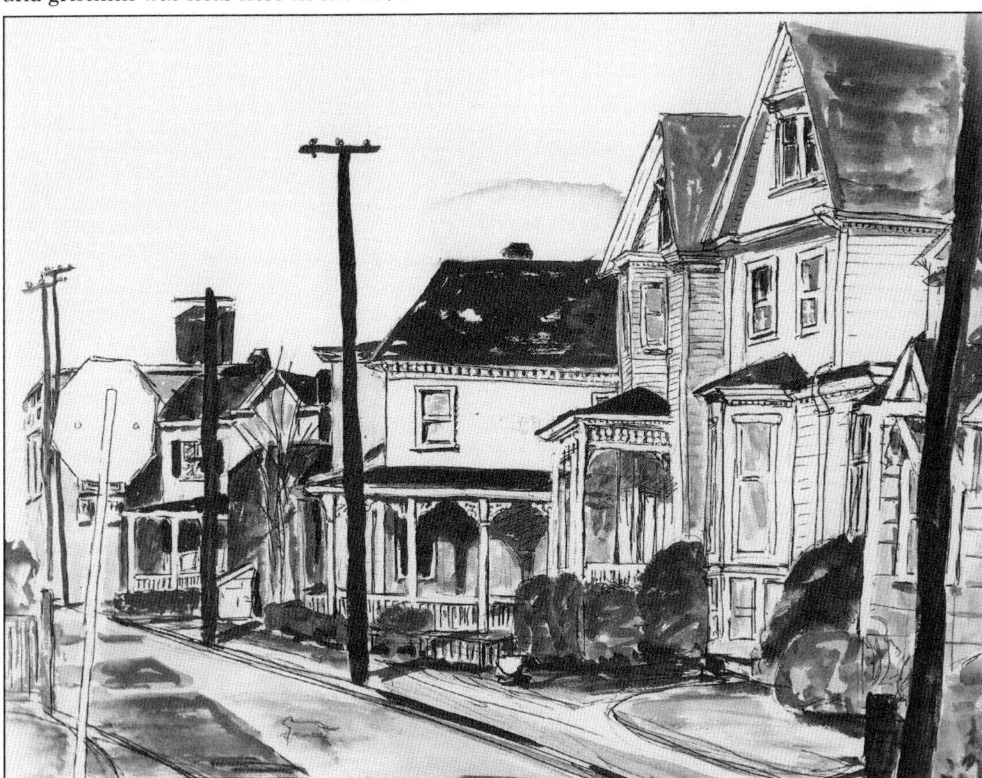

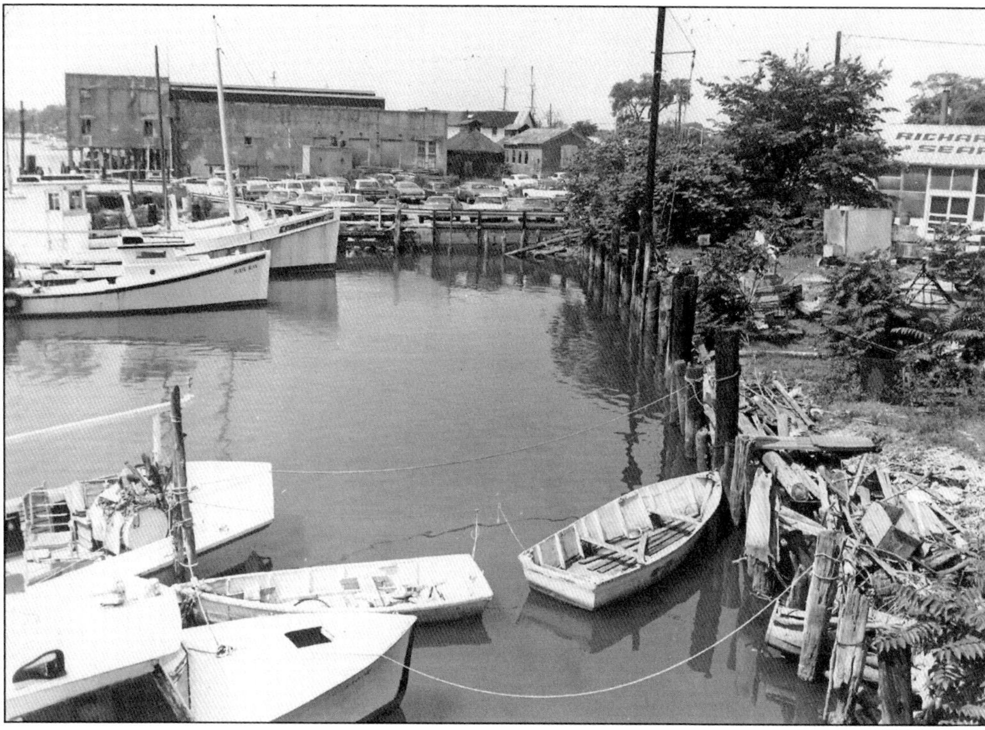

CRABTOWN CHANGING. The Darling oyster pile is gone, replaced by a parking lot, as this 1970s photograph shows. The small, dark, round Darling oyster icehouse, just beyond the cars, is abandoned. The water-line bulkhead has deteriorated, and the shore is littered. Some seafood vessels remain, and while Richardson's Seafood market on East Queen Street (right) seems prosperous, Crabtown is disappearing.

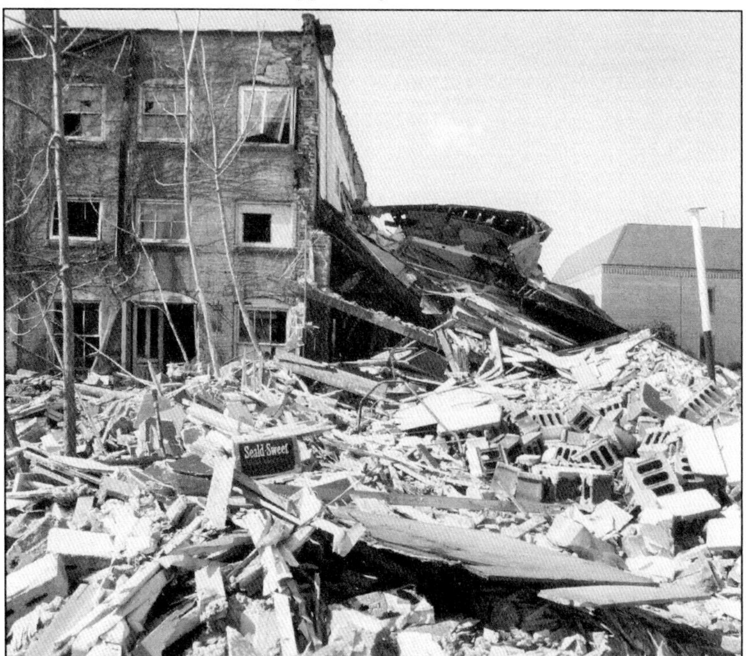

THE PROCESS OF REDEVELOPMENT. The handsome Kecoughtan Building was demolished in the spring of 1975, producing the rubbish pile shown here. Only a few pieces of its copper drain spouts and terra-cotta ornamentation remain. One of the latter has been sited on south King Street as a historic exhibit. The building with the mansard roof now houses the Bank of America.

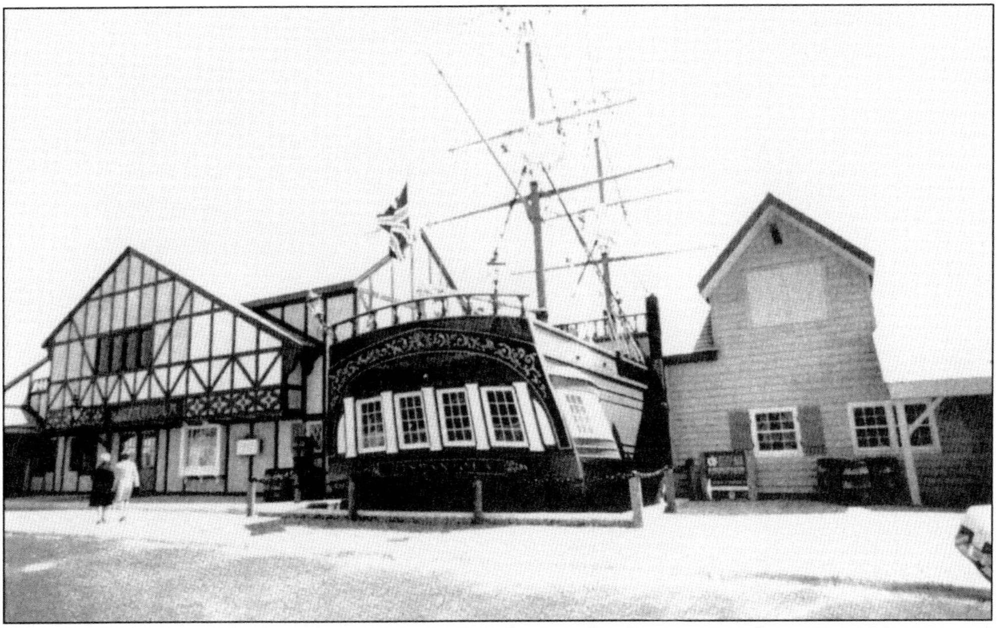

THE HISPANIOLA. Hampton's first effort at waterfront redevelopment in the early 1970s centered on a restaurant partially located in a replica of a ship from the Spanish Main, with a view on Hampton River. The seafood-heavy menu was good, but the venture did not draw enough customers, and it, too, was demolished in the late 1980s.

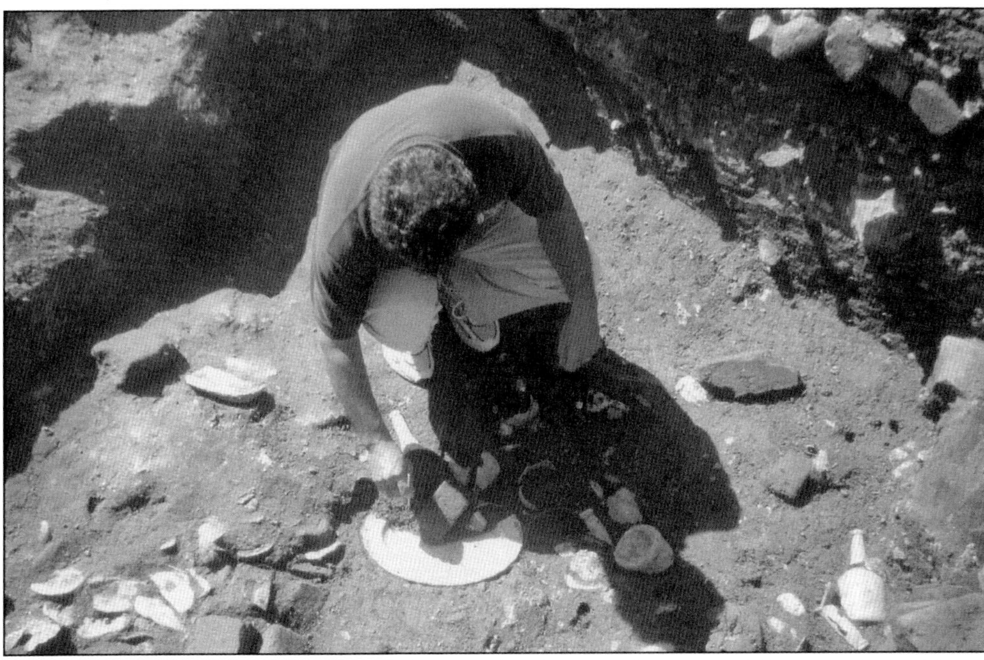

ARCHAEOLOGY. One benefit of redevelopment has been archaeological digs and finds. Almost the whole of Hampton's downtown south of Queen Street has been systematically searched for historical material. Here, amid brickbats and oyster shells in a basement storage pit, Nick Luccketti removes dirt from a fine cream-ware platter. The remnants of several wine bottles can also be seen. Hampton is one of the most extensively excavated urban sites in America.

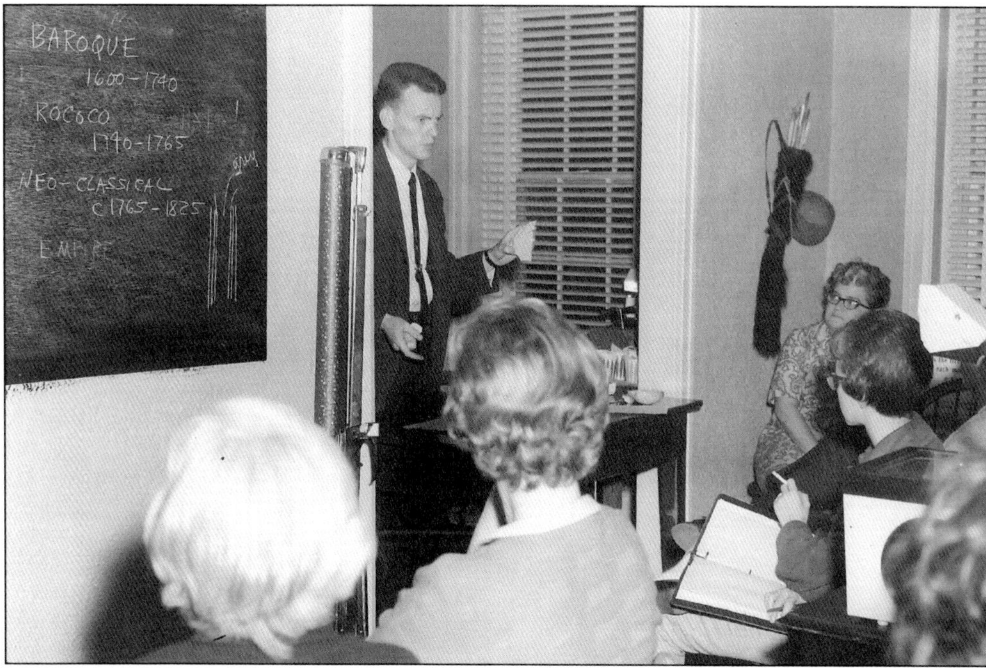

LEARNING ABOUT ARCHAEOLOGY. Dr. Norman Barker of the College of William and Mary is shown in this 1970 image lecturing to a group of interested history buffs. These instructive classes were part of the local emphasis on ongoing Hampton archaeological research and excavations, sponsored by the Hampton Association for Arts and Humanities.

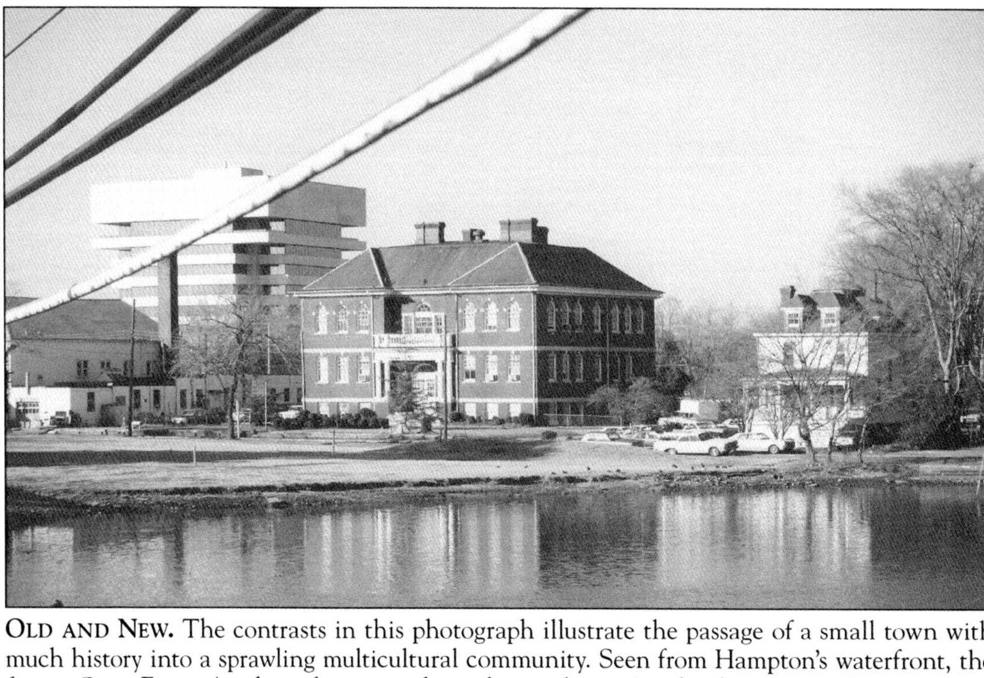

OLD AND NEW. The contrasts in this photograph illustrate the passage of a small town with much history into a sprawling multicultural community. Seen from Hampton's waterfront, the former Syms-Eaton Academy, later torn down during the city's redevelopment, is dwarfed by the ultra-modern, nine-story city hall. Dedicated on January 8, 1977, the new facility was designed to serve the needs of city government into the next century.

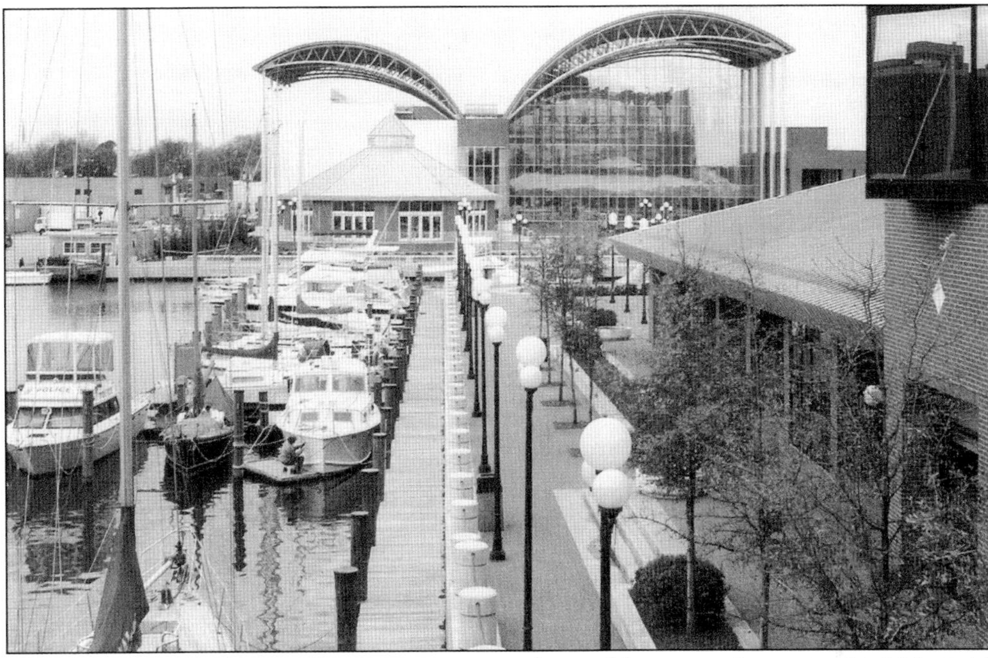

Air and Space. With its roofline meant to remind one of the wings of a soaring bird, Virginia's Air and Space Center anchors Hampton's second downtown redevelopment and attracts many visitors. Seafood businesses lie to its left, the round building houses the carousel from Buckroe's vanished amusement park, and a new restaurant next to a hotel is at right center. (Courtesy of William E. Rouse Research Library.)

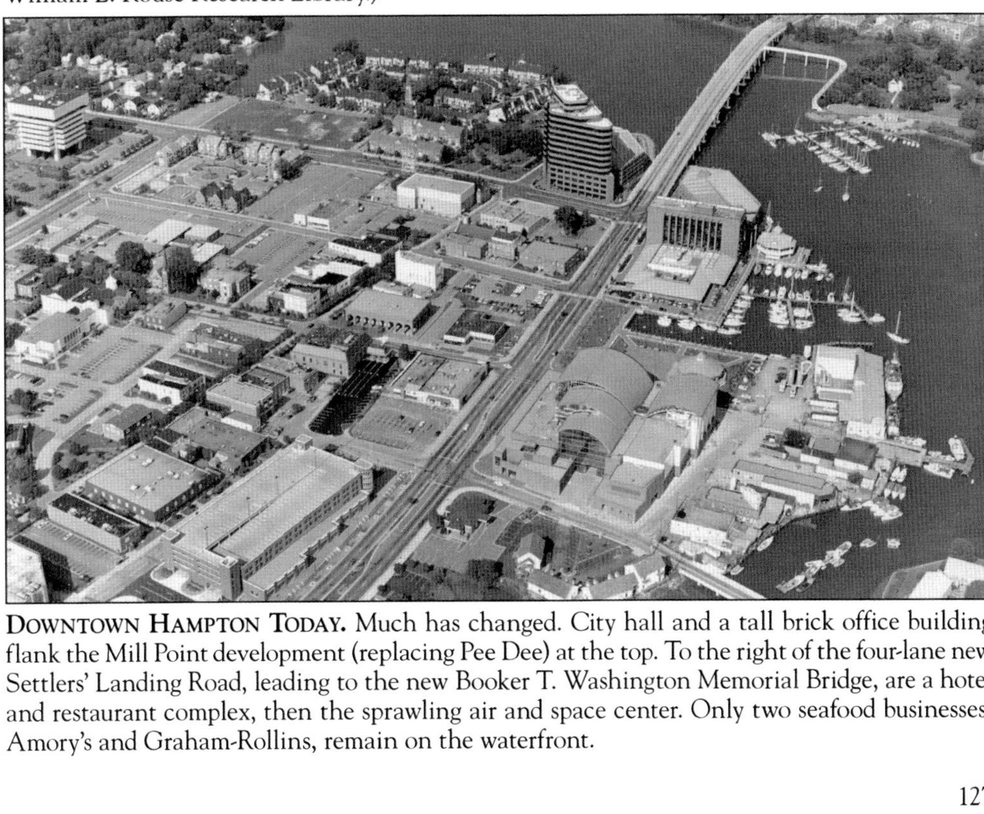

Downtown Hampton Today. Much has changed. City hall and a tall brick office building flank the Mill Point development (replacing Pee Dee) at the top. To the right of the four-lane new Settlers' Landing Road, leading to the new Booker T. Washington Memorial Bridge, are a hotel and restaurant complex, then the sprawling air and space center. Only two seafood businesses, Amory's and Graham-Rollins, remain on the waterfront.